Robert S Hamilton

Present Status of Social Science

A Review of the Progress of Thought in Social Philosophy

Robert S Hamilton

Present Status of Social Science

A Review of the Progress of Thought in Social Philosophy

ISBN/EAN: 9783744669566

Printed in Europe, USA, Canada, Australia, Japan

Cover: Foto ©Suzi / pixelio.de

More available books at **www.hansebooks.com**

PRESENT STATUS

OF

SOCIAL SCIENCE.

A REVIEW, HISTORICAL AND CRITICAL, OF THE PROGRESS
OF THOUGHT IN SOCIAL PHILOSOPHY.

BY

ROBERT S. HAMILTON.

New York:
H. L. HINTON, PUBLISHER,
744 BROADWAY.
1873.

PREFACE.

The present work was prepared for publication seven years ago, and submitted to a few eminent critics and others, for consideration. But portions of it, especially some passages bearing on the late American war, being considered too antagonistical to the prevailing opinion, and the then highly excited state of public feeling in America, it was deemed advisable to delay its publication for a time.

It is now submitted to the public, with the hope that differences of opinion, between the author and a portion of his readers, on questions of merely transient interest, will not prevent a hearty accord between them, on those that are of permanent and enduring moment.

If the intentions of the author should be carried out, the present work will, in a short time, be followed by another, on "THE FUNDAMENTAL LAWS OF SOCIAL LIFE—EMBODYING THE OUTLINES OF A THOROUGH SOCIAL SCIENCE," that will contain the most condensed expression of the author's own observations and reflections, as this contains the most condensed expression of those of anterior thinkers.

October 1st, 1873.

CONTENTS.

INTRODUCTION.

Importance of Clear and Definite Ideas as to the True Ends of a Science—An Important Law of Mental Evolution hitherto unrecognized—Present Status of Social Philosophy defined in Brief—The True Ends of that Philosophy clearly defined—Identity of the Just and the Expedient—The Necessity nevertheless of respecting the Apparent Differences between Them—The Three Existing Systems of Thought in Social Philosophy stated and defined.. 1

CHAPTER I.

The Three Existing Systems of Thought in Social Philosophy, considered by the Experimental Test or from the Practical Standpoint—Their Manifest Insufficiency as thus exhibited.......... 37

CHAPTER II.

The Insufficiency of the Three Existing Systems considered by the Rational Test, or from the Theoretical Stand-point............ 49

CHAPTER III

General Summary as to the Most Essential Significance of the Three Systems—Thus still more clearly revealing their Essential Insufficiency................................... 62

CHAPTER IV.

The Reasons for considering the More Advanced Ideas of Previous Thinkers, before proceeding to develop Those of the Author, which are in entire Accordance with Those More Advanced Ideas. 65

CHAPTER V.

Of the Method and Order to be adopted in considering the New Ideas. 75

CHAPTER VI.

The More Advanced Ideas in Social Philosophy essentially expressed and critically examined in Brief—The Seven Main Propositions that embody Those Ideas 82

CHAPTER VII.

A Brief Retrospect into the Wisdom of Antiquity—As manifested in Confucius and Solon. 132

CHAPTER VIII.

A Critical Review of Guizot and Hallam. 140

CHAPTER IX.

The Valuable Contributions of De Maistre and Chalmers to the Philosophy of Society critically considered 156

CHAPTER X.

Sismondi and Mill—Their Most Essential Contributions to the Philosophy of Society brought prominently into View. 181

CHAPTER XI.

Of Comte and Buckle, and Their Most Essential Contribution to Social Philosophy 207

CHAPTER XII.

Of Comte and Spencer, and What they have done for the Philosophy of Society.. 234

CHAPTER XIII.

The American Contribution to Social Philosophy briefly considered. Webster, Calhoun, and Henry James particularly noticed. The Late Great War glanced at, and the Lessons it inculcates........ 277

CHAPTER XIV.

General Summary—The Present Status of Social Philosophy more explicitly defined in brief—Its Commendable Therapeutics—Its Imperfect Diagnosis—Its Copernican Idea distinctly defined—Its Newtonian Idea suggested rather than defined—Concluding remarks... 308

PRESENT STATUS

OF THE

PHILOSOPHY OF SOCIETY.

INTRODUCTION.

IMPORTANCE OF CLEAR AND DEFINITE IDEAS AS TO THE TRUE ENDS OF A SCIENCE—AN IMPORTANT LAW OF MENTAL EVOLUTION HITHERTO UNRECOGNIZED—PRESENT STATUS OF SOCIAL PHILOSOPHY DEFINED IN BRIEF—THE TRUE ENDS OF THAT PHILOSOPHY CLEARLY DEFINED—IDENTITY OF THE JUST AND THE EXPEDIENT—THE NECESSITY NEVERTHELESS OF RESPECTING THE APPARENT DIFFERENCES BETWEEN THEM—THE THREE EXISTING SYSTEMS OF THOUGHT IN SOCIAL PHILOSOPHY STATED AND DEFINED.

§ 1. A science has already made great progress toward the attainment of its ends, when it has attained to clear perception what those ends really are. It is already far advanced, when it has come at length to clear understanding of the work it has really to perform—to full cognition of its true and proper ends.

It has been well said by an ancient sage, "He has already half finished his work who has begun it."* Rightly enough may it be so said, and in a far wider sense than that intended by the author of the sentiment. For we do not know, we have not yet learned, how to begin our work properly, until we have already half finished it—nay, nearly completed it—in so far, indeed, as human effort ever completes any work. We have to finish our treatise before we discern clearly how it should have been commenced, and then only are we duly prepared to write the introduction, which seldom fails

---

* Horace. Epistles. Book I., Epis. II., line 40. The words are, *Dimidium facti, qui coepit, habet.*

to suggest a remodelling of the whole work. We have to end our lives before we learn truly how we ought to have begun them. Who that has ever undertaken to write a book, or essay, or treatise of any kind, that has not realized the truth of the former observation? Who that has ever come to die, with all his senses about him, that has not realized regretfully the truth of the latter?

Nor less to the same point has it been said by a modern *savan*, "The next thing to having a question solved is to have it well raised."* This is indisputably true. The development of thought requisite to see clearly and state explicitly the problem to be solved, has already proved itself adequate to its solution. Let us but know and clearly perceive the work to be done, in any line, and we have already advanced considerably toward its execution. Let the physician only know what the disease is that he has to treat, and the difficulties of his task are more than half removed.

How much human effort is uselessly expended—alike in theory and practice—in science and in art, from the want of just and clear apprehension how it should be applied—of just, clear and definite appreciation of the ends to which it should be directed and conformed! How often, and how long, are mankind to be seen beating hither and thither in different directions, without any definite idea what it is that they really seek, and with unavailing effort, precisely because they have no such definite idea! But let them rightly attain to the true idea, let them but clearly ascertain what it is that they really seek—that they really want, and they are already far advanced toward its attainment.

When a science has really discovered how to begin its work, how properly to direct and conduct its inquiries *ab initio*—which it can never do until it has attained to just, clear and definite ideas as to its true and proper ends, and which it discovers only at the moment it attains to such ideas—it is already far advanced; it has already progressed so far, and accomplished so much, that

---

* J. S. Mill. See his Dissertations and Discussions, Vol. II., p. 227. Boston Ed., 1865. Article on Michelet's History.

little remains to be accomplished—little indeed of the very little that human effort can ever accomplish, even toward understanding phenomena, much less toward controlling or modifying them. But, by an apparently anomalous law, this is nearly the last discovery that a science makes It is not, however, in reality, by an anomalous law, but by a grand and universal law, hitherto almost wholly overlooked, even by the most profound philosophers.

By a startling paradox, this is the indisputable truth, a mere corollary from that law—stated, indeed, somewhat too strongly, perhaps, that it may be the more forcibly presented and unavoidably seen—THE LAST THING THAT WE LEARN IN ANY SCIENCE IS HOW PROPERLY TO BEGIN OUR INVESTIGATIONS. If it be not indeed the last that we learn, it is so nearly so, that what remains to be discovered amounts to but little—little indeed, except what relates to verifying observations already made, explaining phenomena before observed without being understood, and setting at rest controversy, which before distracted the human understanding, embarrassed its efforts, and prevented its rightly applying practical conclusions, long before attained by the higher intelligences, but not as yet sufficiently established to unite and concentrate general effort in the right direction.

For then, for the first time, do phenomena, which before presented an unintelligible appearance, become clearly intelligible. Then do objects, which before appeared to the mind in an inverted position, assume their true normal position. Then do facts and observations, which before, as it were, stood upon their heads, turn to their feet—the delighted mind is constrained to exclaim EUREKA, and the new science stands before the mental view in all its wonderful simplicity and beauty.

Perhaps, indeed, we should crave indulgence here for somewhat too hasty speech. The result above indicated, we should rather say, follows not immediately from the mere discovery of the true ends of a science, but from *the attainment of those most fundamental truths* to which that discovery directs us. But this attainment follows so naturally and speedily, often indeed so instantaneously, from the discovery of the true ends, to which attention should be immediately directed, that we may reasonably be excused for availing ourselves here of the well-established rule of equitable jurisprudence, that, *what is to be done shall be considered as already done.*

So true is it, as Mill has said, that " the next thing to having a question solved is to have it well raised ;" so strong is the chemical affinity of thought for truth ; so reliable is the human intellect, in its highest forms, at least, in coming to right conclusions when it is once fairly started on the right track ; so sure is it to perform its work when it is once rightly instructed what the work to be performed is, that it is only necessary to let the philosophical mind know definitely, or discern clearly, what are the scientific ends to be attained, and they may be regarded as already virtually attained. In this respect the human mind, at least the philosophical mind, may be compared to the hunter or hound of truest breed, which, once on the right track, never fails to start the game. Nay, it may be compared to the greyhound. Show it the game, and it may be regarded as already caught.

Hence it is that so generally, nay, nearly always, the same mind that discovers what are the true scientific ends of a science, discovers also the great fundamental truths, or laws, to which those ends point, and in the discovery of which consists the attainment of those ends. It was Newton, for example, who first discovered what were the true ends to which astronomical inquiries should be mainly and fundamentally directed ; and it was Newton who first attained those great fundamental truths, or universal laws of motion, which completed the long and brilliant series of discoveries in astronomy. The bare statement of the problem to be solved was, to his mind, tantamount to its solution.

§ 2. The most fundamental truths are generally, if not universally, those which come last into view. Yet these are precisely the truths which every science must attain before it can know how properly to begin its work—how rightly to direct its investigations, or classify its observations. Long before these most fundamental truths are discovered, many highly important ones are brought into view, although until then they are but vaguely perceived and imperfectly appreciated.

This is the obvious reason why we do not know how properly to begin our work of constructing a science, or rightly classifying or even viewing its phenomena, until we have nearly finished our labors, or certainly gone through the most laborious and most protracted portion of them. For then, for the first time, do we attain to those most fundamental truths which afford the only basis upon which we can scientifically build, or systematize our observations and conclusions. Then, for the first time, do we discover that we have been hitherto looking in the wrong direction for obtaining a right view of the phenomena to be explained or otherwise dealt with, and that we must reverse our position, and look in the diametrically opposite direction, in order to obtain the true view, the really scientific view of those phenomena.

In our first, or non-scientific observations we proceed from the superficial to the fundamental. In our next, or scientific observations we precisely reverse our former movement, and proceed from the fundamental towards the superficial—from the general to the particular, from the simple to the complex, from "the homogeneous to the heterogeneous," as a late writer of rare ability* expresses, in part, the same idea. All mental progression or evolution passes through this double movement, this reverse process. In the first of these stages, and before it has attained the most fundamental truths, the movement is non-scientific, tedious, and slow. In the next it is scientific, easy, and rapid—often instantaneous—quick as the electric flash—the electric flash of thought. In the first stage of progression, movement is impeded by the obtuseness and fallibility of the perceptive faculties—always at first seeing objects, in the intellectual realm, only in their inverted position. In the next it is directed by the unerring and infallible guidance of the rational faculties—by pure reason—the Divine light that dwells within the human soul.

This is a law of mental progression, or evolution, wholly unobserved hitherto, although not less important, perhaps, than Comte's law of the three stages—the *theological, metaphysical,* and *positive;* or Spencer's law of evolution, to which he has attached

---

* Herbert Spencer.

such great importance—*that all movement is from the homogeneous to the heterogeneous*—a law obviously included, as we have just now seen, in the more comprehensive one here laid down—more comprehensive, at least, in so far as it applies to mental evolution.*

A great advance in human thought and its modes of philosophizing will have been effected when the philosophical world shall have come to the general recognition of this great law of mental evolution, so obvious in some of its aspects. The law is, that the human mind passes invariably through a double movement in the natural course of its development—that in the first stage or phase of its development it proceeds from the obvious to the obscure, from the superficial to the fundamental, from the apparent to the real, from the subversive or inverted view of phenomena to their true and scientific view; and that in its second stage of development, it precisely reverses this movement, and then, for the first time, sees objects or phenomena in their true aspects and relations. In the first of these stages, it should be obvious, the mind passes from the *heterogeneous* to the *homogeneous*, or from the complex to the simple, and in the second only follows the law laid down by Mr. Spencer, and passes from the *homogeneous* to the *heterogeneous*, or from the simple to the complex.

Vainly, it seems, has nature painted this law, to our sensuous view, on the retina of the eye, where the object is invariably first presented in the inverted position, or upside down—a position which the mind, infallibly guided by instinct in so far as the senses are concerned, immediately rectifies, seeing the object, without the intervention of reason, in its true position.

---

* Mr. Spencer's law is more comprehensive in this, that it is applied by him to universal movement or evolution—in the realm of matter as well as of mind—whereas the law here laid down applies only to mental evolution, as to which it is manifest that it is more copious and comprehensive. There can be no reasonable question as to the truth of Mr. Spencer's law, nor Comte's either. For they very nearly agree; although Mr. Spencer, who belongs apparently to the order of kings in the intellectual realm, who wish to reign not only supremely but exclusively, seems to have deemed it necessary to take exception, in this respect as in some others quite unnecessarily, to the great thoughts of his illustrious compeer the too little appreciated, though certainly not faultless or wholly unexceptionable Comte.

Not less conspicuously, and much more simply, clearly, and palpably, has nature furnished us illustration, in truth an exact illustration, of this great law, in the geological structure of the earth's crust, wherever we are permitted to view it in its true normal state. For the most superficial, and at the same time most complex, most *heterogeneous* rocks are precisely the ones that come first into view. Step by step only do we proceed to the most fundamental, most simple, most homogeneous. But when we have attained to these most fundamental rocks, then, and not until then, do we properly begin our scientific work in Geology. We begin it with those last discovered rocks. Then only can we rightly organize geological science, or discern the true order in which our observations are to be classified and considered.

Whithersoever, in short, we turn our view we find evidence of the great fundamental law here sought to be partially developed, although, of course, apparent contradictions of the law may be detected by those small minds that can only see, in one view, some isolated part of a great truth, and are incapable of those comprehensive views before which apparent discords and discrepancies disappear. Nature is a vast circle which must necessarily have a *dual* manifestation—its convex and concave aspects.

Universal being everywhere presents a dual aspect. The old Janus of Roman mythology, like all the venerable traditions of the race, is profoundly allegorical. It is the true type of universal being. Nature is everywhere Janus-faced. She looks invariably two ways, although inseparably connected ways—ways that are indissoluble counterparts of each other, as the convex and concave, the male and female. She looks TO man and FROM man. In his first observations in the intellectual realm man looks FROM himself, and sees all objects in their inverted position. In his next, or more mature and scientific observations, he looks TO himself—an effort of which he is at first incapable—toward whom all external nature looks, as her grand apex and crowning point, the great outward and visible type of her interior and invisible God ; and then, for the first time, he sees objects or ideas in the right position—their true normal relations.

Did we need further and more practical illustration of the great fundamental law in question, we might find it by appealing, again and more particularly, to astronomical science. Astronomy was already far advanced before it learned from Newton how to conduct its investigations—how even to begin properly its true scientific work. Copernicus, Kepler, Galileo, Tyco Brahe, Gilbert, Hook, Hugyns, Halley, had all contributed their valuable observations and discoveries. But still astronomy was not yet properly presented to the human view. It had not yet learned how properly or scientifically to begin its work. For it had not as yet attained to those most fundamental laws to which all its other laws are conformed, and by which only they can be thoroughly understood.

Not until Newton had discovered those most fundamental laws did sidereal phenomena assume their true aspects to the human view. All former knowledge in astronomy was still in confusion. But when Newton had discovered and explained those most fundamental laws, then, for the first time, order arose out of chaos in the human understanding, in regard to sidereal phenomena. Then, for the first time, were all anterior discoveries in astronomy not only verified, but explained and understood. Then, for the first time, worlds stood upon their feet, and the universe rose before the human view in all its grand and majestic proportions.

§ 3. It need not, then, appear strange that, even at this advanced period of human thought, when so many valuable contributions have been made to SOCIAL SCIENCE, and when many of its great problems have been under consideration for more than two thousand years, this important science has not yet attained to just, clear, and definite ideas as to its true and proper ends, and that, consequently, it has not yet learned how even to begin its inquiries properly, how to direct its efforts, or systematize its observations. For this is precisely the present condition of Social Science, or as we should more properly say perhaps, of the Philosophy of Society. For it is only with very questionable propriety that we can apply the name of Science to a Philosophy as yet so very indeterminate in its reasonings as that which relates to the phenomena of Society.

When we speak of Social Science here, therefore, or, to use its more specific and more scientific title, SOCIOLOGY,* we must be understood to speak prospectively of the science that is to be—of the science that is as yet in its nascent state, and has to be cradled, nay, formed and developed, by a more thorough and sagacious Social Philosophy.

For it should hardly be necessary to say here—although it may not be out of place to do so, concerning terms so vaguely understood in general as Science and Philosophy—that Philosophy stands related to Science as the greater to the less—we might almost say, as the parent to the offspring. As every Art has its correspondent Science, every Science has its correspondent Philosophy. It is the province of Science to form, direct, and advance the art to which it appertains—if, indeed, it be one of the EFFICIENT sciences, or one that has, like Medical and Social Science, any correspondent art. It is the province of Philosophy, in like manner, to form, direct, and advance its correspondent Science. Philosophy is at once a more comprehensive, a more vague, more indeterminate system, or mode, of thought than Science. It is Science as yet in its nascent state—*in embryo*. When ideas have been sufficiently developed to be thoroughly understood, or conclusively established, they pass from the domain of Philosophy

---

* It may be worthy of remark, as a part of the unwritten history of the world of thought, that this word is of the author's own *coinage*, though not exclusively. So recently as September, 1855, he consulted an erudite friend as to the propriety and necessity of coining a new word to express the comprehensive ideas involved in his mode of considering the phenomena of Society, and suggested *Socialitics*, *Socialistics*, and *Sociology*. His erudite friend, however, adjudged that neither of these words would be allowable—that such liberties with language were proper enough with the German, but far less admissible in the Anglo-Saxon tongue. The author, notwithstanding, concluded, upon his sole responsibility, to adopt Sociology. He shortly after learned that the word had been already used, and even as the title of a late work, by Mr. George Fitzhugh, of Virginia, entitled, "Sociology for the South." Shortly thereafter he found that it had been freely used in the last, or *eighth* edition of the Encyclopedia Britannica, under the title of "Communism," and still more recently, that it had been not less freely used by Comte in his Positive Philosophy, published as far back as 1835. This statement will illustrate how different minds, without any concert of action, but acted upon by like necessities, operating extensively in the same epoch of the world, are often led to the same discoveries or inventions, whether of thoughts or words.

into that of Science—from the more indeterminate to the more determinate state. Philosophy, in short, deals with reasonings—Science only with established conclusions.* Very obvious, it should appear, that in dealing with the principles of Society, or the principles on which depend, most fundamentally, the welfare of states, and of the individuals composing them, we are dealing with ideas that belong as yet to the domain of Philosophy rather than of Science. Hence it is that, throughout these pages, the terms Social Philosophy and Philosophy of Society, which are obviously identical in import, will be almost universally employed where to some it might appear preferable to use the less forbidding terms, Social Science or Sociology.

From this brief digression, concerning the true meaning and relative import of the terms Philosophy and Science, we return to the observation, that, strange as it may appear, with all its valuable attainments, the great want of Social Philosophy at present, is the want of just, clear, and definite ideas as to its true and proper ends. Although far more advanced, relatively, in particular ideas, than sidereal philosophy before the time of Newton, it scarcely less needs the PRINCIPIA MATHEMATICA PHILOSOPHLE SOCIALIS, or rather the PRINCIPIA PRIMA. It needs these primary principles, which have not as yet been attained, to instruct it how rightly to direct its inquiries—how properly to begin its legitimate work.

Great practical attainments have, indisputably, been made by Social Philosophy. Many of its subordinate sciences have been carried to a very high degree of proficiency, while the main fundamental science remains almost wholly undeveloped. Its branches have been nearly matured, while its trunk, or rather

---

* As an illustration of the exceedingly vague ideas generally prevalent as to the relative meaning of Philosophy and Science, it may be mentioned that a late writer of eminence, though the author does not remember who—merely remembering vividly the fact—uses the phrase, "the Science of Philosophy." Could any phrase appear more grotesque or preposterous, to one rightly apprehending the true relative import of the words? This is about as grotesque an expression as *the tree of the fruit* would be. We say, very well, the fruit of the tree, and so we may say conversely the *philosophy* of science, but surely not the *science* of philosophy.

roots are as yet but imperfectly developed, nay, almost wholly undiscovered, to the scientific view. For this is conformably to the law of evolution in the *psychological* realm, as we have already seen, which is the exact reverse or counterpart of that which prevails in the *physical*.

Jurisprudence, or the science of JUSTICE, has been nearly perfected. The Justinian code accomplished that for Social Philosophy; and modern wisdom has improved somewhat, if not considerably, upon that justly esteemed and admired system of civil laws.

Political Economy, or the science of WEALTH, has been equally, if not still more nearly perfected. Adam Smith accomplished this great work for Social Philosophy. For he is indisputably the true Newton of Political Economy. Or if, in any essentially important respect, he has erred or failed, the more recent labors of McCulloh, Senior, and Mill have supplied his deficiencies and amended his defects.

The laws of POPULATION, hardly as yet sufficiently reduced into scientific order, have been clearly enough explained by Malthus, despite his exaggerated, and in some respects, erroneous estimate of the bearings of one of those laws. Nor have they really needed the more copious light which subsequent discussion has thrown upon them—except, indeed, in so far as was necessary to correct the too unqualified statement alike of Malthus and Dr. Chalmers, concerning THE TENDENCY OF POPULATION TO PRESS TOO CLOSELY ON THE LIMITS OF SUBSISTENCE, which has been ably and amply done by the later Malthusians—Senior, Mill, McCulloh, and William Thomas Thornton, not to mention Sir Archibald Alison, who can scarcely merit the title of Malthusian, or more than that of *Quasi*-Malthusian.*

Great progress has been made in the science of POLITICS, a

---

* For a more thorough appreciation of the distinctions here taken concerning the various shades of thought, clearly distinguishable in the brilliant train of illustrious thinkers, who have participated in the great discussions to which the essay of Malthus on Population has given rise, reference must here be made to the author's unpublished work on Malthusianism, or part of work, comprising the Part Fifth of this Series.

science, in its largest import, almost co-extensive with the master science of SOCIOLOGY, although, as commonly understood, signifying the science of government in its merely *positive* aspect, as contradistinguished from its far more important *negative* aspects. English and American statesmanship have almost exhausted the capacities of the human intellect in this direction, from the practical stand-point, while, from the theoretical stand-point, the highest intellects of the world, from an early period, have poured copious light upon this important field of inquiry. The writings of Aristotle, Machiavelli, Locke, Montesquieu, De Tocqueville, and the great expounders of the American Constitution, leave but little to be desired in this particular domain of thought in Social Philosophy— little indeed except the discerning and designing mind, that is capable of sifting the grain of truth from the chaff of words and the tares of error, that is capable of deciding what is to be adopted and what rejected, of thoroughly separating the former from the latter,—leaving the latter, which merely obstruct the channels of thought, to drift where it rightly belongs—

> Ad locum umbrarum, noctisque, somnique, saporæ.

Nor has the far more profound and hitherto too little regarded science, or rather philosophy of ETHNOLOGY been wanting in its cultivators and distinguished exponents, who have thrown important light upon this truly fundamental influence in social destiny.

Yet notwithstanding all these important attainments, Social Philosophy has not yet attained to just, clear and definite ideas as to its true and proper ends. It has not yet learned how properly to begin its work—how to direct its inquiries—how to apply its vast and various knowledge—how rightly to shape its jurisprudence, its political economy, its legislation, and, in short, its political action in its largest and most comprehensive extent. Before it can attain to this great discovery—this *last* discovery, which must, however, come *first*, in the true scientific construction of our ideas and efforts—it must discover and clearly discern ONE OTHER GREAT LAW, or rather CONGERIES OF LAWS, equally as fundamental as that of ETHNOLOGY, and far more comprehensive, reverse its mode of viewing the phenomena of society, and remodel its whole system of thought and effort conformably to the plan which will be readily suggested by the disclosure of those great fundamental laws.

Then, for the first time, will social phenomena, hitherto viewed only in their subversive or inverted position, assume their true position, and the social universe will stand disclosed to the human view not less clearly, if indeed less conspicuously and grandly, than did the sidereal universe under the disclosures made by Newton. Then will it be discovered that the social universe is modelled upon the same type with the sidereal, and that both are modelled conformably to the grand conception of Schelling, not less than of the semi-delirious Fourier, THAT THE UNIVERSE IS CONSTRUCTED UPON THE MODEL OF THE HUMAN SOUL, which is doubtlessly the miniature or condensed reflex of the Divine Soul.

In order to attain to this grand and comprehensive view, this truly scientific view, of the system of human society, it is necessary, and only necessary, that Social Philosophy should attain to just clear and definite ideas as to its true and proper ends. Having clearly discerned those ends it can have no great difficulty in discovering those great fundamental laws to which they directly point our inquiries, and which constitute the last discovery to be made by Social Philosophy, and the last that it needs, in order to consummate its efforts, in the establishment of a complete system of Social Science, and the identification of that system with the general system of nature and universal being.

§ 4. It is remarkable, but in entire accordance with the great law of mental evolution already laid down, that among all the eminent philosophers who have hitherto thrown light upon the Philosophy of Society not one appears to have had any just, clear or definite ideas as to its true or proper ends, nay to have discovered the necessity or propriety of having such ideas, of keeping them steadily in view, and of subordinating and conforming all inquiries mainly to those ends.

Even as late and eminent a thinker as Montesquieu, who addressed the world with his valuable thoughts as recently as about the middle of the last century, does not appear to have entertained any such ideas. In his famous disquisition on "The Spirit of Laws," first published in 1748, he has furnished us with not less than THIRTY different books, or parts of the general body of his disquisition, treating of Laws, in reference to as many different ends, and yet not one of all those THIRTY books is in reference to the true or proper ends to which all such disquisitions should be confirmed. Nay, he does not once broach the great primary, and in a truly scientific sense, preliminary question in Social Philosophy: What are the ends, the main fundamental and primary ends, to which all such disquisitions on laws should be directed and conformed? This is the great defect of that so much applauded and altogether overestimated disquisition—a defect scarcely less conspicuous in that work than in the far earlier and very similar one of Aristotle on Politics.

A good many writers have indeed addressed themselves to this great question, but very imperfectly, and partially, and with a very inadequate conception, evidently, of its great importance. One class of reasoners that we often meet with, for example, tells us that the true end of social science, or of government and society, is JUSTICE. So argues Plato in his speculations on the Model Republic, and more recently Mr. Herbert Spencer, in his disquisition on "Social Statics." Another class, more practical and truly sagacious than the former, though not at all more correct, in so far as the philosophy of the former extends—for they are both partly correct, both correct, in short, as far as they go in their philosophy—tells us that the true end of social science, of government and society, is EXPEDIENCY, or, more explicity to speak, the WELFARE OF MANKIND, the protection and promotion of their INTERESTS, as well as their RIGHTS—ideas not entirely co-extensive, although perfectly equivalent as far as they run together, or rather run at all. For it should be obvious that the idea of JUSTICE breaks down, or fails in its application, for all practical purposes at least, long before the idea of EXPEDIENCY.

Both of these two classes of reasoners are just and right, as far as their observations and inquiries extend. But they do not extend their observations and inquiries far enough. They are very imperfect and insufficient in their conceptions as to the true ends of Social Science or Philosophy. Not only are they liable to criticism from the observation of Plato, that " the higher generalities give no sufficient direction,"* of which their proposed ends afford illustration, but they are liable to a far more serious criticism, namely, that they are not sufficiently comprehensive.

They are not only too general, but too little comprehensive. They are at once too inexplicit and not general enough. They are not only too vague in their declaration of purpose, but are manifestly enough too contracted in the purpose which they avow. They are not sufficiently all-embracing in their fundamental aim, which is indispensable to true scientific effort and inquiry. They fail utterly to bring into view a vast field of inquiry, indispensable to be surveyed, and thoroughly considered. They give no attention, or wholly inadequate attention, if any at all, to the great fundamental and primary question: What are the causes that stand in the way of the accomplishment of the ends which they propose—what are the causes that prevent us from attaining justice and expediency, or obstruct our efforts toward those ends—what are the real difficulties in the way of attaining them?

Are those causes, those difficulties, merely of human creation, as superficial declaimers have been ever prone to assert, or are they of nature's own creation? Are they founded merely in the structure of THE GOVERNMENT, or the ORGANISM of the society, as learned fools, or the fools *secundum artem* assure us; or are they founded in the structure of eternal nature and the ORGANISM of the UNIVERSE? If in the latter, in what respects are they so founded? How far do they admit of remedy or countervail? What are the most reliable instrumentalities for seeking such remedy or countervail?

As to these great and evidently most fundamental questions, neither those who tell us that they aim at Justice, nor those who tell us that they aim at Expediency, or the welfare of mankind in respect alike to their rights and interests, nor indeed any school of thinkers as yet in Social Philosophy, give us any sufficient or reliable information. They tell us, indeed, that they aim at

---

* See Plato's Timæus.

Justice, at Expediency; but do not appear to have once thought it necessary to consider what are the difficulties in the way of obtaining those ends.

They are like the superficial doctor who tells us that he is bent on curing the disease, but has not thought it worth while to inquire into its causes, or real nature. Nay, they are like the soldier who tells us he is going to take Russia, but has not given a moment's attention to the great practical question—at once practical and preliminary—what are the difficulties in the way of taking Russia. A true general would readily tell our flippant soldier that before he attempts to take Russia it would be well first seriously to consider what are the difficulties to be encountered in such an enterprise, and how are they to be combated. Not less obviously would a true philosopher tell those superficial reasoners, we had almost said those flippant sophists, who have been telling us, ever since the world began, that they are aiming at Justice, or Expediency, for mankind, that, before seriously undertaking such arduous endeavors, they would do well thoroughly and profoundly to inquire into the causes, or obstacles, which render so difficult of attainment those eminently desirable ends.

§ 5. What then are the true or proper ends of Social Philosophy, or of the science which it is its function to develop? To answer thoroughly this question, we should take a brief general survey of the sciences in general, or of universal science, in reference to the proper ends of each particular science.

All science may be regarded, and should ever be, in two main aspects, or in reference to two grand ends—its purely scientific ends, and its practical or efficient ends. But all sciences do not have any practical or efficient ends, properly so understood. All sciences may, therefore, be properly divided into two grand classes—the purely scientific and the practical or efficient sciences. Those of the former class have but one main end, or order of ends, and that the purely scientific. Those of the latter class have two main ends—the purely scientific and the practical. The main grand end of the purely scientific sciences, as it is indeed the purely scientific end of all the sciences, is simply TO KNOW—to know phenomena and their laws. The two main grand ends of the practical or efficient sciences are, first, TO KNOW; secondly, TO MAKE PRACTICAL APPLICATIONS OF THAT KNOWLEDGE, with a view to controlling or modifying the purely scientific aspects of the phenomena to be considered, nay, the very laws to be dealt with. All sciences, therefore, have a purely scientific end, and this is, moreover, with all sciences the main, and grand primary end.

Mathematics, Astronomy and Geology, for example, are purely scientific sciences. Medical Science, or rather, the great confederation of sciences bearing that general name, and Sociology, are efficient sciences. No one studies mathematics with a view to changing its fundamental laws, principles, or relations—with a view to contriving a new order of triangles or parallelograms, or in any respect varying or modifying its immutable relations. God himself could not do that. It is a mathematical impossibility. Neither does any one study astronomy with a view to altering, or in any respect modifying, the movements or relations of worlds; nor geology with the view of controlling or modifying the great natural laws of terrestrial transformation and development. God, as He is commonly understood, may indeed do that. But it is utterly beyond the power of man.

On the other hand, men do study medical science, or rather, physiology, pathology and therapeutics, not only with a view to the purely scientific end of ascertaining the laws of health and disease, and the possibilities of controlling those laws to some extent, but with a view to the great, practical and efficient end of actually controlling those laws. So, likewise, men do study—imperfectly and superficially enough hitherto, to be sure—the laws of social health and disease, and the possibilities of controlling them to some extent, not only with reference to the purely scientific end of understanding those laws, hitherto indeed shamefully neglected, but with a view furthermore to the great, practical and efficient end of actually controlling them, to which latter end indeed attention has been hitherto almost exclusively directed, by a sort of blind *empiricism* in social philosophy—by a sort of shameful *quackery*, indeed, which undertakes to treat social disease without any adequate consideration of its true DIAGNOSIS—almost without any regard whatever to the great and vitally important sciences—hitherto almost wholly uncultivated—of SOCIAL PHYSIOLOGY and SOCIAL PATHOLOGY.

§ 6. After these brief generalizations and fundamental observations, we are enabled, accurately enough for general purposes, to answer the question—What are the true and proper ends of Social Philosophy, and its correspondent science, SOCIOLOGY? They are, FIRST, to ascertain what are the causes or laws which determine the social condition of mankind; SECONDLY, to ascertain how far, and by what means, can those causes or laws be controlled or modified by human agency—by human intention or effort, purposely and designedly directed to that end. For it is to be borne in mind, that an important distinction is ever to be taken between involuntary and merely *instinctive* human agency, and that which is voluntary and *rational*. The former belongs exclusively to the realm of nature, or pure PHYSICS; the latter alone to MAN, properly so understood, or the realm of PSYCHOLOGY. The one, in other words, we may say, appertains to the *primary* and simple laws of nature; the other, to the *secondary* and more complex laws of nature. For all is comprehended in Universal Nature. There is no valid distinction—no scientific, no truly philosophical distinction to be taken between MAN and NATURE, as Lord Bacon, in common with his prototypes, the Chinese philosophers, has awkwardly done.*

The FIRST of these two main ends is the immediate and more important one. It is the one which, thoroughly apprehended, teaches us how little can be done in respect to the other; but teaches us, at the same time, how most effectively to direct our efforts, with a view to the accomplishment of the little that can be accomplished by human agency, properly so called.

If astronomical science discloses to our view laws that human effort cannot control or modify at all, social science reveals to us laws—natural and universal laws—which such effort cannot control or modify, except to a very limited extent.

---

* The Chinese philosophers, not less than Lord Bacon, have made the awkward and eminently unphilosophical division of all knowledge into three main parts, relating respectively to God, Man, and Nature.

Astronomical science reveals to us two great forces, the CENTRIPETAL and CENTRIFUGAL, from the constant action and reaction of which, or of the antagonism between them, result all sidereal movements. Social science, true social science, not less reveals to us two great forces, precisely equivalent to those of the astronomical realm, if not, indeed, precisely the same forces, transferred from the purely physical realm to the composite realm of physics and psychology combined, from the constant action and reaction of which result all social movements and destiny.

The only noteworthy difference between the two sets of laws is, that in one, both of the two great forces lie *outside* of man, and therefore entirely beyond his control; while, in the other, one of those forces lies *within* himself—nay, one of them he himself constitutes; and therefore, accordingly, and in so far as he can and may control himself, or be in any way controlled, modified, or improved, may he be enabled, to some small extent, to control, modify, or improve his social condition and destiny.

§ 7. To a rightly discerning view, however, it will readily appear manifest, that this great, primary and fundamental question in social philosophy—WHAT ARE THE CAUSES WHICH DETERMINE THE SOCIAL CONDITION OF MANKIND?—divides at once into two more particular ones, which demand particular and separate consideration. For it is only the more particular questions, strictly conformed and subordinated to the most general ones, that can rightly conduct us to any explicit ideas, or practically important conclusions.

These two more particular questions, to which attention should be more immediately addressed in Social Philosophy, are, FIRST, What are the causes that really, and most fundamentally tend to DEPRESS the social condition, or to militate against human welfare; SECONDLY, What are the causes that really, most essentially, and most fundamentally tend to countervail the depressing causes, and to ELEVATE the social condition. In the former we have given the CENTRIPETAL forces of the social COSMOS, or the laws of universal social GRAVITATION—in the latter, we have the CENTRIFUGAL.

Now then we are prepared to judge, rightly and scientifically to determine, how far inquiries in Social Philosophy hitherto, have been well or wisely conducted—how far they have apprehended the true ends to which they should be directed, and how far, therefore, they have tended to really important conclusions, or the most important conclusions.

§ 8. But there is yet another subdivision of thought and inquiry to which attention should be directed, before we shall be enabled to obtain a sufficiently clear and explicit view of the great fundamental ideas to which all inquiry in Social Philosophy should be subordinated, and directed AB INITIO.

For, to a justly discerning mind, the question will immediately arise—on the statement of the great primary question, either in its general form, or its more particular forms, as already indicated—In what respects are the causes which determine the social condition of mankind to be considered or inquired into? What is to be understood by the phrase, *determine the social condition of mankind?* If we are to say that certain causes determine the social condition, *depress* it on one hand, or *elevate* it on the other, in what respects are we to understand that such causes so determine the social condition ?

The answer to this question, thus variously stated, is, that it is in respect to both of the two great ends constantly aimed at by mankind, and to one or other of which Social Philosophy and practical statesmanship, alike, are constantly addressing themselves, in one form or other—JUSTICE AND EXPEDIENCY—both the RIGHT and the USEFUL.

In other words it is the main fundamental end of Social Philosophy to ascertain what are the causes which determine whether mankind shall obtain justice, as well as expediency, their *rights,* as well as their *interests*—whether they shall be neither unduly wronged in their feelings, nor destitute of the proper comforts of life.

And here arises at once for consideration, one of the most difficult questions to be precisely determined, and one of the most exhaustless for discussion, that is to be encountered either in the realm of Sociology or Ethics—for it appertains to both. How far is the JUST, expedient, and the EXPEDIENT, just? Or, rather, how far is the apparently JUST, expedient, or the apparently EXPEDIENT, therefore to be considered just? For this last is really the form, and the only form, in which the question can be actually presented to the human mind.

What human mind, indeed, shall presume to pass final judgment upon these unfathomable questions? What human judgment shall dare to pronounce absolutely upon them? All that human reason can say is, that some things appear to it just and right, for these are identical terms, and that some things appear expedient or useful—nay that some things appear just and right, without any reference to their expediency or utility, and that others again appear expedient and useful, without any reference to their justice or rightfulness. But whether anything is really either right or expedient, or whether only some things are so, and others not, or whether again all things are not both right and expedient, we do not know, and can never know with our finite minds.

We may indeed boldly dogmatize with Pope, and say with him, not less than with Spinoza, and the Sooffee philosophers of modern Persia, who all find their expression in that bold assertion of his—"This much is clear, whatever *is* is right"—an assertion which implies that there is but ONE SUBSTANCE in the universe. Or we may hardly less boldly dogmatize with the Magi of ancient Persia, and declare that there are two different and antagonistic substances or spirits in the universe—two different sets of influences, constantly operating upon the world, and struggling for the mastery—Ormuzd, or the spirit of GOOD, and Ahriman, or the spirit of EVIL—the idea which we find preserved in the more recent stratification of theological opinions, where those two antagonistic spirits bear, in our terse Anglo-Saxon, the familiar and less imposing names of God and the Devil. But we shall never know, with our finite minds, what is the precise truth in regard to these unfathomable mysteries, whatever may be our various opinions, notions or "faiths," concerning them.

§ 9. What rule, then, are we to lay down, or is there any universal or even widely prevalent one, for the guidance of the Ethician or Sociologist, but more especially of the latter, in regard to these two great fundamental ideas of the human mind—the idea of the JUST and that of the EXPEDIENT? Is there any rule, in other words, which can determine to which of these two ideas they should directly or mainly address themselves? Such rules apply for the most part, alike in Ethics and Sociology. For there is but this difference between the two domains of thought, that Ethics deal* exclusively with the idea of the RIGHT, while Sociology deals alike with the idea of the RIGHT and the EXPEDIENT. In this respect Sociology is a wider domain of thought than Ethics. Nay, all things considered, it is undoubtedly a wider domain. But in respect to the idea of the RIGHT—in so far as that idea is to be especially considered, and that only—Ethics is a far wider domain than Sociology. For Ethics deal with many questions of RIGHT which appertain not at all to Sociology. Sociology concerns itself with the rightfulness of human actions, only in so far as they affect others besides the agent himself. But there are many questions, vitally important questions, respecting the rightfulness of human action that affect only the agent himself, and his relations to God, if we may here use that little comprehended name, or what Mr. Carlyle has styled "man's vital relations to this mysterious universe." † With these Ethics has to deal, as well as with all other questions of RIGHT.

What rule, then, are we to lay down, or is there any, for our universal guidance in respect to these great fundamental ideas of the RIGHT and the EXPEDIENT? There is undoubtedly one great rule, of universal application—a rule constituting, indeed, one of the grandest, most beautiful, and most inspiring, of all the great truths that underlie human destiny, alike in the domain of Ethics and Sociology, we might almost say, alike in the domain of God

---

* The author here takes the grammatical license of treating Ethics as either singular or plural, according as the laws of euphony may suggest. Evidently it may be treated either way, although, perhaps, more properly it is a singular noun. But to say "Ethics deals" would be altogether too violative of euphony even for our little euphonious dialect.

† Mr. Thomas Carlyle, in Heroes and Hero-Worship.

and man. It is this—that the two ideas are essentially identical, and that it matters not to which we may directly address ourselves, except, indeed, that sometimes the one idea throws more light upon the question to be determined, and sometimes the other. The RIGHT and the EXPEDIENT are but different phases of the same truth—its inseparable counterparts—the true equivalents of each other. It matters not, therefore, which we may embrace and wisely prosecute. They both conduct us to the same result, to one common end—that which is right and proper, wisely and truly expedient.

The right is expedient, and the expedient, right. This much at least we may know, whatever else we may fail to know. We may not be able to know, to know certainly, or absolutely, what is either right or expedient. But this we may know, that whatever is right is also expedient, and *vice versa.* If we can but be assured, by any means whatever, that a thing is just and right, then we may be assured that it is truly expedient. If, on the other hand, we can but be assured, by any means, that a thing is expedient, is truly expedient, and in the largest sense of that idea, then we may be well assured that it is just and right. The infallible mathematics of human reason, in its fundamental postulates, proclaims this truth as indisputable—this great first truth in moral mathematics.

We may be indeed mistaken, with our contracted views, as to what is expedient, really and in the largest sense, expedient. But not less may we be mistaken as to what is right, or just. He is indeed a pitiably weak and superficial reasoner who supposes that, by adopting the idea of justice or right for his guidance, he has obtained an infallible criterion by which to shape his judgment. On no subject do men more differ or disagree than in respect to what is JUST, or what is RIGHT. On no subject is it really so difficult for the human mind to obtain sure guidance and direction. It is an old proverb among the English lawyers, that " the jurisdiction of the Court of Chancery depends upon the length of my Lord Chancellor's foot."

Unhappy would it be for mankind if they did not differ and disagree somewhat less as to what is EXPEDIENT, than as to what is JUST, if it were not really less difficult to obtain true guidance by appealing to that idea. It must necessarily be so from the nature of things. For the idea of justice appertains to abstract thought, the purely rational ideas, which are very feebly developed, except in a very few minds, while the idea of expediency appertains more to practical thought, the common sense ideas, which are largely developed in the great majority of men. It is often easy enough, for example, to convince a man that it is his true interest to do or not to do a given act, when we should in vain appeal to his sense of justice or right, in the case, which for a double reason is a feeble idea with most men—first, because they have not the brains to comprehend the idea, and, secondly, because they have not the heart to appreciate or respect it, were it even comprehended. In short, most men are open to arguments founded on interest, or the idea of expediency, while but few are open to those founded on right, or the idea of justice.

Hence it is that we find really valuable reasoners, the great practical thinkers, nearly always addressing themselves to the great practical questions of Expediency. It is only the sentimental philosophers, for the most part—we had almost said the school-boy philosophers, and certainly we might say the schoolroom philosophers—who are to be found frittering away their attention on the interminable and indeterminate questions, the delusive and ever-deluding speculations, about JUSTICE or RIGHT, irrespective of their relations to the great practical ends of expediency—questions and speculations which utterly fail to throw any satisfactory light, even for the most superior intellects, upon many of the most important concerns of mankind.

We beg pardon here of the august name of Plato. But what rule is without its exceptions? He who discourses so justly, wisely, and nobly of JUSTICE as Plato, may surely be excused for having expended some time upon a theme so little suggestive of really JUST conclusions, except on questions of pure Jurisprudence. In truth, nearly all Plato's ideas of justice, in respect to government and society, are essentially grounded upon enlarged, sagacious, and eminently just ideas of EXPEDIENCY.*

---

* See Plato's Ideal Republic.

Let us but know what is the EXPEDIENT, with clear full reference to the just, to all well-settled ideas as to what is in itself just and right, even though we may have partially, or, apparently, at least, to some small extent, to sacrifice those ideas—and we have, at the same time, that which is just and right. Nay, moreover, as to very many things, in order to ascertain whether they are just and right, it is imperatively necessary to inquire into their expediency, their utility, their conduciveness to the general good of mankind, in the largest and most comprehensive sense. There is no other sure or reliable criterion by which we can determine whether or not they are just or right.

It matters not what Jeremy Bentham may have said, or intended to say, in regard to the principle of utility as the true foundation of right, nor what shallow reasoners, incapable of understanding him, may have said against his philosophy, and who commence their senseless bellowings whenever his name is either mentioned or suggested by a kindred thought. The principles here enunciated need no Bentham to substantiate them, nor to pervert them—if, indeed, he has done so—to lead men into misapprehension in regard to them, by his defective statement of them, as Malthus has done in regard to his philosophy by his imperfect and faulty presentation of it. Nor have we anything to do here with his statements of or concerning the great truth here laid down.

The writer of these pages is the Rudolph of his own philosophy, and claims for it no higher lineage, however august may be its unknown ancestry. No puny Eclecticism enters into that philosophy, as might be inferred from the great deference with which he so often invokes high authority, nay, courts its approbation. He is but poorly qualified to act the part of an organizer, systematizer, or revolutionizer, in Philosophy, who does not draw for himself, and at first hand, from the great original fountains of truth, as they gush out of the Eternal Mind, through the outlet of human reason.

It is reason, in its most fundamental and indisputable postulates, that declares the RIGHT to be expedient, and the EXPEDIENT, right. They are convertible terms, substantially equivalent expressions, essentially identical ideas. They are but the opposite ends of the same rule, the different poles of the same galvanic battery, the convex and concave aspects of the same circle of truth. Said we not rightly before, Nature is ever *Janus-faced?* So is truth, or nature in her moral aspects, her psychological manifestations. It ever looks in two opposite directions, which, nevertheless, tend to the same common end, and if steadily persisted in, must eventually conduct to the same end—just as inevitably as two men, travelling due east and west respectively, around the globe, must eventually come together. If on one side, therefore, we see the august visage of nature, in her moral realm, looking toward expediency, and indicating to us the EXPEDIENT, we may be perfectly sure, that if we could obtain a view of her other front, we should find it looking steadily toward the JUST—in a direct line toward the throne of eternal justice and right.

Briefly and beautifully has it been said by a late writer, "Nature is harmoniously constructed; that which is just is beneficial."* To the same point, another has said, in reference to the Great Creator, "He has so intimately connected, so inseparably interwoven the laws of eternal justice with the happiness of each individual, that the latter cannot be obtained but by observing the former, and if the former be punctually obeyed, they cannot but induce the latter."† Nor less to the same point has the great poet said in the immortal play—

> "To thine own self be true,
> And it must follow as the day the night,
> Thou canst not then be false to any man."

These are all indisputable truths. If, therefore, men would truly consult their own INTEREST, they must pursue the RIGHT, and do JUSTICE to all men, themselves included. In the grand economy of the moral universe, it is sublimely ordained that MAN'S HIGHEST INTEREST IS HIS DUTY.

---

* Patrick E. Dove, on the Elements of Political Science. Edinburgh and London Edition, 1854. Ch. ii., p. 49.

† Sir William Blackstone, Commentaries on Law, Intro., sec. ii.

§ 10. These great truths, or rather this one great truth thus variously expressed, being indisputably pronounced by the infallible mathematics of human reason in its true normal state, which is the highly enlightened state, it might appear to be wholly immaterial to which of these two great correlative and inseparably connected ideas we may directly address ourselves, either in the realm of Ethics or Sociology. But this would be a grand mistake, just such a grand mistake as the school-room philosophers, we had almost said the SOPHOMORIC philosophers, are constantly committing. No great practical thinker, no truly anointed or thoroughly imbued philosopher will commit any such stupid blunder. On the contrary, in spite of the essential identity of the two grand ideas, of the JUST and the EXPEDIENT, so different are the appearances which they outwardly present to the human view, so often do actions appear just, without any immediate reference to their utility, and expedient, without any immediate reference to their justice, that it is highly important, for all practical purposes, that we should recognize and constantly bear in mind the distinction, or apparent difference, which the mind in its ordinary perceptions naturally makes between them. The observance of this distinction is often important even in Ethics— far more frequently in Sociology. So much more frequently, indeed, is this observance necessary in the latter, than in the former domain of thought, that a different general rule in regard to them arises therefrom. While in the former, the great paramount question to which thought should be immediately addressed, is the idea of the RIGHT, in the latter, precisely the converse is the general rule. In Sociology the great paramount question to which thought, investigation, and effort should be immediately addressed, is, mainly, though not exclusively, EXPEDIENCY.

Here, therefore, we see the great capital error of Mr. Herbert Spencer in his brilliantly written, and in many respects valuable, though in others highly fallacious work, entitled Social Statics—a work which presents us indeed an admirable, and in some important respects original disquisition on Ethical Statics, but a very indifferent, or certainly very insufficient and unreliable one on Social Statics, rightly understood. For, in this work, like his illustrious prototype Plato, in his Ideal Republic, he addresses himself directly and almost exclusively to the idea of JUSTICE. In doing so, he has conclusively shown, not only the insufficiency, but almost inevitable fallaciousness of that mode of investigation in Sociology, which addresses thought all-absorbingly to this idea. His work in question demonstrates the necessity of repeatedly, nay, generally addressing ourselves to the EXPEDIENT,—nay, of consulting the idea of expediency, in order to ascertain that of justice.

For here is the great ground or reason of the necessity for consulting expediency—that it throws light upon the question of justice, just as the question of justice often conversely throws light upon that of expediency. We cannot often see the right except through the spectacles of the expedient. In order to ascertain the just, it is often necessary to bring into requisition all the spy-glasses of expediency. Sometimes we have to use its *telescopes*, sometimes its *microscopes*, sometimes both.

In order to decide what is right, what is best, or what is proper to be done, it is sometimes sufficient to consult simply the idea of the just, sometimes to consult simply that of the expedient. But sometimes again, and in doubtful cases, we have to consult both the just and the expedient, and may deem ourselves fortunate, if even then, with all the combined lights derivable from the suggestions of justice and expediency, in so far as they can be obtained by human intellects, we are enabled to arrive at just, right, or truly wise conclusions. How very fallacious then is the idea that the sense of justice, or the idea of the right, even as expounded and developed on Mr. Spencer's very correct principle, any more than the idea of the expedient, as developed upon that of Bentham, can conduct us uniformly or unerringly to right conclusions!

There is no possibility of obtaining for man any such infallible or perfectly reliable criterion of right. We can only approximate it—can only approximate sure guidance or direction, in relation thereto. Sometimes the idea of the just best directs us, sometimes that of the expedient. Most generally or extensively the former idea best directs us in pure Ethics, the latter in Sociology, except indeed as relates to one department of that wide domain of thought, namely, civil Jurisprudence. For there the idea of the just reigns almost exclusively; yet not entirely so. For how often does even the mere jurist have to appeal to expediency, in doubtful cases, in order to determine what is truly just!

§ 11. While it is true, however, that either the idea of justice or expediency indifferently may be safely applied to for guidance, and that sometimes the one and sometimes the other best directs us, it is to be furthermore remembered, as already intimated, that we have not always the privilege of consulting equally both ideas. They are not always, nor generally indeed, equally presented to our view. In the mystic chain of truth which intertwines human existence sometimes the *links* of expediency only, and sometimes again those of justice alone, are clearly revealed to our view. In the great galvanic battery of universal being sometimes we can observe only the *positive* pole, and sometimes only the *negative*. Or, to use yet another illustration of the same idea, the *Janus-faced* visage of nature, as disclosed to view in the moral realm, sometimes exhibits to our view only her expediency front, and sometimes only that which looks directly toward justice.

We find striking demonstration of the great truth thus sought to be illustrated, in our observations in Sociology. As to a vast variety of matters appertaining to that domain of inquiry we must first ascertain whether they are expedient before we can determine whether they are right. Nay, moreover, as to a vast variety of such matters, there is no question as to their rightfulness or justice, and the only question is as to their expediency, or conduciveness to indisputably proper and eminently desirable ends. He, therefore, who considers the welfare of society only from the stand-point of JUSTICE, as Mr. Spencer has done in his Social Statics, will necessarily omit a great deal that is important, and of the highest importance.

The whole order of social wrongs which Blackstone has properly enough, though not altogether unexceptionably, designated as MALA PROHIBITA,[*] or things to be considered wrong because they

---

[*] See Blackstone's Commentaries on the Laws of England.

are prohibited by the laws of Society, as contradistinguished from the MALA PER SE, or things wrong in themselves, illustrate this general observation. They may all be considered wrong, or opposed to what is right or just, simply because they are ascertained or believed to be inexpedient, or opposed to the interest and welfare of mankind.

What light does the simple question, *what is in itself just or right*, throw upon the great practical question, what acts shall be considered MALA PROHIBITA? Nay, what light does it throw upon a class of questions still more indisputably beyond the reach of the simple idea of justice; questions about which no doubt whatever can arise on the score of justice, and about which the only doubt that can arise is in relation to expediency?

No one, for example, will dispute, no one can doubt, that it is just, right, and proper, nay, eminently so, that all men should be provided with a sufficiency of the primary necessaries of life—with sufficient food, raiment, shelter, and fuel. But how can they be so provided? This is to this day, the *pons asinorum* of Social Philosophy—the great practical question that has not yet been decided, nay, not even thoroughly discussed as yet, even by Malthusian sagacity, with all its important and far-reaching practical conclusions. What light does the idea of mere justice, which is not at all involved, throw—what light can it throw upon this great practical question?

It is true that Mr. Spencer does attempt to grapple with this great question, in his Social Statics, in so far, at least, as the Poorhouse System is concerned. But he commits a vital error in regard to it, and precisely because he attempts to deal with the question mainly, if not exclusively, from the single stand-point of Justice.*

But even in regard to those great questions in Sociology on which the idea of Justice is capable of throwing direct light, how inadequate is it often to the solution of those questions, without the additional light derivable from the most enlarged suggestions of the idea of Expediency! How different, for example, are the

---

* See Chapter XII. of this work, where Mr. Spencer's views on this point are more extensively considered.

reasonings of Plato and Mr. Spencer in regard to justice! What a contrast, in this respect, between the former and the latter Plato!

The former nobly teaches that justice, rightly understood, consists in assigning to each one his DUE, and in ordaining that every man shall pursue his own proper function in the state—that the shoemaker shall make shoes, the hatter shall make hats, the brazier shall deal in brass, the physician shall deal with physic, and the statesman with the destinies of states.*

But hear what our modern Plato teaches in regard to justice. He teaches that justice consists in regarding all men as EQUAL, and therefore, as all equally entitled and qualified to pursue all functions, but most especially the most important, the most difficult, and the least understood functions; that a man who knows nothing about a business has an equal right to manage it with one who is thoroughly acquainted with it, because, argues our modern Plato, all men have equal rights; that this rule applies at least to the highest and most abstruse offices of life, and that a fool has as much right to set the world on fire with his folly, as a wise man has to allay the flames of a disastrous conflagration. He teaches, indeed, that the shoemaker should make shoes, the hatter hats, and the like, but that every one has a right to make laws and rule the destinies of states, or to take an equal hand in the business.

Every one has a right to *vote*, and *suffrage should be universal*, without regard to the fitness of the people for such a dangerous franchise, argues our modern Plato, *because all men have equal rights*. Nay, an illustrious compeer, of the same school of thought, John Stuart Mill, it seems, would abolish the long recognized distinction between the sexes, in respect to this important franchise.

It will only be necessary to go one step farther, to abolish the long-recognized distinction between manhood and *juvenility*, and the ultimatum of human absurdity—to which our modern Platos seem to be fast tending, in their expanded ideas of justice—will

---

* See the immortal work of Plato, entitled the Republic, everywhere.

have been reached at last. In that happy millennium to which they would advance us, we shall reap the fruits of "universal suffrage," as they expound it, when every question, from the highest to the lowest, shall be decided by the ballot-box, and when the children shall every morning take the vote at the breakfast-table, to determine how their parents shall rule the household during the remainder of the day.

Happy would it be for the world if the head of the ancient Plato could reappear on the shoulders of the modern Plato, or, perhaps we should rather say, on the *stilts* of our modern philosopher, which cause him so unduly to estimate his own stature. We might then learn some more just ideas of JUSTICE, as applicable to the great practical issues of the day, than Mr. Spencer has afforded us in many of the weak and superficial reasonings of his Social Statics. Then we might learn that the great DEMOCRATICAL ideas of the age, so little comprehended by many of its unworthy and incompetent exponents, rightly apprehended, lead to very different conclusions from those which are commonly and vulgarly supposed. Then it might be discovered that a true Democracy is not inconsistent with a genuine Aristocracy, and that these two ideas, which are totally inseparable from human society in some form or other, have yet to be harmonized—wisely and justly harmonized, before we shall be able to actualize the best possible condition of human society. Then we might learn that the just harmonizing of those two great and vital ideas of a true "Social Statics," is not to be found in the weak, ridiculous, and palpably false idea, that all men are equally fitted for all offices, or indeed for any office, but in precisely the counter idea, somewhat imperfectly expressed, though nobly appreciated, in part, by the truly great Plato—the idea that different men, different individual men, and different classes, nations and races of men, have their own appropriate functions and parts to play in the grand economy of human existence, and that justice truly consists in assigning to each of these their own appropriate functions.

Then might it be found that true Democracy—a just, enlightened, and truly wise Democracy—does not cherish the low-born idea that Aristocracy is to be either dreaded or despised, but rather the counter and ennobling idea, that it is one of the main ulterior ends of rightly organized human society to develop and cultivate a true aristocracy—an aristocracy of true worth, regardless of extraneous circumstances—an aristocracy to which the humblest son of toil may nobly aspire—an aristocracy which recognizes the great truth that the truly faithful and skilful laborer in any, even the humblest departments of human life, is in his own little sphere an aristocrat, one of nature's own nobility, deserving of universal consideration and esteem.

§ 12. After this perhaps too long digression on the importance of directing inquiries in Sociology to both of the two main ideas of Justice and Expediency, but mainly and most prominently to the latter, we return to the great fundamental observation, that the great primary end to which investigation and effort in this domain of thought, should be directed and conformed, is the discovery of the fundamental causes which determine the social condition of mankind—*first*, of the depressing causes—*secondly*, of the countervailing causes.

Recognizing this as the great primary end of Social Philosophy we shall be able the more readily, as well as more clearly and justly to estimate the efforts that have been hitherto made in this realm of inquiry, and what is now mainly needed in order to complete those efforts. As already observed, no writer as yet appears to have duly appreciated this great primary end or aim of Social Philosophy, and but few have even directly addressed themselves to it, while a great many have not addressed themselves to it at all, except, indeed, by implication, and not unfreqently by very remote implication.

The multitudinous contributors to Social Philosophy may all be regarded as belonging to one or other of two grand divisions— of those who have, either directly or by manifest implication, addressed themselves, however imperfectly or erroneously, to the great primary end to which all such inquiries should be directed, and of those who have not. The latter may be dismissed from all consideration here, as of too little significance to merit any

2*

particular consideration. The former division again may be regarded as belonging to one or other of two other main divisions, or subdivisions, namely, of those who essentially appertain to some organized or clearly distinguishable system of thought, and those who do not. It is proposed in the present disquisition to consider both of these two last named divisions, and more particularly the last of them, as being by far the more important division, and embracing classes of thinkers whose reasonings are too large to be comprehended in either of the systems of thought that may be regarded as organized, or, at least, clearly distinguishable.

There are three clearly distinguishable systems of thought, to one or other of which nearly all the noteworthy contributions to Social Philosophy hitherto may be referred, in whole or in part. These three different systems may be designated respectively, and will be in these pages, as the Political, the Politico-Economical, and the Malthusian.

The distinguishing idea of the reasonings of the first named system, or of the Political school, is that they, either positively or negatively, directly or indirectly, expressly or by implication, attribute the social ills of mankind which demand consideration, to some defect or deficiency, some error or omission in the Government, or political organism, or, in a yet larger sense to speak, in the social organism of the society. The distinguishing idea of the second, or the Politico-Economical school, is that they indirectly and by implication, rather than directly or expressly, attribute those ills to some misapprehension of the laws of Wealth, and a consequent deficiency of Wealth. The distinguishing idea of the last, or the Malthusian school, it should hardly be necessary to say, is that they directly and explicitly attribute those ills to a misapprehension and disregard of the laws of Population, and a consequent excess of Population.

It can scarcely be necessary to add here, that the founder of the Malthusian school was the Reverend Thomas Malthus; that the true organizer, rather than founder, of the Politico-Economical was Adam Smith, and that the Political school has no known author or organizer—running back to a remote antiquity, and constituting the first school of thought, as being the most superficial, which inquiries in Social Philosophy would naturally embrace. For here again we find our great fundamental law of mental evolution clearly illustrated—*the most superficial ideas come first into general recognition.*

While, however, the Political school cannot show any known author, or extensive organizer, it can at least present one preeminently conspicuous exponent, a cotemporary of Malthus and Adam Smith, one William Godwin, who may justly claim the unenviable distinction of having carried the fundamental error of this school of Social Philosophy to its most extreme and absurd applications. The absurdities of this ridiculous sophist, as displayed in his notable work, entitled Political Justice, were the immediate occasion of the ever memorable Essay on Population. To the absurdities of Godwin, therefore, we are immediately indebted for the wisdom of Malthus. So true it is that evil is often, if not generally, the parent of good, that absurdity breeds wisdom, and truth springs even out of the very heart of falsehood. As the expiring lamp often gives out its brightest flame towards the very last, so the waning and sickly Political school of Social Philosophy emitted its most glaring absurdities in the reasonings of Godwin's Political Justice. That ghostly flicker of expiring absurdity was not in vain. It started the spirit of Malthus, which has accomplished much, but not all that was needed, by a great deal, in this domain of thought. He has penetrated more deeply, than any other enlarged or systematic inquirer, toward the fundamental causes, but not deeply enough. He has indeed struck down into the upper crust of the great PRIMITIVE FORMATIONS of social geology, so to speak; but he has not disclosed to view the whole, nor even the greater part of those grand formations.

It should be further observed that, under the title of Politico-Economical school, is not embraced every writer on Political Economy, and that, as the science of Population is one thing and Malthusianism another, so is the science of Political Economy one thing, and the school of Social Philosophy to which most political economists, though not all, belong, quite another. John

Stuart Mill, for example, has written ably on Political Economy; but he is much more a Malthusian, than an exponent of the Politico-economical school of Social Philosophy, although to some extent both. Dr. Chalmers, too has written avowedly on Political Economy; but he is essentially and exclusively a Malthusian.

Many reasoners again, who are no political economists, and who have not brain enough to comprehend so abstruse and great a science, nevertheless belong to the Politico-economical school of thought, as here intended and defined; for the whole of their philosophy is comprised in plans for merely *increasing the wealth, or available wealth of society.* Such petty theorists we find in those who expect to accomplish great things for the destitute classes of society by merely abolishing tithes, diminishing the expenses of the civil list, reducing taxes, reclaiming wastes, or abolishing the extensive parks and pleasure grounds of the rich, and converting them into productive fields. Poor, contracted, short-sighted reasoners! What do they know of the causes which really determine the social condition of mankind? For their shallow philosophy that of Malthus is amply sufficient and more than sufficient. But we need a deeper and more comprehensive philosophy by far than that of Malthus. Toward that Philosophy let us proceed.

It is proposed, in the present work, to show the total insufficiency of the three existing systems of thought in Social Philosophy, as already defined,—their inadequacy to solve the great fundamental problem in that Philosophy demanding solution, *as to the causes which really and fundamentally determine the social condition of mankind,* and then to indicate the tendencies toward that larger system, which it is the aim of the present inquirer to organize and systematize. In executing the former part of this work, we shall be brief, as that part has been already fully executed in three separate works, or parts of the series to which this appertains, not as yet submitted to the world, and of which the reasonings here presented on that head are merely recapitulatory. In executing the latter we shall be more particular and more elaborate.

CHAPTER I.

THE THREE EXISTING SYSTEMS OF THOUGHT IN SOCIAL PHILOSOPHY, CONSIDERED BY THE EXPERIMENTAL TEST OR FROM THE PRACTICAL STAND-POINT—THEIR MANIFEST INSUFFICIENCY AS THUS EXHIBITED.

§ 1. WHEN the great astronomer [*Newton*] undertook to ascertain the fundamental or mathematical principles of Natural Philosophy,* he directed his inquiries, primarily and immediately, to the great fundamental question, What are the causes or laws which determine the movements of MATTER, whether in the form of pebbles or of worlds. In like manner, when we undertake to ascertain the fundamental or primary principles of Social Philosophy, we must direct our inquiries, primarily and immediately, to the great fundamental question, What are the causes or laws which determine the movements or conditions of MAN, whether in the form of the individual, or of the nation?

So imperfect, however, has been the development of ideas hitherto in this domain of thought, as we have already seen,† that very few, if any, of the many eminent thinkers who have sought, in one way or the other, to illustrate it, have directed their inquiries, immediately, or otherwise than indirectly and by implication, to this great primary and fundamental question. In so far as thought has been systematically so addressed, or with any considerable approximation toward system, as already shown,‡ it may be referred to one or other of three different systems or schools, which may be respectively designated as the Political, the Politico-economical, and the Malthusian—the first of which schools, either directly or indirectly, attributes the social ills demanding consideration to *political causes*, or to some misapprehension or disregard of the true principles of GOVERNMENT—the second to some misapprehension or disregard of the principles or

---

* His immortal work is entitled *Philosophiæ Naturalis Principia Mathematica*, or Mathematical Principles of Natural Philosophy.
† See Introduction.   ‡ See same, § 12.

laws of WEALTH, and the third to some misapprehension or disregard of the laws of POPULATION.

A very little consideration must be sufficient to show the insufficiency of each one of these three systems, and their inadequacy to form the basis of a thorough Philosophy of Society, or a complete science of Sociology—the meagreness of the expositions they present of the laws which determine the social condition of mankind—their inadequacy to meet the requirements of the great social problem to be solved, HOW IS A PROPER SOCIAL CONDITION FOR MANKIND TO BE INSURED?—their failure to discern the radical or fundamental causes which depress the social condition, or to indicate, clearly, intelligently, and consistently, the aims to which attention should be mainly directed, with a view to counteracting, and, so far as possible, eradicating those causes.

It is true, indeed, that considerable progress has been made by the latest of those systems, the Malthusian, towards a full discovery of the aims to which attention should be mainly directed, or the *practical* ends to be aimed at by the social philosopher, which constitute what may be termed the remedial policy of Social Philosophy, but without a full or just appreciation of the reasons for that policy, or adequate cognition of the CAUSES of those social ills which it is sought to remedy.

As a right appreciation of the causes of the phenomena, coming within the scope of its observations, is one of the most important requisites for every science, indispensable to a rational and consistent vindication of its remedial policy, however just or wise that policy may chance to be, and without which a consistent adherence to that policy cannot be relied upon, we must adjudge the Malthusian, as well as the two other systems or schools of Social Philosophy, very imperfect and insufficient to form the basis of a thorough system or science of Sociology. Accordingly, and as might be expected from its imperfect and meagre induction of causes, we find that Malthusian philosophy, while it rightly aims at the noble end of ELEVATING THE MORAL STATUS OF MANKIND, does so only on a very limited scale, and with almost exclusive reference to counteracting what it erroneously regards as the main cause which depresses or degrades the social condition of mankind—the too great tendency of the human species, in common with all animated nature, to multiply its numbers.

§ 2. It is only when a science has thoroughly apprehended the causes of the phenomena with which it has to deal, that it can be expected to frame a remedial policy, fully adequate to the control or modification of those phenomena, in so far, indeed, as they may admit of control, or modification, by human agency. In this mainly consists the great insufficiency of the existing systems of social philosophy. They are all too superficial and contracted in the scope of their induction and reasoning as to the CAUSES which determine the social condition, while only one of them has made any important advance toward thoroughly correct views as to the proper modes of attempting to improve it. Their *diagnosis* of causes is very imperfect, if not absolutely erroneous, while only one of them has attained to a tolerably correct *therapeutics*, for the social maladies which it is sought to cure.

The Political system, the most superficial of them all, as already before shown, attributes the ills of the social state, which it is proposed to remedy, to some defect in the Government, or political organism of society, and vainly looks to some reorganization of that organism, or to some action or other on the part of government, for their removal or correction. The Politico-economical system impliedly, though not avowedly, attributes those ills, or all the ills that it seems to regard as worthy of any serious consideration, to some mistake or misapprehension in regard to the laws of Wealth, and not much less vainly seeks to remedy those ills by disseminating correct views in regard to those laws, and, more particularly, by actually increasing the aggregate or general wealth of society. The Malthusian system, much less superficial and unphilosophical than either of the other two, attributes those ills to the tendency of all animated nature to press too closely upon its means of subsistence, thus striking down, it is true, to the very ROOTS of the matter, as exhibited in THE PRIMITIVE AND INEVITABLE LAWS OF NATURE, but confining its attention only to one root of a manifold cluster of roots, and that too not the TAP-ROOT—attributing, justly indeed, the ills of the social state to the primitive and inevitable laws of nature, but taking altogether too partial and contracted a view of those laws, in their tendency to determine, and more particularly to depress, the social or economical condition of mankind.

§ 3. That neither of these causes, to which these three different systems or schools of Social Philosophy respectively direct their main attention, is the true cause, or main true cause, of the social ills which they seek to remedy, or the main true cause to which attention should be mainly directed, may be demonstrated by considering what effect would be produced by the removal of those causes. Nor does the insufficiency of these several systems really need any more conclusive demonstration than is afforded by the illustration which may be thus obtained, how little is effected, for the welfare of society, by accomplishing for it all that they severally seek to accomplish, or, rather, how lamentable the accomplishment of the ends they aim at, fails to remedy the ills complained of.

If the idea of the Political school were correct, then it would follow that under political institutions conformed to their views, in the main, if not entirely, the social ills complained of would no longer exist, or not at least in anything like nearly the same proportion as under political institutions diametrically opposed to their views. If the idea of the Politico-economical school were correct, then it would follow that in those countries in which the science of Wealth had been cultivated with great success, and in such a manner as to cause wealth to abound to an extraordinary degree, those ills should not exist, or at least only in a very mild and mitigated form. If the idea of the Malthusian school were correct then it would not less follow, that, in those countries in which population is scanty, and much in request, as in colonial settlements, or other newly settled countries, like California and Australia, those ills would not exist.

§ 4. But there is abundant evidence, experimental as well as more purely rational, that no such result is obtainable from either of the conditions indicated, nor indeed from all combined. Thus it is found, that, in the United States, where the political institutions are conformed to the most approved ideas of the Political school, in the main, if not exactly and completely, those social ills which have ever formed the subject of complaint since organized human society began, exist, to almost as great an extent as under the anti-republican governments of Europe, which are essentially antagonistic to their ideas, and to very little, if any, less extent than is sufficiently explained, and accounted for by the far less density of population in those states—by the fact that they are new, while the European states are old countries.

In the United States, just as in European countries, we find, although in a much less marked degree—as in all new, or rather young societies,—the same tendency to the formation of a broad line of demarcation between the capitalist and laborer, which has been the subject of complaint ever since the formation of civilized society, the same tendency of the rich to become richer and the poor poorer, the same tendency of one portion of society to become altogether too rich and of another to become or to remain altogether too poor, the same tendency of the workings of the social organism, or, rather of the organism of the Universe, as manifested in that part of universal nature which the social organism constitutes, to throw off a large number of its component members from all opportunity of earning a competent livelihood, and dooming them to the sorrowful condition so touchingly described in the melancholy language of Holy Writ, "the foxes have dens and the birds of the air have nests, but the son of man hath not where to lay his head."

Thus, in like manner, it is found that in England, where the science of wealth has been cultivated with extraordinary success, and where it is generally and justly conceded that wealth more abounds than in any other country in the world, social distress, in its various forms, also prevails to an extraordinary degree, and, in fact, to a much greater extent, and in much more aggravated forms, than in far less wealthy countries, in relatively poor countries, such as Switzerland, Norway, Sweden and Denmark—thus conclusively demonstrating that it is not to a mere increase of national wealth, nor to a just apprehension of the laws of wealth leading to such increase, that we are to look for a removal of the causes which depress the social condition of mankind.

Thus, also, it is found that, in new colonial settlements, as Australia, California, and many of the more recently settled states of the American Union, where the great want is more population, an increase of labor, there is not, by any means, an absence of the social distress which forms the subject of general complaint in human society, as should be the case if the Malthusian idea were strictly correct, but, on the contrary, a widespread and almost universal want of the proper comforts of life—thus conclusively showing that it is not to a mere reduction of population that we are to look for an improvement of the social condition, nor to a mere excess of population that we are to look for the cause which most fundamentally and extensively depresses the social condition.

It is true, indeed, that, in such states of society as we find in these newly-settled countries, there is very little of the kind of suffering that forms the most prominent subject of complaint in human society, and which is so glaringly manifest in older societies,—very little of the inability of able-bodied laborers to obtain employment—very little of that ruinously low rate of wages which is one of the greatest banes of society—very little of absolute pauperism, or abject want, on the part of any considerable class or number of the community.

This exemption from the most prominent ills of the social state, however, is dearly purchased, for such states of society, by the sacrifice of the general comfort of the society at large. For while such states of society are eminently favorable to the lower classes, they are eminently unfavorable to the higher, and, what is more important, eminently unfavorable to the general welfare of the community—building up the fortunes of one important class, but pulling down those of another, and lowering the general condition and average comfort of the society —affording, indeed, a paradise to the laboring man, but rendering existence impossible, to a class scarcely less indispensable to a model condition of human society, than a well-conditioned labor class, a highly educated and refined affluent class.

§ 5. This exemption, nevertheless, which such states of society enjoy, from the most prominent and probably most serious ills of the social state, bears suggestive and conclusive testimony to the truth of the Malthusian idea, to a considerable and very important extent—thus conclusively showing, also, that it is much nearer the truth, the whole truth, that we are in quest of, than either of the other two systems. For truth is ever consistent with itself, in spite of apparent contradictions, sometimes to be encountered; and in as much as the Malthusian idea is, to a considerable and very important extent, true, inasmuch as over-population is in reality one of the immediate causes which depress and degrade the social condition, whenever that circumstance is removed, we find the social condition materially improved, in respect, at least, to the most prominent ills that demand redress. But inasmuch as over-population is not the sole cause, nor indeed the main cause, of social degradation, its removal fails to effect the removal of all the ills that demand redress, or to insure the end proposed—a proper social condition.

Inasmuch as the leading ideas of the Political and Politico-Economical schools have little or no truth in them, except, indeed, indirectly and remotely, inasmuch as what they respectively regard as the main causes that depress the social condition, are not in reality among the IMMEDIATE causes at all, but only among the INDIRECT and REMOTE causes leading to that result, the removal of those causes, we find, accordingly, does not exert any sensible influence whatever in improving the social condition, in respect, at least, to those more prominent ills observable in the social state to which philosophical attention is and ought to be most generally directed—the lamentable poverty of the poor and the scarcely less lamentable affluence of the rich.

§ 6. Thus it appears that we may accomplish for human society all that each one of the existing schools of Social Philosophy seeks to accomplish, and yet manifestly fail to attain the end proposed—a model condition of human society, or more simply to speak, A PROPER CONDITION OF HUMAN SOCIETY, which may be defined, in brief, as that in which the comfort of all is insured, and the affluence of a large class.

Not much more difficult is it to demonstrate, that we may accomplish for human society all that these three schools combined seek to accomplish, and yet fail to attain the desired end— that, in short, what each one of these schools singly fails to accomplish they all combined fail to accomplish.

That this is so we may find conclusive illustration and demonstration, experimentally, in the example of the United States of America, already cited. In those states we find actualized, to a very great extent, and to a far greater extent than anywhere else, or ever before, all the three conditions which the three existing schools of Social Philosophy make their controlling ends respectively, and yet we find, as before remarked, a sad failure to actualize the desired end—a model or proper condition of human society—a condition, in short, in which few are perniciously wealthy, many are affluent, all comfortable, and none, therefore, destitute.

In the United States we find almost perfect government, or almost as perfect as the nature of man allows, an average of national wealth scarcely if at all second to that of England, and a general scantiness of population actually, and more especially in relation to the ultimate capacities of the country to support population, so great as to make an increase of population one of the greatest wants of society everywhere throughout those states. But the desired end has not been attained. A proper condition of human society has not been actualized. On the contrary, throughout the United States, as well as throughout the states of Europe, although of course in far less proportion, one of the most glaring ills observable in the social condition, GAUNT PAUPERISM, stalks abroad.

From every state of the American confederacy the cry of destitution audibly and systematically arises, which is always and everywhere trivial in comparison with that which is stifled by the sentiments of an honorable pride and proper self-respect, or is only uttered in the half-suppressed sighs and groans which poverty will wring even from the noblest soul when struggling too hard with its grievous trials.

In the State of New York, which is in many respects the most favorably circumstanced of the United States, there were, in 1843, not less than 82,754 regular paupers, or about one in thirty to the total population; and, in addition to these, there were 62,047 paupers temporarily relieved by the public officers, making an aggregate of 144,801 paupers, or about *one* to every *eighteen* of the inhabitants of this eminently fortunate state.*

In Massachusetts, a state even more favorably circumstanced than New York, every respect being considered, and decidedly the most favorably circumstanced of all the American states in respect to its political institutions, there were, during the same year, 15,655 regular paupers, or about one to forty-eight of the total population,† showing a much smaller proportion of pauperism, indeed, than in New York, where the proportion is doubtless increased largely by the larger percentage of foreign immigration, but sufficiently large to indicate that even in this, the most favorably circumstanced of all the highly favored American states, one of the most glaring and aggravated of the ills, observable in the social state, exists to a very grievous extent.

§ 7. Conclusive as is the demonstration thus practically afforded, by the condition of society in the United States, of the insufficiency and fallaciousness of all the three existing schools of Social Philosophy, to some portions of the political school, to those who belong to what we have elsewhere designated as the THIRD CLASS of that school,‡ this demonstration will not be satisfactory. Having no other stock in trade than the pitiful idea, that GOVERNMENT is the cause of all the ills experienced by human society, to this idea they adhere with incorrigible tenacity. Like the doleful bird, known to the poetical world as "Poe's Raven,"

---

* See American Almanac for 1845, p. 226. Upon a point so indisputable, it has not been deemed necessary to invoke any more recent statistical reports.

† See same authority, p. 241. The number of paupers temporarily relieved in Massachusetts is not stated.

‡ See Part III. of this Series, Chapter 3, not yet published.

whose only stock in trade was the single word, it had somewhere picked up, and which constituted its sole response to every question,—"nevermore,"—these senseless declaimers, against the injustice of GOVERNMENTS, have no other response for any and every question concerning the causes which depress or injuriously affect the social condition, under any circumstances, than that it is owing to some wrong, or fault, or error on the part of GOVERNMENT, to which alone they direct their contracted views. In Europe, indeed, they make this response in relation to the condition of things there, with some show of reason, some color of justice. But they are not less pertinacious in making it, also, in regard to the condition of things in America, where there is no justification or excuse for such stupidity.

In Europe, these contracted theorists of the political school, are for ever crying out for a government like that of the United States. Regardless of the existing state of society there—profoundly ignorant of the important truth that governments do not form society, but society governments—profoundly ignorant that governments are the mere *outgrowths* of society, which is itself but the *framework* of the existing ideas and habits of the people composing it, and that if any other government were *manufactured* for a people, or attempted to be set up over them, than such as is the spontaneous and natural *outgrowth* of the existing state of their habits and ideas, it could not permanently stand, could not take root or thrive—these unwise revolutionists are forever striving to subvert the existing governments of Europe, and substitute in their stead such government as exists in the United States of America. Give us but such government as they have in the United States, cry these short-sighted reformers, and we shall regenerate society in Europe, and cure all its serious maladies.

Well, they have such a government granted to them, in America, as they are constantly praying for in Europe, as the *panacea* for all their woes. But what does it avail them? They are still not satisfied with the government, nor of the fallaciousness of their theory, respecting the causes which depress the social condition, and which have to be countervailed in order to elevate it. They still insist that it is owing to some fault in the *government,* or existing social *organism,* that the desired condition for mankind is not actualized.

In the language of one of their organs, from an American standpoint, Mr. Stephen Pearl Andrews, who has been before alluded to, in a preceding part of this work,* it is owing to "some subtile and undiscovered cause of manifold evils lying hid down in the very foundations of our existing social fabric," and which he, in the plenitude of his simplicity, proposes to remedy by allowing every man to manufacture money as he wants it, by issuing his own notes of hand,—a prescription about as wise and efficacious as that which should declare that every man shall be at liberty to fix the state of the thermometer for the climate he lives in, and to ordain, if it so please him, that the mercury shall never fall below *seventy*, nor rise above *seventy-five*.

But what this "subtile and undiscovered cause" is, these sage Solons have never been able to determine satisfactorily either to themselves or others. While some opine, doubtless, with Mr. Stephen Pearl Andrews, that the cause is the inability of every man to impart the same credit to his notes of hand that any other man has—his inability, in short, to convert his own private pocket into a bank of circulation—some assert that it is the want of "free trade," others that is "too much free trade," others again, that it is "land monopoly." Nor is it at all uncommon in American society, to find some seedy gentleman, who, from some one or more of the manifold causes, either positive or negative, which really depress the social condition—possibly because he he was too lazy to work, or lacked the judgment to work judiciously, has been unsuccessful in business—who, discoursing largely on the errors of government, slaps his hand emphatically upon his thigh, assures the company that he has given the subject his profound attention, and that his own misfortunes and those of the rest of mankind, are all owing to "class legislation."

With this class of thinkers, however, we have already dealt sufficiently in a former part of our work,† or the series to

---

* See Part III., Chap. 3d of this series. † Part III., Chap. 3.

which this belongs, nor would it be profitable to waste more time with them, now that we are hastening towards, and are nearly arrived at, the grand conclusions, and all-embracing, all-harmonizing ideas, of the system to be proposed, in which every system, and every class of ideas, will find themselves distinctly recognized, in so far as they are true, and in respect to their proper relations to the grand science of Sociology.

CHAPTER II.

THE INSUFFICIENCY OF THE THREE EXISTING SYSTEMS CONSIDERED BY THE RATIONAL TEST, OR FROM THE THEORETICAL STAND-POINT.

§ 1. However unsatisfactory, to the visionary class of thinkers alluded to in the foregoing chapter, may be the demonstration, practically afforded by the condition of things in the United States, of the insufficiency and fundamental erroneousness of all the three existing schools of Social Philosophy, to all truly scientific or truly philosophical minds, it must appear conclusive; for it merely ratifies and confirms the conclusions of reason. It is merely an EXPERIMENTAL verification of a RATIONAL deduction. It is entirely in accordance with what reason, aided by general observation, adjudges to be true.

REASON, aided only by general observation, if not in its strictly *a priori* conclusions, pronounces—what in the condition of things in the United States we find specially tested and verified—that each one of the three existing schools of social philosophy is insufficient and fundamentally erroneous; that they are, each and all, in error as to the real CAUSE or CAUSES which depress the social condition of mankind, and that we might, therefore, accomplish for mankind all that they severally and jointly seek to accomplish, and yet fail to actualize the desired end—A PROPER CONDITION OF HUMAN SOCIETY.

§ 2. Reason adjudges that government, or, in a yet larger sense, the organism of human society, cannot properly be regarded as the cause of the social condition existing under it, and that, therefore, any attempt to change that government or organism, as a means of improving the social condition—except, indeed, in so far as such attempt may be in aid of the spontaneous movement of the society itself—must be unavailing and delusive, because government, or the organism of society, is not, by any means, so much the CAUSE as the EFFECT of the social condition.

Government is the foliage, not the root of the social condition. It is but the natural outgrowth of the state of society in which it exists, and although it may be modified to a considerable extent, by culture, and influences *ab extra* brought to bear upon it, it can never be essentially changed, or rendered radically different from what the existing state of society tends to make it. It can no more be so radically changed, than the vegetation natural to certain soils and climates—no more, indeed, than oranges or pine-apples can be made to grow in Norway or Russia. Nor is it any less true, that if it could be so changed, as it could only be by influences *ab extra*, it would not materially change that social condition from which the existing government had sprung, as an indigenous growth.

To seek to change the social condition of a people, therefore, by merely changing their government or social organism, is like seeking to remove the CAUSE by attacking merely its EFFECTS—like seeking to cure the DISEASE by treating merely one of its SYMPTOMS. It is like seeking to affect the roots of the tree by merely clipping or dressing its branches, which may be indeed, under some circumstances, beneficial, but must always be superficial and very limited in its influence. Nay, moreover, we may say, it is like seeking to change the very soil and climate of a country, by merely changing the character of its vegetation, as by introducing new grasses or cereals, which indeed, we know, may exert some influence on the soil, at least, and very faintly also on the climate,* but must always be trivial in its effects, in comparison with the influence which those natural conditions exert, in determining the character of its flora.

As the flora or vegetation of a country reacts on the character

---

* It would be a great mistake to suppose that the climate of a country cannot be at all affected or modified by a change of its *flora*. Though no appreciable effect may be so produced upon its *thermometrical* character, a very decided one may be produced on its *hygrometrical*, and what is perhaps more important, on its *hygienic* character. There seems to be no doubt that the climate of Egypt, in respect to the moisture discharged by its atmosphere, especially in the form of rain, has been materially changed by the great number of trees planted by Mohammed Ali. It rains now copiously in parts of that country where before it never rained. (See Mitchell's Geography. Title Egypt.)

of the soil and climate from which it originally sprang, and as the introduction of a new flora, by *ab extra* influences, may modify that soil and climate, so, and to no greater extent whatever, may government react on the social condition from which it spontaneously sprang, or modify that condition, when it is introduced by extraneous or foreign agencies.

For government, as we have before had occasion to remark, while reviewing Roman Sociology,* may be likened to the BANYAN-TREE, which, although its growth, like that of other trees, is originally occasioned by the character of the soil and climate in which it flourishes, yet, when it has once attained its full development, reacts powerfully on the soil, and somewhat also on the climate, overshadowing the ground, and influencing to a considerable extent, the vegetation around it. But you cannot make the BANYAN-TREE grow in England. Nor can you make some kinds of government thrive among some kinds of people: as, monarchy, properly so called, that is, absolute monarchy, among Anglo-Saxons; democracy among Frenchmen; or good government of any kind among Hottentots or negroes.

The endeavor to improve the social condition of mankind by merely tinkering with their political institutions, which is, to this day, the controlling aim of statesmen in general, not less than of popular reformers, and their auditory, the populace—this endeavor to remove the *cause* by attacking merely its *effects*—to cure the *disease* by treating merely one of its *symptoms*—to change the very *climate* of a country, as it were, by merely introducing a new *flora* —is, in short, about as unavailing and preposterous as would be the endeavor to cure the Asiatic cholera by merely applying a smelling-bottle to the patient's nose, to relieve his nausea; or the endeavor to change the climate of Kamtschatka by introducing into that country the bananas, the palm-trees, and orange groves of a tropical clime.

Quite evidently, it is in some other direction, than that in which the political school point us, that we are to look for the causes which really depress the social condition of mankind, and the in-

---

* See Part II. of this series, Chap. III.

fluences that are to countervail those causes, and elevate that condition.

§ 3. Reason adjudges, also, although in less strong and energetic terms, that the mere knowledge of the laws of Wealth, or rational perception of the processes by which it is created, cannot properly be regarded as the CAUSE of the social condition of a people, in respect to the degree of wealth they may possess, nor the mere increase of their aggregate national wealth resulting from such knowledge; and that, therefore, any endeavor, like that of the Political Economists, to disseminate correct ideas in regard to those laws, and thereby, moreover, to increase the aggregate national wealth, as a means of improving the social condition, must be delusive, or of little avail; because the acquisition of wealth does not so much depend on a RATIONAL PERCEPTION of the processes by which wealth is produced, as on the possession of those energies, physical, moral, and intellectual, by which those processes are carried on. Nor does a proper social condition, by any means, so much depend on the mere aggregate mass of national wealth, as upon the *manner* in which that wealth is *distributed*, which can only be effectually determined and controlled by the same agencies by which wealth is *produced*—by the requisite energies, in the different individuals composing the nation, for diverting, from the aggregate mass of the national wealth, a proper share for their own requirements.

The error of the Politico-Economical School is, in short, very nearly akin to that of the Political. It is the same error, though in a less aggravated or palpable form, of mistaking the EFFECT for the CAUSE—of endeavoring to reach the CAUSE by operating merely on the EFFECT. For Political Economists evidently do not so much regard MAN as the cause and creator of Wealth as they regard WEALTH as the cause and creator of man. Such, at least, to all practical intents and purposes, appears to be their view. Instead of treating Wealth as a mere incident and appendage to Man, they constantly treat Man as a mere incident and appendage to Wealth. They make Wealth, in short, not Man, the primary object of consideration. This is the great fundamental error of the Politico-Economical School—an error which involves all their reasonings, misguides all their aims, vitiates all their conclusions.

Obviously enough, it should appear, the Political Economists have committed the blunder of putting the cart before the horse. Nor need we wonder that, in such an awkward procedure, they have made so little progress towards the desired end, the amelioration of the human condition. In the method of their philosophy they have exalted the incident above the principal, the CREATURE above the CREATOR. It was in reference to this great fundamental error, of this school, that Sismondi, himself one of the school, whose mind, however, had expanded beyond the measure of the contracted ligaments which restrain the inquiries of that school, exclaimed—"What, then, is wealth everything, and man nothing?"*

§ 4. It is remarkable how mankind are constantly committing this error, in their advance towards the truth, in every Science. Their constant proneness to this error may afford some verification of Comte's somewhat obscure law of the three stages, through which the human mind ever passes in its advance toward true science—the theological, metaphysical, and positive. But it more manifestly affords verification of the more obvious and indisputable law, or truth, that mankind are always caught and deceived, at first, by the more obvious and superficial view of things, and are only, slowly and by degrees, advanced towards the less obvious and more profound view, which is invariably the more important and more suggestive of the whole truth.

Thus, in Astronomy, we find them for a long time regarding the earth as the stationary centre of the Solar system, and not until the time of Copernicus definitely ascertaining that the very reverse of this, the apparent view, was the true one. Thus, too, in Geology, we find them beginning their observations, as is very natural, with the rocks lying on the surface, which, in most countries, are either the *tertiary* or *secondary* formations, and only

---

* See the translated Essays of Sismondi on various Political and Politico-Economical questions. London Ed., 1847, p. 43, also *postea* Chap. X, § 3.

at a later period of their investigations, striking down into the more fundamental and *primary*.

Perhaps, indeed, the geological stratification of the Earth, and the order in which it is gradually unfolded to the human view, may be accepted as a perfect type and illustration of the order in which the human mind naturally, if not necessarily, proceeds towards a thorough knowledge of the external world, in all its aspects—*an inverted order*—as we see illustrated, furthermore, in the order in which external objects are presented to the mind, by a picture painted, or daguerreotyped, as it were, on the retina of the eye—*upside down*.*

However this may be, as a universal law, there can be no doubt of its very extensive applications. We find it verified in Astronomy, in Geology, and in Sociology. As in astronomy and geology, so in Sociology, we here find that mankind have been until now, with the exception of some vague and disconnected suggestions of the reverse method, and some imperfect approximation toward it, in practice, on the part of the Malthusians, confining their attention to the mere *surface* of human society in quest of the causes which determine its condition—to the most *obvious* and *superficial* view of the social condition for a solution of its most abstruse problems—to the mere EFFECTS of the social condition, for a discovery of its CAUSES.

Thus it is that we find Social Philosophers, until now, almost exclusively directing their attention either to the mere political institutions which Man throws around him, or, somewhat less superficially, to the mere wealth which he creates with his own hands, for the real causes of his prosperity, or the reverse, and never as yet fixing their attention directly, and most prominently, if not exclusively, on MAN HIMSELF, who, under subjection to

---

* As may readily be detected, here the idea first suggested itself to the author, which, in the Introduction to this work, has been so much more fully developed. That introduction, like most introductions, being written last, the author was best prepared, in that part of his work, to do justice to the idea. For this is in accordance with the great law itself, so little understood or considered. The most important ideas come last, in the order of discovery, though they should come first in the scientific order of considering them. The last, then, becomes first, and the first last.

some control from the laws of his NATURAL ENVIRONMENT, is, and must ever be the real Architect of his fortunes, the true Creator of his destiny*—to MAN, HIMSELF, who is, ever has been, and ever must be, the "Alpha and Omega, the beginning and the end, the first and the last," of all that concerns his Social destiny.

§ 5. In addition to this great fundamental error of the Politico-economical school, of supposing that the improvement of the social condition of mankind is to be effected by fixing attention directly on the laws of wealth, instead of the laws of man's own nature, physical, moral and intellectual, two other more particular errors of their system, nearly allied to this fundamental one, if not its natural offspring, may claim some more particular notice here. These are, *first*, the general idea, implied in their mode of reasoning, that a knowledge or rational perception of the laws of wealth is necessary, or at least essentially conducive to its acquisition, and, *secondly*, the more particular idea, not less manifestly implied in their philosophy, that an increase of the aggre-

---

* The author must beg to be here explicitly understood, in pronouncing man the architect of his fortunes and creator of his destiny, as speaking in a *physical* and practical sense, merely, not in a *metaphysical*, or strictly philosophical, strictly correct, sense. For, strictly speaking, man is neither a creator nor architect, but a mere *instrumentality*, a mere *manifestation* of some unseen, unappreciated REALITY. He is but a part of the grand machinery of the universe; in all his acts, like every other part of that grand machinery, conforming to laws, fixed, inevitable, mathematically certain, and necessary, laws—even in his *volitions*, which, though superficially and vulgarly supposed to be, unlike other mental phenomena, self-created and independent of law, are, in reality, as much governed by law as any other phenomena, either mental or physical. GOD, himself—if the atheistic tendencies of recent science will allow such a term —GOD, himself, cannot WILL, except in conformity, in rigid obedience to law, fixed, inevitable, mathematically certain, and exact law. How absurd, then, to talk about the volitions of man being *free?* Admitting it to be true, as asserted by the weak adherents of the free-will school, or free-agency school, of Ethics, *that a man can do as he wills*, which is true only as to a very few things, still it remains to consider, *can he will as he wills;* or, rather, can he *will*, except in conformity to law, to law inevitable and beyond his control? Can he *will*, except as his natural propensities, as modified by the whole train of circumstances by which he has been surrounded from his birth, and as influenced by all the surroundings of the moment, prompt and imperatively ordain?

gate national wealth is, *in itself* beneficial. Neither of these ideas is correct, except to a qualified and very limited extent.

A knowledge of the laws of wealth is not necessary to its acquisition—not any more so than is a knowledge of the laws of health necessary to the possession of health—not any more so than is a knowledge of the laws of physiology necessary to the right movement of the human frame. A man does not require a knowledge of physiology in order to know that he should step forward instead of backward, nor to teach him how to contract his muscles, in order to leap a fence or dodge a stone. All these things, and many more, he learns to do instinctively and unconsciously, and so he does also, to a qualified extent, and certainly to a far less extent, in regard to the acquisition of wealth. He instinctively, and almost unconsciously, follows the suggestions of those physical, moral and intellectual activities of his nature that are the real producers of wealth, without concerning himself at all with rational considerations as to the mode in which his exertions tend to the production of wealth.

Many of the healthiest and most robust men are profoundly ignorant of the laws of physiology, as well as of therapeutics, and hygiene, while many of the most delicate and unhealthy are precisely those who are most conversant with those laws. Nor is it any less true that the men who are most successful in producing or acquiring wealth are often those who know least about its abstract or scientific principles. The bee amasses wealth without any knowledge of the laws of political economy, and so does man.

Of what great avail, then, is the dissemination of knowledge respecting those laws—respecting the merely abstract and scientific principles of wealth? Of some avail undoubtedly it is—of some importance, as already remarked in a former part of our work. It is important, however, only as is the influence of government important—*indirectly and remotely*—but having little or no direct or immediate bearing on the social condition of a people. It is important, undoubtedly, with a view to preventing governments from so acting, through ignorance of those laws, as to be the occasion of positive injury to the industrial or economical interests of society.

§ 6. Quite as little truth is there in the more particular idea of this school to which their more peculiarly specific aim is conformed, that an increase of the aggregate national wealth is, *in itself*, beneficial. For general observation and experience clearly enough indicate, what reasoning from analogy would infer, THAT IN SOCIOLOGY AS IN ASTRONOMY, GRAVITATION IS TOWARDS THE LARGER BODY—a law which finds its expression in Sociology in the constant tendency of the rich to become richer and the poor poorer, after the society has attained a certain development, or density of population, as a density varying according to circumstances, from one hundred to two hundred to the square mile—in the constant tendency of an increase of the national wealth in such societies to aggravate this two-fold evil of the social condition.

Thus it appears, that what this pretentious school of Social Philosophy is constantly striving for and makes the grand specific aim of its philosophy, is, in itself, rather a curse than a blessing, unless indeed it be properly qualified and checked in its natural tendency. Malthusianism has already demonstrated that the attainment of this their grand specific end, is simply nugatory, inasmuch as the mere increase of wealth tends only to the mere increase of population to consume the wealth—a proposition of original Malthusianism, it is true, which, as we have before seen, has been justly subjected by the later Malthusians to some important qualifications. But of what great value is a school or system of Social Philosophy which thus blunders, mistakes, and misdirects its inquiries? Evidently enough, it is in some other direction than that in which they point attention, that we must look for a satisfactory solution of the great social problem to be solved.

§ 7. Reason adjudges, also, although in less strong and energetic terms, than in respect to either of the two before-noticed errors, that the mere excess of Population cannot properly be regarded as the true cause, or at least the main true cause, that afflicts the social condition of mankind, and that an endeavor to improve that condition by merely reducing population would be of but little avail in any case, of doubtful utility in many, and of undoubted injury in some.

Among the many causes which may, with some degree of propriety, be assigned for every phenomenon, that is evidently to be regarded as the true cause, or main true cause, and therefore, in common parlance, THE TRUE CAUSE, or, *par excellence*, THE CAUSE, which most essentially and immediately contributes to produce the phenomenon, and the removal of which will insure its disappearance. Now, very plainly to the eye of reason, it must appear that the mere excess of population cannot properly be regarded as such a cause, in reference to those phenomena of the social state, which are antagonistic to the realization of a proper social condition, and which it is or should be the main aim of Social Philosophy to remove or to mitigate. Very obviously, excess of population is not THE CAUSE, the removal of which will insure the desired social condition.

It is obviously a very poor plan, and certainly a very imperfect and insufficient one, for affecting the removal of any ill to diminish the force, or any one of the forces, by which it is to be combated. But this is precisely the nature of the plan which Malthusian philosophy proposes for the removal or mitigation of the most deplorable ills that have been hitherto found inseparable from human society—the poverty of the poor, and the painful stringency and difficulty of earning a livelihood experienced by many not properly to be regarded as of the poorer class. It is a very poor plan, in short, for insuring a right supply of wealth in the right places, namely, in the hands of those who really need it, to diminish the main force by which wealth is created, namely, LABOR, or, in other words, POPULATION.

Labor, or population, which constitutes or supplies labor, is the main force that creates wealth. Nay, in the eye of Political Economy, which regards only *values* and not *utilities* however important, that have no *value*, or exchangeable price, it is the sole creator of wealth. For capital, which must generally, if not invariably, co-operate with labor in the production of wealth, is itself but the product of anterior labor, and may be elegantly termed merely CRYSTALLIZED LABOR. Yet it is precisely this

Labor, or Population, which is, with some important qualifications, its convertible term, the excess of which Malthusian philosophy regards as the main cause that afflicts the social condition, and by the removal of which alone, it proposes to improve that condition.

§ 8. Very manifestly, the effect of a mere reduction of population, under most circumstances, if not indeed under all, must be to lessen the aggregate productive force of the society, and by consequence the aggregate production of wealth, resulting therefrom, by diminishing the incentives to industry, and relaxing the severe tension, which excess of population tends to give, to every nerve and muscle and sinew of that productive force.

This relaxation may indeed be beneficial, and undoubtedly is so, under many circumstances, but must always be of but partial influence, and must, under most circumstances, only confer benefit in one form, to take it away in another—only improve one portion of society, to injure another portion—only raise up the labor-class, to lower the affluent class. Hence it is, in entire accordance with what reason thus inculcates, that we find in very sparsely-populated countries, as before remarked,* a paradise to the laboring man, while existence is rendered extremely difficult, if not impossible to an affluent class, without which a proper condition of human society is not less impossible, than without a well-conditioned labor-class.

However desirable and important, indeed, may be the *reduction of population*, under many circumstances, it must be apparent to the higher order of intellects, on a little reflection, that an *excess of population*, not less than the tendency of population to increase beyond the *proper* means of subsistence, which occasions such excess, is, upon the whole, beneficial in its effects—is, in short, one of the necessary forms of evil, which we could not take away without incurring some still greater evil.

This idea, as we have before had occasion to remark,† is not exclusively the idea of the author, but has been before expressed also by McCulloh, in his Principles of Political Economy, al-

---

* See Chapter I., § 4.
† See Part V., Chap. IV., in which McCulloh's views are critically examined.

though not quite so distinctly and emphatically. Thus, indeed, do we find a triumphant proof of the truth of the Malthusian idea, so much railed against by shallow declaimers, on the very ground on which they have planted their main objections—the wisdom and goodness of the plan of Providence. Thus do we find that the very tendency to *excess of population*, which, they argue, cannot exist, because it is opposed to that wisdom and goodness of design, is, in reality in harmony therewith. Thus, moreover, do we find, at one and the same time, conclusive illustration of the truth of the Malthusian doctrine, and of the futility of its aims, in so far as they are directed to the specific end of removing that which they erroneously regard as the *main* evil to be combated in the social state.

§ 9. What sort of scheme, indeed, for improving the social condition of mankind, is that, which, for the most part, only improves that condition in one way to injure it in another—only takes away one form of evil to impose another—which, in order to remove one of the partial forms of social evil, seeks to abolish one of the very conditions which are indispensable to the highest attainable state of human society, one of the conditions that are indispensable for successfully combating the combined force of all the ills that afflict humanity?

Such is the scheme which Malthusian philosophy proposes, which in order to remove the partial evils resulting from the tendency of population to increase beyond the *proper* means of subsistency seeks to abolish that tendency altogether—and thus to deprive society of the incalculable benefits resulting from that tendency, when not too much aggravated in its form—thus to deprive society of all the GOOD resulting from this form of EVIL.

Quite evidently, must it appear, that it is in some other direction than that in which Malthusian philosophy points us, or, at least, with a somewhat more searching gaze, that we must direct our attention, if we would clearly and thoroughly discern the causes which determine the social condition of mankind—the causes which, most essentially and inevitably, tend to depress that condition, on one hand, or to elevate it, on the other.

§ 10. Thus do we discern, both experimentally and rationally, the manifest insufficiency of all the three existing schools of Social Philosophy. Thus do we find that we may accomplish for mankind all that these three schools, severally and jointly, seek to accomplish, and yet fail to actualize, that which is the proper aim of all Social Philosophy, A PROPER SOCIAL CONDITION.

Thus do we find that we may bestow on mankind the best political institutions,—that we may instruct them thoroughly in the laws of wealth, and endow them with the largest abundance of "national wealth," resulting from such instruction,—that we may deplete population, to any extent we please—that we may do all these things, and still fail, lamentably fail, to attain the desired end.

Very obviously, therefore, it is in some other direction than that in which either of these schools point us, that we must look for solution of the great problem to be solved.

CHAPTER III.

GENERAL SUMMARY AS TO THE MOST ESSENTIAL SIGNIFICANCE OF THE THREE SYSTEMS—THUS STILL MORE CLEARLY REVEALING THEIR ESSENTIAL INSUFFICIENCY.

§ 1. That the insufficiency and positive meagreness of the three existing systems or schools of thought in Social Philosophy may be made yet more manifest, by still greater condensation of their most essential ideas, let us yet more succinctly than before recapitulate those ideas.

The all-absorbing idea of the Political school is, How shall mankind be GOVERNED, or, at most, how shall they be ORGANIZED ; that of the Politico-economical is, How can mankind be ENRICHED, or, expressing their idea at once more clearly and more accurately—*How can two blades of grass be made to grow where only one grew before ;* that of the Malthusian is, How can the tendency to over-population be prevented, or, in other words, *how can two persons be prevented from growing where only one grew before, whensoever two blades of grass are made to grow where only one blade grew before.*

§ 2. When it is duly considered to how small an extent mankind ought really to be governed, that is to say by political authority—when it is duly considered that the best way of so governing men is, in fact, for the most part, to let them alone—that, in short, the proper function of government, as already before shown,* is to *let mankind alone*, itself, and insure their being *let alone* by others, or, as Herbert Spencer has expressed the same idea, is simply to grant *protection* to men, and that, whenever government is allowed to do more than this, there is always danger of its becoming a special cause of mischief, always danger of its doing more harm than good to society—when these considerations are duly weighed, how small, how comparatively insignifi-

---

* See Part 3, Chap. I.

cant, appears this grand, this all-absorbing idea of the Political Doctors of the world—How shall mankind be governed politically, or by the public authority of states!

§ 3. When, again, it is duly considered of how little utility is the mere increase of National Wealth, at least after a nation has once attained a proper density of population, as some *two hundred* to the square mile—of how little utility is the realization of the much-vaunted endeavor to make two blades of grass grow where only one grew before—when it is duly considered that the natural tendency of this increase of *grass*, or its equivalent idea, *wealth*, is, for the most part, merely to increase the population to consume the *grass*, how insignificant and even paltry appears this the grand aim of the Political Economists and their entire school of Social Philosophy!

§ 4. When it is duly considered, yet again, of how little utility, of how limited influence, under any circumstances, must be the mere REDUCTION OF POPULATION—that such reduction must inevitably tend to diminish the aggregate productive force of society, at the same time that it diminishes, undoubtedly, the severe pressure of the social machinery on the labor class—that this prescription for the sufferings of society, if applied too freely, is calculated indeed to operate like the policy that holds on at the *spile* and lets out at the *bung*—is calculated to do more injury to the society at large, than it does good to any particular class —how very partial and limited must appear the absorbing aim of Malthusian philosophy, greatly in advance, as it unquestionably is, of the other two schools of Social Philosophy!

§ 5. The Political School, in short, in their reasonings on the social condition, and in their endeavors to improve it, have directed their attention only to the *bark* and *branches* of the TREE OF KNOWLEDGE, appertaining to Social Science; the Politico-Economical, somewhat less superficial, has penetrated the *trunk* and examined critically its *vital circulation;* the Malthusian, far more discerning than either, has struck down into the very ROOTS, but unfortunately for the cause of Social Science hitherto, has seized upon only one root of the manifold cluster of roots demanding attention, and has missed the TAP-ROOT.

Nay, moreover, Malthusian philosophy has not only failed to bestow proper attention on the whole cluster of roots, from which the social condition of mankind springs, as a natural growth, but it has utterly failed, not less than the other two Philosophies, to bestow due attention on what are scarcely less important, the SOIL and CLIMATE, in which those ROOTS are to be developed, and from which they are to derive their nourishment. In short, while Malthusian philosophy has, with eminent propriety, bestowed its attention directly on MAN, it has not only failed to take a sufficiently comprehensive view of him, in his manifold ramifications of himself, but has also failed to bestow any attention whatever on the LAWS OF HIS ENVIRONMENT, which are to man, both in his individual and aggregate development, precisely what the soil, climate, and other natural conditions are to the plant, or the seed and roots from which it is developed.

This brief *exposé*, by metaphor, of the essential significance of the three existing Philosophies of Society, clearly reveals their lamentable deficiencies. Quite evidently we need a Philosophy that shall supply these deficiencies. Quite evidently we need a Philosophy of Society, which, founding itself upon MAN and the laws of his NATURAL ENVIRONMENT, as primary fundamental principles, shall construct, upon these foundations, the frame-work of a thorough and complete Social Science, subordinating to these fundamental principles, whatever is really valuable in other, and more superficial systems of thought respecting the principles of Society. To organize such a Philosophy, to lay the enduring basis of such a Science of Society, is the paramount aim of the author of the present undertaking.

CHAPTER IV.

THE REASONS FOR CONSIDERING THE MORE ADVANCED IDEAS OF PREVIOUS THINKERS, BEFORE PROCEEDING TO DEVELOP THOSE OF THE AUTHOR, WHICH ARE IN ENTIRE ACCORDANCE WITH THOSE MORE ADVANCED IDEAS.

§ 1. IF the author of this work were, like the greater number of discoverers in Science, or founders of new systems of Philosophy, more ambitious to appear the sole discoverer of truth than to do full justice to the valuable contributions of those who have preceded him in the world of thought, he might here end his REVIEW of the thoughts of others and proceed at once to the development of his own—he might here abandon the office, he has assumed, of the critical historian of the Philosophy of Society, and assume at once that of its constructor and architect, an office far less laborious, and for which he is, in many senses, far better qualified.

But such a course would be incompatible with the thorough execution of the task he has undertaken, of presenting to the world the combined result of all anterior researches, and reasonings on the Philosophy of Society, before proceeding to the promulgation of his own, which would, indeed, be but little worthy of attentive consideration if he had not thus availed himself of the benefit of all anterior investigations. Having undertaken this task, it is his purpose to discharge it faithfully, to execute it thoroughly.

The task is eminently worthy of the undertaking, not less as a proper, if not, indeed, a requisite preliminary to his own peculiar views, than as a valuable and much needed contribution to the History of the WORLD OF THOUGHT, which, philosophers seem, at last, to be coming to understand, is far more deserving of consideration than that which has hitherto almost wholly engrossed historical consideration—the History of the WORLD OF ACTION.

An eminent thinker has well said : " It is a great proof of our respect for the human species, when we dare not address it from the suggestions of our own minds, without having first conscientiously examined into all that has been left to us by our predecessors, as an inheritance."* It is with a deep sense of this respect, which is due to " the human species," and more especially to the eminent thinkers who have preceded him in this important field of inquiry, that the author now addresses the scientific world.

A much more eminent thinker, Victor Cousin, in his great work, on the Philosophy of History, by a singular misnomer, entitled, " Introduction to the History of Philosophy," has still more forcibly said, to the same point : " Whosoever, in the study of any science, neglects its history, deprives himself of the experience of centuries and places himself in the situation of the first inventor ; and he thereby needlessly places in opposition to himself the same chances of error which his predecessors were obliged to encounter ; yet with this difference, that as the first errors were necessary, they were useful, and consequently more than excusable ; whereas a repetition of the same errors, being unnecessary, would be useless, and unproductive of any benefit to others, and therefore disgraceful to himself. Human Science, like humanity itself, should be progressive : and a real progress in science is made, only when a new work represents all that preceded it, as well as what is peculiar to its author, when an author resumes all anterior labors, and adds to them the fruits of his own."† This is precisely what the author of the present work proposes to accomplish, by the great preliminary work which he has undertaken, and of which that now submitted to the world is but a fraction, or seventh part.‡

§ 2. Having now demonstrated the insufficiency of the three existing systems or schools of Social Philosophy, and which are the only ones that can, with any propriety, be regarded as organ-

---

* Madame de Stael, in her work on Germany.

† Cousin's Introduction to History of Philosophy, Lecture XI., p. 330. Boston edition of 1832, as translated by Linberg.

‡ More properly we should say, the Sixth part, because the *Seventh* part of this Series, or that immediately succeeding the present, is designed to present the fundamental ideas of the author's own system of Social Philosophy, and its general outlines.

ized systems of thought in regard to the Philosophy of Society, it might, indeed, appear that nothing rightly remained for the author to do, but to proceed at once to the development of his own plan, or system, for organizing thought and directing endeavor in this vast and momentous realm of Science.

But, by adopting this course, we should omit notice and lose sight of the most valuable contributions, by far, that have been as yet made to the Philosophy of Society—contributions which place the contributors beyond the pale of either of the three well-defined systems of thought on Social Philosophy, by reason of the very largeness of their thoughts and comprehensiveness of their views—thoughts too large, and views too comprehensive, to be embraced by the circumscribed confines of those contracted systems.

Evidently enough, the human mind is rapidly expanding beyond the measure of the contracted systems of thought that have heretofore circumscribed it, in this field of science. Of this expansion many evidences have been afforded by late eminent thinkers. Can we consistently or properly omit notice of these evidences? To do so would be to expend attention on antiquated and nearly worn-out systems of thought, such as we have already considered, and withhold it from thoughts tending toward, and clearly appertaining to, more enlarged and more correct systems, to be hereafter organized.

The intellectual world, not less than the physical, has its transition epochs, of which the present century is pre-eminently one. Long before any new system of thought, in any science, is duly organized, evidences of a tendency toward it may be clearly discerned. Without such evidences, indeed, the proposer of any such new system might well doubt as to its correctness, nor would it be scarcely less than presumption in him confidently to propose it. Nothing is at the same time invented and perfected. No thoroughly organized system of thought concerning any science, can be exclusively the product of one human brain. Hence, it was well said by the sage of antiquity, "In a multitude of councillors there is safety."* Nor much less correctly has it been

---

* Solomon.

said by a modern savan, "That is a hazardous precedent which has not as yet been approved by the example of worthy men."*

Is it to be supposed that the new System of Thought in regard to the Philosophy of Society, which the author of this work proposes to introduce, if it is true, has never as yet been recognized, however imperfectly, by any other mind; that no testimony to its peculiar doctrines has yet been afforded by any of the eminent thinkers to whom the present age has given birth; that none of the new ideas, or rather, not commonly received ideas, which appertain to that system, have as yet been expressed, nay, urgently insisted on, by any of those eminent thinkers? Can it be supposed that the contemplated system does in reality accomplish, for the Philosophy of Society, what the combined result of the teachings of Copernicus and Newton accomplished for the philosophy of the stars, and that no evidences of a tendency toward it are as yet, in this advanced period of human science, to be discerned? It would be the height of presumption and of folly to suppose so.

Even the Copernican theory of the solar system had been before conjectured by Pythagoras, and somewhat approximated by Philolaus, Aristarchus, and other ancient astronomers. Nay, the grand and conclusive discoveries of Newton, in regard to the laws of Gravity and the universality of their operation, had been almost attained previously by Kepler, Gilbert, and Hooker. One of the too extravagant eulogists of Newton has justly said concerning him, "An alliance indeed of many kindred spirits had been long struggling in the combat, and Newton was but the leader of the mighty phalanx—the director of their combined genius—the general who won the victory, and wears its laurels."†

If such were the truth in regard to the most loudly-bruited and really most valuable discoveries in Astronomy, still less can it be supposed that any one mind can have advanced very greatly beyond all others in Sociology—a science far more practical, far more nearly related to the immediate interests of mankind, and which

---

* Sir Edward Coke.
† Brewster's Life of Newton. Vol. I., Chap. XI., p. 251. Edinburgh Ed., 1855.

has engaged, to a considerable extent, the attention of the most superior minds in all ages. If it is true, as undoubtedly it is, of all other sciences, still more must it be true of this, that no individual mind can throw itself very greatly in advance of all others. The most that any one mind can accomplish, as a leader in science, is to step somewhat in advance of the grand army of advancing humanity, or its great central column, THE PHALANX OF SCIENCE, and gently urge forward the mighty and ever slowly-moving mass. This is all that the greatest discoverers or leaders in science ever do. The author of this work certainly does not expect, nay, dares not even hope, to do more.

§ 3. For these reasons, a consideration of those evidences of a tendency toward a higher system of thought in Social Philosophy, is not less due to the author of this work himself, than to those eminent thinkers by whom those evidences have been manifested, and moreover, to the task which he has undertaken, of presenting to the scientific world a brief *exposé* of the combined result of all anterior investigations in Social Philosophy, as a PRELIMINARY to the presentation of his own. If such evidences do not exist, or if, existing, they do not tend to establish the system proposed, serious doubts may well be entertained as to its correctness. If they do exist, and tend to establish that system, they are strong testimonies to its truth. For every human mind is, to a certain extent, an ORACLE of nature—an ORACLE of the truth, in regard to the most essential condition or nature of things. More especially is this true of superior minds, of the independent or original order of thinkers.

Every independent human thinker—every thinker who has enough of the CENTRIFUGAL force of mentality, in himself, to gyrate in an orbit of his own, or rather, to move as a PRIMARY body in the intellectual realm, and not as a *secondary*—not as a mere *satellite* of some other thinker—is a credible witness, affords *competent* testimony, however inconclusive, to the truth of that which he proclaims, or claims to have discerned, in the course of his own independent *revolutions*. When many such independent thinkers concur in proclaiming the same truth, how strong becomes that testimony!

If the irregular motions or perturbations of a single world, like Uranus, were sufficient to indicate to astronomers the probable existence of another world not yet discovered, and lead them to the discovery of this world, in the person of the planet Neptune, how much more should the like motions of many such worlds indicate the momentous truth? If, in like manner, the testimony of a single human mind to the existence of new truths, not embraced by any of the existing systems of Social Philosophy, and requiring another and more comprehensive system to embrace them, be competent testimony to the probable existence of such truths, how strong becomes that testimony when many minds concur in sustaining it—how potent does it become when many of the most eminent thinkers of the latest and most advanced period of human thought are found bearing testimony to the same truths, and emphatically proclaiming them!

§ 4. Desirous of obtaining the support and co-operation of such eminent thinkers, the author of the new system rather courts than rejects their concurrence of opinion. Unlike the greater number of discoverers in science, whose main ambition seems to be to appear original and therefore different from all anterior inquirers, it is rather *his* aim to appear to be in harmony with the most approved thinkers that have preceded him, and, indeed, with all anterior inquirers—nay, not to *appear* to be in harmony with them, merely, but actually to be so. It could not be otherwise, indeed, consistently with his own fundamental ideas in Philosophy. For, entirely agreeing with Victor Cousin, "that there is no total error in an intelligent and rational being,"* he is compelled to adopt a yet larger postulate, which may indeed be regarded as a corollary, or unavoidable deduction from that of Cousin, that HE ALONE IS THE TRUE PHILOSOPHER WHOSE SYSTEM COMPREHENDS AND HARMONIZES ALL SYSTEMS.

That the system which he proposes to introduce does this, for all anterior systems of thought in regard to the Philosophy of Society, and more especially for those more enlarged ideas that

---

* Cousin's Elements of Psychology, as translated from the French, by Rev. C. S. Henry. Chap. ix., p. 240.

have not as yet been reduced to system, is, to his mind, the grand and conclusive proof and verification of its truth.

The proposer of this system does not appear before the scientific world as a fomenter of controversy, but rather as a harmonizer of discords. He does not come as an innovator or, in any sense, AN AGITATOR, but rather as the composer of strife, and the adviser to QUIETUDE, alike in the world of thought and of action. Still less does he come as one claiming to be wiser than all other men, but simply as one who has extended his observations a little further and somewhat more comprehensively than any other inquirer. He does not come, indeed, so much as an ORIGINATOR, as an ORGANIZER, in the world of thought.

Entertaining these views and proposing these ends, the author does not feel regret at the discovery that many of those ideas which had originated with him, and which had, indeed, been almost completely organized into their appropriate system, before he was aware that they had ever been expressed before, or had even heard of the authors, or some of them at least, by whom they had been expressed, had, nevertheless, been before distinctly and emphatically announced by eminent thinkers. Instead of feeling regret at this discovery, he is rather rejoiced to find this response of accord from other and eminently superior minds. He might, otherwise, have felt doubt or mistrust as to the correctness of his views, and more especially as to their important significance. But how can such doubt or mistrust exist, when on every side he finds response of accord breaking forth into utterance, when, from many different points, he discovers the human mind, as manifesting itself through its greatest thinkers, moving in the same direction, although, as yet, without any due concert of action or organization of purpose.

§ 5. It has been justly noticed, as remarkable, by one of the multitudinous historians of the world of action,* that all the different bodies of the grand army of Napoleon which had left the Niemen, in the ever-memorable Russian campaign, by different

---

* See Count Philip De Segur's Narrative of the Russian Campaign. Book iv., chap. 7.

routes and at different times, notwithstanding innumerable obstacles, after a month of separation, and at the distance of a hundred leagues from the point of their departure, all found themselves concentrating at the village of Bezenkowiczi, a little to the westward of Ostrowno, on the same day and at the same hour. With so much precision had their march been directed. What an impression must such a wonderful concentration of armies have excited in a thoughtful mind! Could the beholder of such a spectacle fail to be impressed with the conviction that some great movement was in progress, and that some great designer was directing the combined movements of so many different hosts?

Such is the impression that has been made on the writer of these pages by the like spectacle which has been disclosed to his view in the world of thought. When he has contemplated the number of writers, who, without any concert of action, without taking suggestion from him or from one another, are moving in the same direction with himself—concentrating their attention on the same points—emphatically proclaiming the same great truths, on the promulgation of which he is mainly bent, and which have hitherto remained almost wholly unknown or unnoticed—he has been struck with amazement, if not, indeed, with awe, at the apparent disclosure of the OCCULT FORCES by which the world of mind, not less than that of matter, is governed and directed.

Whence comes this remarkable accord of thought—this simultaneous concurrence of so many minds in proclaiming the same truth? Does it not disclose A GREAT UNSEEN DESIGNER, who directs the movements of the world of mind, not only as imperiously as he directs those of the world of matter, but somewhat more directly and immediately—whose planning and direction are conspicuous here? Or shall we say that this accord is only the natural result of the established laws of mind, operating under like circumstances, in the same epoch of the world, in the same stage of intellectual development?

It matters not, for the purposes of the present work, which view we may take of this momentous question—whether we adopt the theory of a designed and *consciously* intelligent direction of events, or that of a mere functional or organic direction, devoid of design and *conscious* intelligence—whether, in short, we adopt the THEISTIC or the ATHEISTIC view of Nature, and her eternal laws.

Whichsoever of these two views we may adopt, this wonderful accord of minds, from whatever cause resulting, must be regarded as bearing strong testimony to the truth, as well as to the important significance, of the ideas which they unite in proclaiming, which are, many of them, identically those which the author of this work desires to bring into prominent view, and to make the basis in part of a more enlarged system of thought in regard to the Philosophy of Society.

May he not, in view of such concurrence of authority, such accord of thought, without impropriety, entertain increased assurance of the correctness, as well as importance of his design? May he not, without the imputation of arrogance, attempt to organize the disconnected forces of this battle-field of science, with which he finds himself unexpectedly allied, and direct their combined movements toward the accomplishment of the end proposed by all—THE AMELIORATION OF THE HUMAN CONDITION? May he not, in short, venture to attempt such an organization and discipline of the "grand army" of advancing humanity, as may, at least, secure it adequate provisions and comfortable winter quarters, in the dreary regions it has to traverse, if they do not, indeed, insure to it victory, in so far, at least, as victory is possible, in the feeble attempt of man to combat THE LAWS OF HIS NATURAL AND INEVITABLE ENVIRONMENT?

For he would be an unsafe leader, in this arduous campaign of human existence, on this uncongenial planet, who should rely too confidently on victory, least of all, on easy victory. Such a leader would resemble too much the Godwins, the Owens, the Fouriers, and other extravagant and deluded adventurers, who have undertaken to conduct this perilous enterprise.

He would be an unsafe director, in this realm of science, who does not inculcate, from the beginning, that the expedition of human life in this world must ever be found a Russian expedition, abounding in difficulties and dangers, having to cleave its way, in a harsh Russian climate, across grim Russian wastes—battling continually with the hostile forces of nature and of man—who does not inculcate that the utmost prudence will be necessary to insure success, and, that there is no hope of success except, moreover, at the price of toil, of hardship, of self-denial, of constant vigilance, and hard valiant fighting—who does not, in short, inculcate that it is requisite to success, in this stern enterprise, that every man should possess, within himself, those energies, physical, moral, and intellectual, which can alone qualify him to withstand the fierce elements to which he must be exposed, and to triumph over the antagonistic forces of nature, and opposing man, amid which, and against which, he must ever have to fight his way.

CHAPTER V.

OF THE METHOD AND ORDER TO BE ADOPTED IN CONSIDERING THE NEW IDEAS.

§ 1. COMING now to consider the evidences of a tendency towards a higher system of thought in Social Philosophy, we encounter two preliminary questions of method, or order, or rather, the one of *method*, and the other of *order:* FIRST, what method shall we adopt for considering these evidences? Shall we consider primarily the ideas, and incidentally only the authors by whom they have been announced, or shall we bestow primary attention on the authors, incidentally only illustrating their ideas? In other words, shall we adopt the synthetical or analytical mode of treating the subject? SECOND, what order shall we adopt for considering the authors, if the latter method of treating the subject be adopted, either in whole or in part? Shall we follow the chronological order of the development of their ideas, or the logical order, or shall we adopt an order conformed to the nationality of the authors, or yet an order differing from all these, either wholly or in part?

These are questions of some importance. Attention to method and order is always important, though generally too much neglected. The only difference, indeed, between the scientific treatment of a subject and the unscientific—the vulgar, or, so-called, popular mode of treating it—consists in the method and order which prevail in the one, are wanting in the other—in the fact that the facts and ideas of the former are methodically arranged, or systematized, while those of the latter are loosely and disconnectedly thrown together. Science is but the classification of knowledge, or systemization of thought.

If history can ever be reduced to a Science, as many of the most eminent thinkers have been, of late, attempting to render it, it can only be by strict attention to method and order, in the presentation of its facts or events. Whether this can ever be accomplished for the History of the World of ACTION, or not, the attempt to accomplish it is highly creditable to those master minds by whom it has been made. If such attempt can be made, with any propriety, or prospects of success, in regard to the world of ACTION, with much more propriety, with much better prospects of success, may it be made, as it ought to be made undoubtedly, in regard to the world of THOUGHT, the history of which, in part, we are endeavoring here to unfold. If, indeed, the history of the world of ACTION can ever be reduced, even approximatively, to the character of a Science, it can only be by making it a counterpart to that of the world of THOUGHT—by subordinating facts to ideas—by considering *facts*, as Cousin recommends,* only in so far as they represent IDEAS.

§ 2. How then shall we decide upon these two preliminary questions? Which of these methods, and which of these orders shall we adopt? Either might be the more correct, according to circumstances. And accordingly, in preceding parts of this work, or of the series to which this particular work appertains, we have adopted the one or the other, or both, either wholly or in part, as appeared more appropriate under all the conditions and surroundings of the subject to be considered.

As to the FIRST of these two questions, or, that relating to METHOD—the question whether we shall adopt the synthetical or analytical method of treating the subject, whether we shall give the main prominence to the ideas or the authors of those ideas—there can be no difficulty in deciding or defining what course we are to adopt, for we shall adopt both, as there is obvious propriety in doing. So important are the ideas, and so eminently meritorious the authors, that they are both deserving of primary and particular consideration. We shall, therefore, in the first place, particularly consider the ideas claiming attention, and, thereafter, in subsequent chapters, consider more particularly the authors by whom they have been respectively announced.

We have adopted this course, in other parts of this series, in

---

* See Cousin's Introduction to History of Philosophy, Lecture VIII., p. 236. Boston. Edition of 1852, as translated by Linberg.

respect to ideas of no value and authors of no merit. Much more proper, surely it is, that we should adopt it, in respect to ideas of great value and authors of eminent merit. We have adopted this course in treating anti-Malthusianism, devoting an entire chapter, of many pages, to the exposition of its whole stock in trade of puerile and absurd ideas, and then another entire chapter, of still greater bulk, to the more particular consideration of the insignificant writers by whom those ideas have been urged.* This was certainly bestowing a degree of attention on ideas and writers of no intrinsic merit, which might appear wholly unnecessary, if it were not duly considered how much more difficult it often is to expose the folly of fools, than to demonstrate the wisdom of the wise, and how prominent a part that folly plays in the world of thought as well as of action.

The doctrine of Malthusianism itself is, at the best, of but small essential significance, as we have before seen, however valuable may be, and undoubtedly are, many of the observations and conclusions to which it has incidentally given rise.† But anti-Malthusianism, which controverts the important and indisputable truths of the Malthusian doctrine, which pitifully attempts to disprove the valuable exposition which it has presented of the Laws of Population, is contemptible—is disgraceful to the human understanding.

Yet upon this pitiful and contemptible system of thought, or rather of error, of stupidity intolerable, we have, in deference to folly, and the part it undoubtedly plays in the grand drama of human existence, bestowed the double mode of consideration—the synthetical and analytical—holding up to prominent view the whole train of its absurd arguments, and thereafter passing in review the most notorious, or most essentially noteworthy, of its exponents. If we have adopted this course, with any propriety, in regard to these *pigmies* of the world of thought, and their pitiful ideas, with much more propriety, surely, shall we adopt it in

---

* See Chapters 8 and 9 of Part V. of this Series.

† For a full view of these observations and conclusions, see Part V. of this Series, and more particularly the X., or last chapter of that Part.

regard to those GIANTS of the intellectual world, those colossal intellects, that we are now about to contemplate.

§ 3. As to the SECOND of the two questions, or that relating to the ORDER in which the authors, now about to be reviewed, shall be considered, it is not so easy either to decide, or to indicate, what course we are to pursue, as we shall not adopt either of the orders specially indicated, but rather a *composite* order, partaking somewhat of the character of each, but not wholly that of either. We shall not pursue strictly the chronological order, nor the logical order, nor yet an order wholly conformed to the nationality of the different authors, but an order which has some respect to each one of these orders. Either of these orders might properly, under some circumstances, be entirely conformed to. But under most circumstances, as in the present, each one of these orders has some merit, some special propriety, which cannot be obtained without sacrificing, to some extent, the other orders.

For many purposes the strictly chronological order of History, whether of the world of thought or of action, is the most proper; for other purposes the strictly logical order is preferable; for others, again, an order comformed to nationality, or to RACE, which is but a higher order of nationality. All of these orders will be blended in that which we are to pursue in regard to the authors now about to be reviewed.

The chronological order, in the consideration of events, either in the world of thought or of action, ought undoubtedly to be somewhat observed under all circumstances, and strictly conformed to, wherever overruling considerations do not ordain a different course. But we can not safely accept the extravagant assertion of Cousin, that, " In fact, every other order is an insult to humanity, a sort of philosophical impiety."*

This assertion may serve very well for a French philosopher, like Mr. Cousin, who hesitates not to bend and cut the facts to

---

* Introduction to History of Philosophy, Lect. XII., pp. 375-6. Boston Ed., 1832.

suit his theory—a great FAULT naturally resulting from the great VIRTUE which characterizes French intellect, the strong propensity to systematize all knowledge, to be mathematically exact in all its conclusions and reasonings. It suits the purposes of a French philosopher, very well, who, like Mr. Cousin, does not care to take notice of any facts except such as harmonize with his theory, as accord with his understanding of the true significance of events. For this is manifestly the state of the case with this eminent philosopher, which he feebly attempts to justify by remarking, " You will please to remark that if a people does not represent any idea its existence is simply unintelligible."* That is to say, in other words, as is manifest from the whole scope of his reasonings, " If a people does not represent any idea that is intelligible to me, Victor Cousin, that is not conformable to my theory, as to the order of human development, alike in the world of Thought and of Action, it is unintelligible, and, therefore, not worthy to be noticed at all."

But this assertion will not answer the purposes of the philosopher, who, with a more true philosophical spirit, will accept and note the FACTS, whether they accord with his theory or not, who will bend, shape, and modify his theory to make it conformable to the FACTS, and who will more especially conform his method and order of considering facts and events to the essential significance and importance of those facts and events, whatever may have been the chronological order of their development.

We shall presently have occasion to notice the propriety of this more truly philosophical mode of procedure. For we shall presently, in deference to the *logical* order of events, have to bring again under review illustrious thinkers who have been already considered, conformably to the *chronological* order. We shall have occasion again to bring under review the profound observations of Confucius and Solon, who, more than two thousand years ago, have announced ideas in regard to the Philosophy of Society, that, logically and essentially, take their place side by side with the most advanced ideas of the present age—ideas, in-

---

* See same work, Lecture IX., p. 255.

deed, of which, many of the leading statesmen of this advanced period of human thought appear to be profoundly ignorant.

§ 4. The authorities who will be selected, for particular consideration, from the illustrious throng who have contributed essentially valuable ideas to the Philosophy of Society, and ideas decidedly in advance of those which properly appertain to either of the three systems of thought heretofore particularly considered, are Confucius and Solon among the ancients, Guizot, Hallam. De Maistre, Chalmers, Sismondi, Mill, Cousin, Buckle, Auguste Comte, and Herbert Spencer, among the moderns, of European society, and Webster, Calhoun, and Henry James, of American society.

These authorities will be considered in the order in which they are here mentioned, and grouped in pairs, formed in accordance with affinities, either of resemblance or of contrast, in relation either to their ideas themselves, the time of their promulgation, or the nationality to which they appertained. Thus Confucius and Solon will be considered together, and in a chapter devoted to them exclusively, as belonging to antiquity, and as both speaking from the stand-point of lawgivers, not without considerable accord, moreover, in the essential significance of their ideas. Guizot and Hallam will, in like manner, be considered together and in a chapter by themselves, because of their resemblance in respect to the mode of delivering their thoughts, and the essential significance of those thoughts, rendered only the more striking and noteworthy because of the contrast between them in nationality, the one belonging to the French, and the other to the English nation. For the like reasons De Maistre and Chalmers will be in the same manner grouped together. Sismondi and Mill—Cousin and Buckle—Auguste Comte and Herbert Spencer.

Webster, Calhoun, and Henry James will be grouped together by reason of their national affinity, and because they stand almost alone in American society as profound thinkers, or, at least, as the only American magnates that have contributed any specially or prominently noteworthy ideas in regard to the Philosophy of Society.

§ 5. If the new system of thought, which it is proposed by the writer of these pages to introduce, should be found to harmonize entirely, with the most essential ideas of these eminent authorities, with the greatest thoughts of these greatest minds—if it should be found to harmonize all their discords, as well as those of less profound thinkers—if it should be found to explain the difficulties which they have left unexplained, to solve the problems which they have left unsolved—if, without contradicting any of their most essential conclusions, but, on the contrary, fully sustaining and carrying forward those conclusions, it yet arrives at still more advanced and comprehensive conclusions—conclusions that embrace the whole range of facts or phenomena demanding consideration, then it must be admitted that it is not without some valid grounds that this system claims to embody, in however rude and imperfect outline, the true PRINCIPIA MATHEMATICA PHILOSOPHIÆ SOCIALIS.

CHAPTER VI.

THE MORE ADVANCED IDEAS IN SOCIAL PHILOSOPHY ESSENTIALLY EXPRESSED AND CRITICALLY EXAMINED IN BRIEF—THE SEVEN MAIN PROPOSITIONS THAT EMBODY THOSE IDEAS.

§ 1. In pursuance of the method indicated in the foregoing chapter, we come now to consider those more advanced ideas in regard to the Philosophy of Society—whether announced in ancient or modern times, although almost exclusively in the latter, and within a very recent period—which do not properly appertain to either of the three systems of thought that have been already considered, but evidently to a larger and more correct system that is yet to be organized.

In the present chapter it is proposed to consider especially those ideas, with some incidental reference only to the authors, or authorities, by whom they have been most prominently set forth, although they will again come under review, in subsequent chapters, while considering more particularly the eminent authorities by whom they have been so set forth.

So suggestive and important are those ideas, that the bare statement of them in their right order, or in an order conformed to their true logical connections, cannot fail to carry the mind greatly beyond the confines of the existing systems of thought in Social Philosophy, if indeed they can fail to carry it forward, to the discovery of the true system to which they manifestly appertain. They could not fail so to carry forward the mind of the present inquirer, if he had not already arrived at that system by a somewhat different route, and one more immediately suggested by the intuitions of his own mind. Nor can it be reasonably doubted that it would in like manner carry forward other minds.

But thrown out disconnectedly, as those ideas have been at different times, and in different connections, one by one author, and another by some other, without any due connection or relation between them being pointed out, without their ever having been even placed in juxtaposition with each other—no one author having as yet grasped, or apparently comprehended all those ideas—they have failed hitherto to be duly appreciated, either in themselves, or, what is more important, in their relations to the true and much needed SYSTEM OF THOUGHT to which they point, almost as unmistakably, as many concurring *magnets* to the *pole*.

Many of those ideas indeed have not merely failed to be duly appreciated. They have failed even to arrest attention, except perhaps to a very limited and insignificant extent. Lying scattered, as many expressions of them do, through masses of extraneous matter, not designed nor calculated to give them prominence, they have remained unobserved, like unsuspected jewels in a rubbish pile. Nay, authors of eminent merit have sometimes picked them up, either from their own *cabinets* of thought, or from those of other thinkers, and after regarding them indifferently, or but for a moment, have laid them aside again, or actually thrown them away, little suspecting the valuable treasures of thought they were thus trifling with, like the astronomer Gilbert, for example, who little imagined, no doubt, when he compared the moon and the earth to two mutually attracting *loadstones*, that he was toying with the law of UNIVERSAL GRAVITATION and developing that germ of truth which has subsequently expanded into the grand conclusions of the Principia Mathematica that have shed imperishable lustre on the name of Newton and the human understanding.

The author of the present work may, therefore, lay claim to some credit, for the service he will have rendered to Social Science, by simply collecting together, and laying before the scientific world, in their due logical order, as he now proposes to do, the valuable ideas which have been already expressed, but which have been hitherto only disconnectedly, and in some cases even casually, rather than designedly, thrown out by different authorities. If, indeed, his labor of life should stop at this—if his career of unrequited toil should be cut short here, and he should not be permitted to bring before the world any more of the results of his arduous and unappreciated labor of years, it will not have been wholly in vain, that he has devoted himself to self-immolation for the CAUSE OF KNOWLEDGE, to which, from an early period, he has, with devout reverence, devoted his energies of head and heart.

With the combined result of all anterior investigations in Social Philosophy, in this little volume condensed, with the most advanced thoughts of the most advanced thinkers, in this realm of inquiry, set forth in their due logical order, it is not to be doubted that some other mind, if his should fail to execute the work, would, in a short time, carry them forward to their ultimate tendencies— the discovery of the true Philosophy of Society. For it is but little, at best, that any one mind can do for the advancement of human knowledge—little enough, indeed, that all combined can do.

§ 2. If, instead of writing out his own independent and conclusive reasonings on the laws of motion, with special reference to the planetary system, Newton had presented to the scientific world a condensed and connected statement of the result of all anterior researches in Astronomy, in their most essential import— of the suggestions, as well as discoveries, of Copernicus, Kepler Galileo, Bouilland, Borelli, Gilbert, Hooke, Huygens and Halley —there can be but little doubt that the human mind would, in a short time, have moved up to all the conclusions of the Principia Mathematica.

Still less is it to be doubted that all the conclusions, to which the present inquirer in this realm of science can hope to advance the human understanding, beyond what is actually expressed in the condensed result of all anterior investigations, which he here attempts to give, would, in a short time, be attained by some other mind, in default of his own, by the aid of the important suggestions derivable from that result.

Happy would it have been, however, for the present inquirer, if he had adopted the far easier task of Newton,—if instead of ransacking the libraries of the world, at vast inconvenience, labor, and expense—to him the most uncongenial of tasks—to discover, analyze, and condense the thoughts of others, he had been content simply to systematize and present his own, which logically comprehend, within their own proper scope, those of all anterior inquirers. But, whether from an unnecessary respect for the thoughts of others, or from an overweening propensity to do his work thoroughly, by condensing all anterior thoughts of essential value into combination with his own, or from both causes combined, he has undertaken this arduous task. And now that it has been undertaken, and has progressed so far, let it proceed—onward to its completion, which happily seems now to be near at hand.

§ 3. What, then—let us proceed forthwith to inquire—are those more advanced ideas, in regard to the Philosophy of Society, the bare statement of which, in their due logical order, must carry the mind far beyond the contracted limits of the existing systems of thought in regard to that Philosophy, and advance it, in a short time, to the true and much-needed system? They may be briefly and sententiously expressed in the following seven propositions.

I. It is not the GOVERNMENT, or, in a larger sense, the ORGANISM of society, that determines the condition of the people composing such society, but it is, rather, the condition of the people in its largest sense, their physical, moral, and intellectual condition, that determines the character of their government, and, in its largest sense, their social organism. Government, the social organism, or framework of society, is the EFFECT, rather than the CAUSE, of the social condition existing under it. Government is the effect—MAN, the CAUSE. Government is the creature—MAN, the CREATOR.

II. MAN is not only the creator of his government, and whatsoever appertains to the framework of his society, but he is also the creator, or architect, of his destiny under that government, and within that society. It is the COLLECTIVE WILL of any class of society that determines its condition in that society, and it is, as it would seem, by an obvious corollary, the COLLEC-

TIVE WILL of the society, or nation, that determines its condition in the great society or family of nations.

III. MAN, and not his government, nor any institution that he has framed; MAN, and not his wealth, nor anything else that he has created, but MAN HIMSELF, is the primary object of consideration, in every scheme for the improvement of society, or the amelioration of the human condition.

It is only by elevating his MORAL and INTELLECTUAL STATUS, or, in other words, by elevating the COLLECTIVE WILL of society, or any given class of society, that any essential or permanent benefit can be conferred on humanity, even in respect to its mere material condition.

IV. It is the NATURAL ENVIRONMENT of man, mainly in respect to climate, soil, and geographical configuration, that primarily determines, to a great extent, if not exclusively or mainly, his real character, and therefore, secondarily, determines the character of his political institutions and social condition.

V. A scarcely less important primary influence than Natural Environment, with all its combined circumstances in determining the character of man and his institutions, is the single influence of RACE, or inherent natural predisposition, intellectual, moral, and animal. But whether RACE is itself the result of the influence of Natural Environment, exerted through successive generations, is a question as yet by no means definitively determined, nor even thoroughly or ably discussed.

VI. The most fundamental laws which govern human society, and control its destinies, are precisely those which are never *written* but which belong to the grand code of the LEX NON SCRIPTA of universal being. These laws are not less fixed, necessary, and inevitable, than those which govern the material universe, although to a far greater extent modifiable and therefore difficult to be estimated. They comprise a part of the immutable laws of nature; and human society is but a part of the framework of universal nature.

The science of SOCIOLOGY is therefore to be regarded as one of the natural sciences, to be studied in connection with all other sciences, physical as well as moral; and as MAN is the last and highest attainment of universal nature, the crowning point of all creation, so is SOCIOLOGY, or the science of human society, the apex and crowning point of all other sciences resting for its support on the pedestal of all anterior science.

VII. MAN being the immediate architect of his own fortunes, and controller of his own social destiny, he works best toward that end when least obstructed in his activity, and with the least possible interference on the part of others—the great law being everywhere applicable, subject of course to some important qualifications, that EVERY MAN KNOWS BEST HOW TO ATTEND TO HIS OWN BUSINESS.

Government, therefore, which is the mere creature, servant and instrument of MAN, should have as little to do as possible with his business. Its proper business is simply to afford protection to its rightful MASTER, and legitimate SOVEREIGN—MAN. Its true function is negative, not positive, and consists in the LET-ALONE POLICY, to be observed by itself, and enforced on others. Its legitimate office, most essentially expressed, is to guaranty the largest play to individual activity that may be consistent with the interests of society, that is to say, of individuals in general.

The tendency of all true civilization, of all real progress in humanity, is, accordingly, to give importance to the CITIZEN, and insignificance to the state—to enlarge the MAN, and dwarf the government—to fix attention on the INDIVIDUAL, and withdraw it from the society, or aggregate mass. Its tendency is, in short, toward the ultimate triumph of the INDIVIDUAL over SOCIETY.

These seven propositions, it must readily be discerned, embrace a vast amount and variety of thought, and, in their combined results, go very far toward suggesting the whole outlines of a complete Philosophy of Society. The propositions have been here stated, for the most part, in the words of the present writer, and they have been, it is true, somewhat freely *translated*, so to speak, from the various and widely disconnected texts from which they have been rent. They have been, indeed, distilled in the author's own brain, from the products of many widely separated fields of thought. Yet it is believed that they will be found to embody nothing more than is essentially involved, if not distinctly expressed, in the thoughts from which they have been extracted, as may presently appear from the very words of the authors by whom those thoughts have been expressed.

It is true, indeed, that a very slight variation in the mode of stating a proposition often effects a great change in its apparent meaning, or rather brings its real meaning and significance so much more clearly into view that it scarcely appears to be the same proposition. This we may find strikingly illustrated in the proposition of the astronomer Gilbert, already alluded to,* comparing the moon and the earth to two mutually attracting loadstones, which, somewhat differently stated, and with only a few additions, becomes the Principia Mathematica of Newton. Perhaps it may be somewhat so with the rendition here given of the most advanced ideas heretofore announced in Social Philosophy; and it may be that the author has unconsciously added somewhat of importance, to that which may be strictly regarded as the real result of all anterior reasonings in regard to that philosophy.

§ 4. It would, undoubtedly, convey a very erroneous impression as to the actual STATUS of the Philosophy of Society, at the present time, to suppose that it comprehends entirely, or in any one combination of thought, all the foregoing ideas, or all that is in them embraced. The entire mind of humanity, as it has heretofore rendered itself, may indeed be said to have comprehended them, but no one individual mind has done so—no one separate work, no one system of thought. No one mind, no one united system of thought, has ever as yet comprehended all these ideas, or even brought them together, if only for the purposes of a mere review. These ideas have hitherto lain scattered and disconnected over vast and widely separated tracts of thought, like the separate forces of a grand army not yet concentrated, or

---

* See § 2 of this chapter.

organized. Here they are collected together with some order, some rude approximation to due organization.

It is a noteworthy fact, moreover, not generally or at all considered, if indeed generally or at all known, that this is, to a very great extent, the case with all heretofore unknown truths, or unknown systems of thought, as they are commonly regarded. What we call great discoveries in Science, or grand achievements in Philosophy, do not so much consist, if at all, in the discovery of any truth which no one knew, or had ever conceived of before, as in the more clear and distinct perception, recognition, or appreciation of the importance and essential significance of some truth hitherto but little noticed, and mainly in its relations to other truths, already recognized and appreciated*—nay, moreover, as in the *combined* perception of many truths, which had been before, only separately discerned, or in a much more limited extent of relations.

The greatest of discoverers, or founders of systems, is not, in reality, so much an originator, as an organizer or condenser of thought. The proverb of Solomon was therefore, after all, substantially true, even for his own times, much more for ours, "There is nothing new under the sun"—a proverb which has perhaps found a somewhat more correct expression in the aphorism of one of our modern Solomons, Victor Cousin, which declares that "the first man was as much in possession of necessary and essential truths, as the last comer into the human family."†

In accordance with the same idea it has been justly said that the true mission of the Philosopher, as well as Poet—who may both be regarded as the true Prophets and High Priests of every age of the world—is to *interpret* for his race or age the fundamental ideas which it represents, and which it is its mission to

---

* See Chapter IV. of this work, § 2, where this idea is before expressed—also, and more particularly Chapter V., Part V., of the series to which this work appertains, in which the idea is much more thoroughly and extensively elaborated, in reference to the claims of Malthus to be regarded as the discoverer or founder of Malthusianism.

† Introduction to History of Philosophy, Lec. II., p. 38, edition before cited.

propagate.* He does not, accordingly, so much present any new idea to his race or age, as *represent*, and render more distinct and emphatic, the ideas which already slumber unconsciously in their mind, or are only partially and imperfectly discerned. The philosopher may, therefore, with more or less propriety, always address his fellow-men, as did the great apostle of Christianity when addressing the Athenians, "The TRUTH which you ignorantly or unconsciously recognize, that proclaim I unto you."

In endeavoring to express, as the author of the present work has here attempted, the combined result of all anterior reasonings on the Philosophy of Society, he has undesignedly, yet necessarily, had to trench somewhat upon the rightful province of the philosopher, and he may have expressed somewhat, if not a good deal, which anterior reasoners have unconsciously and impliedly expressed, rather than intentionally or expressly avowed.

In thus endeavoring to render audible and distinct the combined result of all anterior expressions of the human mind in this branch of Philosophy, the author has, indeed, necessarily had to perform one of the most arduous labors of the Philosopher—that, indeed, to which, according to Victor Cousin, the whole life of Socrates was devoted, and also, in the same sense, the life of many other philosophers. This preëminent thinker, whom we have already so often quoted, and whose transcendent sagacity constrains us still to quote him, says, "To listen to and understand ourselves; to be manifest to ourselves; to know what we truly say and think; this was the object of Socrates: a negative object undoubtedly; but this was only the beginning, not the consummation of philosophy."†

---

* The author is not able to cite the authority for this idea, which he has somewhere encountered in his reading. It is probably Mr. Thomas Carlyle. It smacks decidedly of his style of thought, and that of Germany, with which, happily for the Anglo-Saxons, Mr. Carlyle is deeply imbued. The idea, indeed, could hardly have come from elsewhere than from Germany, and if so, Carlyle is probably the medium through whom it has been transmitted. To him belongs the merit of having imported the deep thinking of Germany into Anglo-Saxondom, where the purely intellectual *mould*, which is naturally shallow, only by slow degrees can admit of very *deep ploughing*.

† Introduction to History of Philosophy, Lecture II., p. 44. Boston Ed., 1832.

Now this observation of Cousin's may serve precisely to indicate what it is that the author of this work is here attempting. To listen to the many-tongued voice of humanity, as it has hitherto declared itself; to understand its true meaning and report it back; to make manifest to mankind what it has truly said and thought on this great problem of universal Science, or rather this great CONGERIES of problems, respecting the laws which determine the destinies of human society, before proceeding to develop what he has himself, more particularly, to suggest in relation thereto—this is the object of the author of the present undertaking.

Having, in former parts of this Series, the THIRD, FOURTH, and FIFTH parts respectively, reported what has been thought and said appertaining to one or other of those systems which we have designated as the Political, Politico-Economical, and Malthusian, he is now endeavoring to report what has been thought and said, that appertains to a larger system of thought than either of these.

In executing this more difficult task the author may have failed to discharge so correctly the duties of the faithful historian or reporter, and may unconsciously, in the seven propositions just now announced, have expressed somewhat that appertains to the future, rather than the past, of human thoughts, or audibly expressed reasonings. Nay, whether he has really done so or not, he will be very likely to appear to have done so. The faithful mirror of human thoughts, or deeds, which it is the province alike of the philosopher and poet to hold up to human view, rarely fails to excite astonishment, if it do not also to give offence. The representation which Socrates thus made to mankind gave so much offence that he was put to death.

There is this difference, however, or apparent difference, at least, between the representation or report of Socrates to mankind, concerning the essential significance of their thoughts and words, and that which is here made. Socrates was condemned because he faithfully represented to mankind how little they really thought or said—how little of real significance there was in their supposed knowledge and imposing words—which, indeed, most essentially considered, is ever the truth. But the author of this work is more likely to be condemned because he has represented to mankind how much they have thought and said—how much, at least, that is opposed to commonly received opinions, on account of which opposition his report will be most likely to be condemned or objected to; on which account, moreover, the difference between his report and that of Socrates is less real than apparent. That his report, however, is substantially correct, and, on most, if not all points, amply sustained, will presently be made manifest by special reference to the authorities themselves, and, on many points, by the citation of their precise words.

§ 5. The FIRST of the seven foregoing propositions, or that which asserts substantially that the people make their institutions, rather than the institutions the people, has been so often and so emphatically asserted, and from so early a period in the lifetime of humanity, that it may be regarded as matter for astonishment, that it has not as yet been more generally received, if not, indeed, definitively settled. We find it distinctly and emphatically asserted in the famous aphorism of Hume, that, "All governments are founded in opinion." Nowhere else, indeed, has the idea been so well, so admirably stated in brief. Nowhere else has it been at once so simply, so tersely, so precisely, and so copiously expressed.

What a world of meaning, of thought, and suggestion lies imbedded in that little sentence! Yet how little have mankind heeded its suggestions, or comprehended its import! Nay, how little did the illustrious author himself comprehend the full import of that immortal sentence! How often, indeed, are men inspired to utter truths the full import of which it is not given them to comprehend!

In that little sentence is embodied nearly one half of the whole Philosophy of Society. It is the germ of the Copernican idea of Social Science. He who shall prove himself the true Copernicus of SOCIOLOGY, will be he who shall do but little more than simply unfold this grand idea of Hume's into its legitimate, and true logical expansions. The germ of it all, or nearly all, lies there—in that grand yet simple aphorism, "ALL GOVERN-MENTS ARE FOUNDED IN OPINION."

We find the same idea somewhat less distinctly expressed, though clearly enough for even ordinary comprehension, in the somewhat celebrated remark of Sir James McIntosh, that "Constitutions are not made, but grow," a remark which Herbert Spencer, in commenting on it, has happily amended into the assertion that "Government is a growth, not a manufacture."*
We find it expressed by Guizot, Hallam, De Maistre, Comte, Buckle, and a host of eminent thinkers in modern times. Nay, we find distinct recognitions of the idea, if not direct assertions of it, in remote antiquity, among the Greeks, and even the Chinese—in the profound observations of Solon and Aristotle, among the former, and of Confucius, among the latter.

How happens it, then, that, in spite of these repeated and emphatic assertions of the idea, it is not only not commonly received, but is almost totally unrecognized in the practical statesmanship of the world? Nay, how happens it that the very authorities, by whom the idea is asserted, are not unfrequently to be found totally ignoring it in their reasonings, if not flatly contradicting it?

The true reply to this question reveals nothing, so clearly, as that, which it is one of the main objects of the present undertaking to demonstrate, the necessity of a total reorganization of thought in the Philosophy of Society, and the reëstablishment of it upon new principles, new modes of thought—a reorganization as radical and thorough as that which was introduced into Astronomy by Copernicus and completed by Newton. In no other way can we get the minds of men practically to recognize the very truths which they have theoretically asserted in this domain of science. In no other way can we bring the human mind to a practical realization of the great truth under consideration in common with many others, than by disengaging it from those yet more fundamental and general ideas to which it is still wedded—

---

* See Spencer's miscellaneous work, entitled, "Illustrations of Universal Progress." Essay on the Social Organism.

than by changing its very habits and fundamental modes of thought.

On this point we cannot do better than quote the admirably just words of Comte, confirmatory of the general observation above made, and in reference to the very idea now under consideration. " Desultory indications," he says, " more literary than scientific, can never supply the place of a strict philosophical doctrine, as we see from the fact that from Aristotle downwards, and even from an earlier period, the greater number of philosophers have constantly reproduced the famous aphorism of the necessary subordination of laws to manners, without this germ of sound philosophy having had any effect in the general habit of regarding institutions as independent of the co-existing state of civilization, however strange it may appear that such a contradiction should live through twenty centuries. This is, however, the natural course with intellectual principles and philosophical opinions, as well as with social manners and political institutions. When once they have obtained possession of men's minds, they live on, notwithstanding their admitted impotence and inconvenience, giving occasion to more and more serious inconsistencies, until the expansion of human reason originates new principles of equivalent generality and superior rationality."*

These new principles of superior rationality, and more than equivalent generality, are what we need, in order to revolutionize so completely men's thoughts, that we shall no longer find them incapable of adhering consistently to those valuable ideas which they repeatedly assert, that we shall no longer find them one moment asserting a great truth, and the next flatly contradicting, or, at least, palpably disregarding it. Such are the shameful inconsistencies which the critical reviewer of the development of thought in the Philosophy of Society is compelled to observe, in respect to the great truth now under consideration, as well as many others.

Thus we find as eminent a thinker as Hallam, in his justly

---

* Comte's Positive Philosophy, as translated from the French by Miss Martineau. Book IV., ch. 3.

celebrated work on "The Middle Ages," in his *second* chapter, distinctly asserting or recognizing the truth, and in his *eighth* chapter, flatly contradicting it. In his second chapter, treating of the Feudal System, he very justly regards the anarchy then prevailing in Europe as the CAUSE rather than the EFFECT of feudal tenures—thus distinctly recognizing the idea that men, or their existing moral and intellectual condition, habits, and opinions, make their institutions, not the institutions the men. Yet, in his eighth chapter, or that which treats of the constitutional history of England, we find him committing the palpable inconsistency, and unpardonable blunder, of attributing " the characteristic independence and industriousness" of the English people " to the spirit of its laws." Had Mr. Hallam been consistent with himself, nay, had he thoroughly apprehended the idea which he had somewhat feebly uttered in his second chapter, he would readily have discerned, that, in this latter assertion, he was palpably inverting the true order of things, was bunglingly placing the cart before the horse, and that he should have attributed " the spirit of its laws," very obviously, to " the characteristic independence and industriousness" of the people. But of this inconsistency of Hallam's we shall have more to say in a subsequent chapter.

A not less palpable inconsistency, of the same kind, may be noted in a somewhat notable, if not noteworthy, agitator, in American society, more known to the world by his speeches than by any more formal disquisitions—Mr. Wendell Phillips. This worthy fanatic, and eminently contracted reasoner, has said, in one of his many speeches, and with a sagacity highly creditable to his understanding, " Governments are not formed by man, but are the gradual accretions of time, circumstances, and human exigencies. They grow up like the trees; and man may cultivate, train, and aid their growth and development, but cannot make them entire."* Yet, so little does Mr. Phillips comprehend his

---

* The author is indebted for this valuable thought of Mr. Phillips, to the work of Mr. George Fitzhugh, entitled, "Cannibal All," and published in 1857, where it is quoted approvingly, and referred to a speech of Mr. Phillips delivered at New Haven, some time previously.

own text, or so little does he adhere to it, that we find him, a mere man, vainly endeavoring, conjointly with other mere men, *to form a government*, for the negroes—such a government as never *grew*, and never can be made to *grow*, never can be made to take root, or to flourish, in the soil of negro character. If Mr. Phillips thoroughly comprehended the idea which he has only somewhat imperfectly expressed—if he were, moreover, a thorough Sociologist, he would discern that he would be as profitably employed in endeavoring to set out a cotton plantation in Iceland, or an orange grove in Kamtschatka, as in endeavoring to implant upon NEGROES the political institutions of the Anglo-Saxons.

§ 6. The SECOND of the seven main propositions, or that which asserts that the COLLECTIVE WILL of Society, or any given class of it, determines its condition, and which is, indeed, to a considerable extent, a corollary from the first proposition, is almost exclusively the idea of the Reverend Thomas Chalmers. The idea is, indeed, very nearly approximated by Mr. John Stuart Mill, but it is not fully attained by him, as we shall, presently, more clearly see, much less is it distinctly asserted. It is also very nearly approximated by De Maistre, the eminent Italian savan, whom we have associated with Dr. Chalmers, for consideration in the same chapter, but still less distinctly asserted by him.

The Philosophy of Society has made no higher attainment than in this grand idea of Dr. Chalmers. Indeed, it may be safely asserted that this is decidedly the highest attainment it has yet made. Well does the illustrious author of the idea, who, very manifestly, had not entirely compassed its significance, nor fully comprehended its import, say in regard to it, " However simple and obvious this consideration may be, yet the most important, and as yet unnoticed conclusions are deducible therefrom."* This passage seems to intimate that he had some faint prophetic view of the full significance of his assertion and the grand con-

---

* Chalmers' Political Economy, Apperdix, on Profit, pp. 403-4. Columbus, Ohio, Edition of 1833.

clusions ultimately deducible from it. But, very evidently, as we shall more clearly see in a subsequent chapter, he had but an imperfect actual conception of its extensive applications and full significance. For here again we find verification of the remark before made in regard to Hume, that men are often inspired to utter truths which they do not fully comprehend. To one prophet it is given to let fall some great oracular utterance among men. To another it is given to catch up the grand utterance and carry it forward toward its practical applications.

Vaguely impressed evidently was Dr. Chalmers, when he uttered the words last quoted, that the idea which he had announced was one of highly momentous import. But little did he imagine, doubtless, that in announcing that idea he was virtually announcing the DIVINITY OF MAN—that he was attributing to man some of the highest attributes of God—that he was proclaiming man, in his limited sphere of action, in his little world of toil—a MINIATURE GOD. Yet so he virtually did, and none the less truly, for having done so unintentionally. For so it even is.

What is the highest attribute of God, according to the highest and most approved human conception? Is it not his creative WILL? HE WILLED IT, AND IT WAS DONE! HE SPAKE THE WORD, AND THERE WAS LIGHT! Is not this truly expressive of our highest conception of the attributes of God? Yet, these attributes, says Dr. Chalmers, are even in man, and he says truly. Let mankind but WILL, alike in their individual and collective capacity—let them but WILL, with the appropriate energies and activities of purpose, what is within the realm of human possibilities, and it is done. This is the essential significance of what Dr. Chalmers has asserted in regard to the COLLECTIVE WILL of society, or rather of the different classes of society, although he did not lay down the proposition by any means so broadly as we shall presently see, and in a subsequent chapter.

What a world of thought and meaning is there in this idea. It is a kindred idea to that of Hume, already commented on—"all governments are founded in opinion." But it is a larger idea, a more definite and precise idea also, and therefore more valuable to the Social Philosopher. How much does it imply! The destinies of human society depend upon its COLLECTIVE WILL. In order to actualize for mankind, therefore, the best possible condition, or what we may properly enough term, A MODEL CONDITION, it is only necessary to obtain their collective will that such a condition shall exist.

Alas! and is it not possible to obtain this collective will—this general desire of mankind to be truly happy, and blessed in their estate, as far, at least, as in human life is possible? It is not to be hoped. It is by no means possible. To obtain such a collective will requires that mankind in general should be both wise and good. This they will never be. For the fools are many and the wise are few. So it has ever been. So it will ever be. Men cannot really WILL wisely—except to a very limited extent. They have not the wisdom to do so. And, if they had the wisdom, they would fail in the virtue. What man is there, for example, who does not know that the path of virtue is the path of wisdom—the path of true happiness? Yet, how many are there, who knowing this, yet wilfully prefer to follow that which they know is not the path of virtue, or true happiness.

Let no delusive dreams of human perfectibility, therefore, be cherished by him who would lay any valid claim to the title of Social Philosopher, or true philosopher of any kind. We may approximate a model condition of human Society, or, in other words, a model COLLECTIVE WILL—attain it, never. Let madmen, and their near kinsmen, dreamy visionaries, feed on the vain hope to render the estate of man angelic, and his earthly abode a paradise. True philosophers should know that this world must ever be a stern battle-field—a battle-field of principles, in which wisdom and folly, virtue and vice, truth and error, good and evil, must ever continue, while BEING lasts, to wrestle together in mortal agony, and shake the moral world with discords, convulsions, and devastations, analogous to those which shake the terrestrial.

§ 7. The THIRD of the seven propositions, or that which asserts that MAN himself is the primary object of attention for the Social Philosopher, is so manifestly a corollary from the two preceding ones that it can scarcely need any amplification or illustration.

And, yet, the distinct or direct assertion of the proposition is nowhere to be found, outside of these pages, so far, at least, as is known to the writer of these pages, although very near approximations to such an assertion are frequently to be met with. The nearest approximation to such a distinct assertion of the idea is to be found in the writings of Sismondi on Political Economy, whose reported exclamation—" What then! is Wealth everything, and MAN nothing?"—has already been alluded to,* and whose views in relation to the idea will again and more particularly come under review, in a subsequent chapter.

It is to be furthermore remarked, however, that this THIRD proposition is divisible into two, though substantially convertible ones, and is, in fact, stated in the double form, accordant with such divisibility. It asserts, not only that man is the primary object of attention for the Social Philosopher, but that it is only by elevating his moral and intellectual *status*, that any permanent improvement even of his economical condition can be effected.

Now, strange as it may appear, while there have been no direct or distinct assertions of the former of these two single propositions, hitherto, there have been many of the latter. The idea expressed in this latter proposition has been prominently put forward and emphatically asserted by the Malthusians, and constituted their most essential contribution to the Philosophy of Society. We find it most distinctly and emphatically asserted by Dr. Chalmers, John Stuart Mill, and other eminent authorities, as will be presently seen, and has been heretofore more fully shown.† It is noteworthy, however, that neither of these two intimately associated ideas, embodied in our THIRD main proposition, has been arrived at, or approximated, through the intervention of the two preceding main propositions, from which, very obviously, they are logically deducible. So little of true logical order does the human mind observe in its progress towards truth. It proceeds, nearly always, in a desultory manner, arriving *per saltem*, hither and thither leaping forward, at important ideas,

---

* See Chapter II., § 3 of this work.
† See Part V. of this Series, or the Part on Malthusianism, not yet published.

without discerning their connections or true logical relations, until some more comprehensive and systematic thinker arises, to point out those relations and combine them all into their appropriate system of thought.

Thus we shall find that Sismondi approximated the idea, which we have attributed to him, from the stand-point of the mere Political Economist; that Dr. Chalmers and Mr. Mill arrived at the idea, which is undoubtedly theirs, from the stand-point of mere Malthusians, and neither of them through the intervention of those higher ideas hereinbefore expressed, of which they are but the logical extensions, or, at most, but the logical co-efficients.

It is true that Dr. Chalmers, as we have already seen, was the author of the SECOND main idea, as well as one of the authors of the THIRD; but, as before remarked, he did not fully apprehend the idea, nor state it so broadly, by any means, as it has been here laid down. Still less did he, from a full apprehension of that idea, advance, by due logical sequence, to the THIRD. He rather arrived at them independently of each other. He may be said, indeed, to have stumbled upon them both, as men so often do upon important discoveries. But we should rather say, of so great a thinker as Dr. Chalmers, that he leaped forward to both conclusions, to both ideas, from the stand-point of the mere Malthusian.

§ 8. The FOURTH of the seven propositions, or that which asserts that the NATURAL ENVIRONMENT of man determines, to a great extent, or exerts a powerful modifying influence upon, his character, and consequently upon his political institutions and social condition, has been asserted, more or less distinctly and directly, by a great many eminent authorities, in modern times, although it seems wholly to have escaped the notice of the ancient philosophers. It is noticed by Montesquieu in his celebrated work on the Spirit of Laws, although rather feebly, and almost exclusively in reference to the influence of CLIMATE. It is noticed by Comte, although altogether too vaguely and imperfectly. It is noticed emphatically enough by Herbert Spencer, one of the latest authorities, and somewhat too prominently, or at least relatively so, inasmuch as he makes it a more primary and fundamental influence than RACE, and, in fact, superficially enough, regards it as the origin of RACE.* By various other authorities, it has been also noticed.

The authorities, however, by whom the idea has been most prominently advanced, most clearly and emphatically expressed, are Victor Cousin and Henry Thomas Buckle—by the former, in his publication entitled, "Introduction to the History of Philosophy," and by the latter, in his immortal work on the "History of Civilization in England." It is an account of the strong accord between those two transcendent intellects in respect to this particular idea more especially, as well as on account of the general accord between them in the character of those immortal works which they have bequeathed to mankind, that they are to be associated, in the same chapter, for more particular consideration.

§ 9. The FIFTH proposition, or that which relates to the influence of RACE, although it has been more or less distinctly asserted by many authorities, and has been, indeed, recognized and asserted, to a considerable extent, even in the channels of ordinary or popular thought, does not appear to have been ever asserted with anything like the prominence and emphasis to which its importance is entitled. Indeed, there is no idea, appertaining to the Philosophy of Society, not entirely new, or peculiar to himself—in so far, indeed, as any human thought can properly be regarded as new, or peculiar to any one individual—which it more peculiarly or prominently devolves upon the author of the present work, as it appears to him, to rescue from unmerited obscurity, and to bring into prominent view before the scientific world, than this great idea, as to the paramount and overshadowing influence of RACE, or inherent ineradicable natural traits, in determining the social condition, and general destiny, alike of individuals, nations, and families of nations. It is with this great truth as with others, that the most important are precisely those which

---

* See Spencer's work entitled, "Social Statics."

are the last to be recognized. The most important truths, being always the most fundamental, lie too deep to be readily detected, or to be apparent to the superficial view, as we see illustrated in Geology, as before alluded to in a similar relation, where the primary and most fundamental rocks, in the undisturbed natural order of things, are the last to be discovered, and in the actual order of things are so likewise, except where violent *disturbing* causes have thrown the primary rocks to the surface, or *exceptional* causes of some kind have prevented the natural superimposition of either the secondary or tertiary formations.

Among the most distinguished authorities who seem to have duly estimated the influence of Race on natural destiny is Michelet, the justly renowned historian of France. But he has *recognized* the idea merely, rather than formally asserted it. He has recognized it practically, rather than theoretically, and from the stand-point of the historian, rather than from that of the philosopher. But though an historian he has proved himself an eminently philosophical one, despite his altogether too partial leanings toward the Celtic race, natural enough in a Celt, which he doubtless claims to be. In the third and fourth chapters of his History of France, he has fully recognized the paramount influence of Race, although without formally asserting it, and has shown himself to have been fully imbued with the eminently just idea, lately expressed, that "all history, in its ultimate analysis, is a history, not of kings and laws, but of races."*

It is strange that so great a thinker as Cousin, the countryman and contemporary of Michelet, has not also recognized, and, indeed, positively asserted the idea, in his great work on the Philosophy of History, misnamed "History of Philosophy," so often before cited. On the contrary, he has virtually ignored the idea, in one of his most pregnant, and, in the main, most eminently just passages, that in which he asserts, with rare felicity and force, the great primary law as to the influence of Natural Environment, and which he lays down so broadly and exclusively, after the charac-

---

* See Harper's Magazine of May, 1856, article on "The Rise of the Dutch Republic."

teristic manner of Frenchmen, as to exclude the idea of the yet more important primary law, as to the influence of Race. But, as this eminently valuable, though somewhat objectionable, passage will be more particularly set forth, and examined, in the chapter devoted to the joint consideration of this greater thinker, and his illustrious compeer in the Philosophy of History, Buckle, any further consideration of it here would be superfluous.

When we cross the Channel from France into England, where, as Cousin very justly observes, " everything is insular, everything stops at certain limits,"* and where, he might have added, all thinking is superficial, with some few exceptions, we need not expect to find any more emphatic or prominent assertions of the great idea under review. If the bold and penetrating thought of France has failed us, in regard to the adequate expression of this great idea, we need not hope much from the far more timid and superficial, though, at the same time, far more practical, thought of England. We look in vain to the deepest and most recent thinkers of England, and, in a yet larger sense, of Anglo-Saxondom, for any adequate or justly appreciative expression of the great and paramount influence of RACE, in determining alike individual and national destiny. Of all the great thinkers that have rendered themselves prominent in England during the present century, by their contributions to the Philosophy of Society, the greatest, in many respects, without doubt, may be regarded Henry Thomas Buckle, John Stuart Mill, and Herbert Spencer. Yet not one of these eminent thinkers has done justice to the important influence of Race, or the inherent natural peculiarities of man, whether considered in the individual or the aggregate. The first named of these savans has almost totally ignored the influence, the second has equivocated in regard to it in a very discreditable manner, and the last has so imperfectly appreciated the

---

* See Introduction to History of Philosophy, Edition before cited, p. 380. Quere : Might we not venture to suggest here, the inquiry, whether it would not be better for our beloved brethren in France, if things in France could only be got to stop "at certain limits?" Should we not be less likely to see attempts at Republicanism, there, so invariably degenerating into *Sansculottism*, or *Street-Barricadism*, subversive of law, order, and liberty?

real significance and nature of the influence, that he has pronounced it ultimately resolvable into the manifold influences of Natural Environment.

It is the only noteworthy deficiency of Buckle's great work on the History of Civilization, that he does not duly estimate, and, avowedly, not at all, the influence of Race, in explaining the phenomena of History, which are often to be explained only by this influence. Thus we find him grappling with the peculiarities of Spanish and Scotch civilization, and of their respective historical developments, and attempting to explain them entirely by their respective physical geographies, and various accidental influences, of a political or military nature, without taking any notice of the respective inherent natural traits of the two nations. But in doing so, he not only fails to give a satisfactory explanation of the phenomena of their respective histories, but is betrayed into a palpable exposure of the imperfectness of his theory, and the insufficiency of the influences which alone he recognizes as explanatory of the various and manifold phenomena of human society.

Thus we find him attempting to account for the gross superstition which has ever disfigured the Spanish character, by the geographical position and aspects of the country. Tropical countries, he maintains, and not without much good reason, are the natural seats of superstition, because there men are most exposed to the mysterious influences and uncontrollable destructive forces of nature, as thunder storms, hurricanes, earthquakes, pestilences, and the like.* "Now, it is an interesting fact," he says, " that, in these respects, no European country is so analogous to the tropics as Spain. No other part of Europe is so clearly designated by nature as the seat and refuge of superstition."† And thus he undertakes to account for the known superstitiousness of the Spaniards.

But, unfortunately for the sufficiency of his theory, he presently has to encounter the fact, that another people of Europe, under a very different physical geography, away to the north, far

---

* Buckle's History of Civilization, Vol. I., Ch. I., and Vol. II., Ch. I.
† Same, Vol. II., Ch. I., p. 2, New York Ed., 1862.

removed from tropical influences, where there are no hurricanes, earthquakes, dreadful pestilences, nor the like—the people of Scotland—are almost if not quite as superstitious as the Spaniards, although their superstition is of a somewhat more manly character, and not accompanied by the same "loyalty" to princes, the same disposition to bow to the authority of man. Hear him, on this point: "While, however, in regard to loyalty," says Mr. Buckle, "the opposition between Scotland and Spain is complete, there is, strange to say, the most striking similarity between those countries in regard to superstition. Both nations have allowed their clergy to exercise immense sway, and both have submitted their actions, as well as their consciences, to the authority of the church."*

So striking a similarity between two different nations, so widely distant in geographical position, and so differently circumstanced in other respects, should have suggested what undoubtedly exists, an inherent natural similarity between them, in respect to the superstitious element in human nature, however widely dissimilar in other respects. But Mr. Buckle has, very unsatisfactorily, attempted to account for this similarity by other and external influences.

Nor should the striking dissimilarity between Scotland and Spain, in other phenomena of their respective histories, despite this "most striking similarity," and their respective dissimilarities from other nations of Europe, which have both excited Mr. Buckle's attention, have any less suggested dissimilarities and peculiarities of inherent natural traits, in the two different nations. For he not only notices, emphatically, the great difference between the Scotch and the Spanish, in respect to the indomitable spirit of the former in civil and political affairs, but he notices, still more emphatically, the differences between each of those people and the other nations of Europe.

He notices, most emphatically, what he pronounces "the apparent paradox, and the real difficulty of Scotch history," namely, "that knowledge should not have produced the effects which

---

* History of Civilization, Vol. II., Chap. II., p. 125. New York Edition, 1862.

have elsewhere followed it ; that a bold and inquisitive literature should be found in a grossly superstitious country, without diminishing its superstition,"* and the like. He notices, not less emphatically, what so many others have noticed, as remarkable, the apathetic stupor of Spain, that, "while Europe is ringing with the noise of intellectual achievements," " Spain sleeps on, untroubled, unheeding, impassive, receiving no impressions from the rest of the world, and making no impressions upon it."†

These remarkable phenomena of natural life, he vaguely and imperfectly attempts to account for, by a variety of *external* circumstances, which, as sketched by his matchless hand, serve indeed to delight as well as distract attention, but utterly fail to satisfy the exact and truly philosophical mind. But he fails to strike into the main explanatory cause—the INTERNAL one. With the characteristic superficiality and shallowness of Anglican thought, even as exhibited in its most brilliant intellects, which is for ever seeking to explain everything by referring to *ab extra* influences, without any regard to the far more important AB INTRA influences, he totally *fails* to recognize the main explanatory cause, that which, like the unseen and silent forces of nature, that are ever the greatest, lies beyond the reach of human ken, and can never be explained or accounted for—the original, inherent, distinctive peculiarity of natural predisposition.

Those remarkable anomalies in national life, which distinguish Scotland and Spain alike from one another and from the rest of mankind, after all that Mr. Buckle has said and left unsaid, are to be explained, and only to be explained, by adding to all he has said the additional and far more expressive remark which he has failed to make—that in Scotland the people are Scotch, and in Spain they are Spaniards.

It is true that this explanation leaves a good deal to be explained, just as all other explanations do. For what does any explanation, even the most satisfactory, in common estimation, but land us squarely upon the foundation of some inexplicable diffi-

---

* Vol. II., Chap. II., p. 126. † Vol II., Chap. I., p. 121.

culty or mystery, so manifestly inexplicable, that nobody but a madman attempts to explain it. The foregoing explanation, it is true, leaves still to be explained the problem, how the people of Scotland came to be Scotch, and those of Spain to be Spanish—why they were not both Scotch or both Spanish, or, in other words, both alike in their natural traits.

The solution of this abstruse problem is just about as simple and easy, as is the solution of the equally abstruse and profound one, how came Jack to be one kind of boy and Bill to be another and different kind—how came the one to be a smart boy that learns his lesson readily, and the other a dunce that cannot learn to spell and takes no interest in his schooling? Nay, it is about as simple and easy a problem as that which attempts to account for Shakespeare or Milton.

Pray, ye wise and learned philosophers, who must explain and account for everything, or else reject it as unworthy of your profound, or rather profoundly shallow consideration, explain to us this!—How comes it that Shakespeare alone writes as Shakespeare, and Milton as Milton, while the author of the "Fredoniad" writes in a manner so manifestly different from either? How happens it that they have not all written alike, and could not possibly, by any system of training ever have been brought to write or think alike? How happens it, in short, that one man is a knave, another a virtuoso, one a coward, another a hero, one a dunce, another a demigod? Explain to us all this, or else accept the explanation here given, as the only one possible, of the difficulty encountered by Mr. Buckle in his History of Civilization, just now alluded to, and of many like difficulties. Let it be accepted as the explanation that admits of no further explanation, as the reduction of the phenomenon to the most elementary facts of which the powers of human analysis are capable—to the respective inherent natural *traits* of the two nations and their respective *environments*—conventional as well as natural—to the fact that Scotchmen were Scotchmen, and thought, felt, and acted as Scotchmen, under all the circumstances, moral as well as physical, that surrounded, influenced, and constrained them, and the further fact that Spaniards were

Spaniards, and thought, felt, and acted, as Spaniards, under all the circumstances, moral as well as physical, that surrounded, influenced, and constrained them.

Somewhat different, and far less consistent than that of Mr. Buckle, has been the action or speech of Mr. John Stuart Mill, in regard to this great and paramount idea, as to the influence of RACE on national destiny. He has not, like Mr. Buckle, merely ignored the idea, but has directly assailed it, with the language of contempt, and then, at another time, and in other contributions of his thought, he has very clearly and emphatically asserted the idea, and thus turned his former contemptuous language upon himself.

In the ninth chapter of the second book of his justly renowned work on Political Economy, while speaking of the deplorable condition of the Irish peasantry, a condition, which, as he represents the case, leaves them no motives to industry or prudence, he uses this language, "Is it not, then, a bitter satire on the mode in which opinions are formed on the most important problems of human nature and life, to find grave public instructors imputing the backwardness of Irish industry and the want of energy of the Irish people in improving their condition to a peculiar indolence and *insouciance* in the Celtic race? Of all the vulgar modes of escaping from the consideration of the effect of social and moral influences on the human mind, the most vulgar is that of attributing the diversities of conduct and character to inherent natural differences."*

Very well said, indeed, for an Anglo-Saxon philosopher. And since complimentary language appears to be the order of the day, just here, and in this connection, perhaps we may be excused for saying in reply, that of all the manifestations that have been so often made of Anglo-Saxon *mud on the brain*, this, which is afforded by one of England's greatest thinkers, is decidedly one of the most conspicuous and remarkable. John Stuart Mill—one of the most comprehensive, accurate, sound, and practical thinkers of England, and of the age—one who has made more important

---

* Mill's Political Economy, Book II., Ch. IX., § 3, p. 379. Boston Ed., 1848.

practical contributions to the Philosophy of Society than any man in England, except only Malthus and Chalmers—such a man attempting to throw contempt upon the most primary, the most fundamental, the most essentially important, and all-pervading of all the influences which combine to determine the destiny of MAN, whether considered in the individual or the aggregate! It is a lamentable, though suggestive reflection. It suggests an unanswerable argument of the truth of the idea which Mr. Mill has assailed. It demonstrates the force of the influence of Race in determining opinions and habits of thought, as manifested in Anglican intellect. It shows how strongly marked is the Anglo-Saxon mind with that coarseness of vision and dullness of apprehension, which renders it so slow in appreciating the most fundamental ideas, because they are always the least obvious to the outer sense, the least discernible to "the vulgar modes" of thought—if Mr. Mill will pardon the application of his own words in this connection. It betrays the never-failing *mud on the brain*, if we may so speak, which so strongly adheres to the Anglo-Saxon, and which nothing, it seems, will wash off, but copious ablution in the deep wells of German thought.

If "the backwardness of Irish industry and the want of energy of the Irish people" be not owing largely and mainly to some inherent defect or deficiency in Irish character, to what is it owing? Very evidently it is in Mr. Mill's opinion owing to the *condition* in which they are placed, and mainly in respect to the kind of land tenure which prevails in Ireland. "Almost alone among mankind the Irish cottier is in this condition," says Mr. Mill, "that he can scarcely be either better or worse off by any act of his own."* And pray how came the Irish cottier to be in this condition? How came he to be almost alone among mankind, in being so deplorably circumstanced?

If cottier tenancy be so deplorable a kind of tenancy, as Mr. Mill represents, and need not be denied, how came the Irish tenantry to have so generally acquiesced in it? Does it not take two to make a bargain in Ireland, as well as in other countries?

---

* Political Economy, p. 378-9, of edition last cited.

How comes it that the Irish tenantry, "almost alone among mankind," have come to make such a wretchedly bad bargain for themselves? Do not men, for the most part, make their own *conditions*, in Ireland, as they do everywhere else? Is it not as true of the Irish, as of the Greeks—that which Byron has so nobly said—

> Hereditary bondsmen, know ye not,
> Who would be free themselves must strike the blow?

What other satisfactory or correct explanation can be given of this most significant fact, so misapprehended and misapplied by Mr. Mill, as to the deplorable condition in which the Irish people have allowed themselves to live for so long, than to attribute it to that improvidence, giddiness, recklessness, and thoughtlessness of the morrow, which everywhere distinguishes the Milesian Celt, whether we find him in Ireland, America, or Australia?

But why argue this question longer with an author whom we can so triumphantly quote, in his own subsequent as well as anterior reasonings, against that which is here excepted to? In his review of Michelet's History of France, first published in the Edinburgh Review for January, 1844, and subsequently published, in a more formal manner, in the collection of his various writings, entitled, "Dissertations and Discussions," after taking some exception to Michelet for overestimating somewhat, as he argues, the influence in question, Mr. Mill says, "But of the great influence of Race in the formation of national character no reasonable inquirer can now doubt."*

Still more strongly, because in contrast with another influence, almost universally admitted to be highly potential, has Mr. Mill, in the same essay, borne testimony to the potent influence of Race in determining national character, where he says, "Next to hereditary organization (if not beyond it) geographical peculiarities have a more powerful influence than any other natural agency in the formation of national character."† Very well expressed, in-

---

* See Mill's Dissertations and Discussions, Vol. II., p. 223. Boston Ed., 1865.
† Same, p. 227.

deed, and needing no qualification whatever. One would hardly imagine, however, that such was the language of the very same author whom we found but a little while ago asserting, that, "Of all the vulgar modes of escaping from the consideration of the effect of social and moral influences on the human mind, the most vulgar is that of attributing the diversities of conduct and character to inherent natural differences." We here find him placing the lately despised influence of Race, higher, in the scale of influences that mould national character, even than the potent influence of natural geography. It is gratifying, nevertheless, thus to find that so justly renowned a thinker as Mr. Mill is not insensible to the high place which the influence of Race holds among the many natural influences which combine to mould national destiny, and we may hail, with joy, his full accession to the ranks of the true Philosophy of Society.

Herbert Spencer, a far more bold and comprehensive thinker than Mill, although on that very account, perhaps, a less practical one, less accurate in respect to the practical applications of knowledge, has not failed to recognize the vast diversities of mankind, or the peculiarities of Race, but he has evidently failed, and to a greater extent even than Mill, to appreciate fully the nature of those peculiarities, the obscurity of their origin, and their comparative imperviousness to modifying or controlling influences. He evidently labors under the great error of supposing that they are referable to circumstances, or "conditions," lying open to human intelligence, and that they may be modified, controlled, or effaced entirely, by varying those circumstances, or "conditions."

In his work on "Social Statics," in his chapter on "The Evanescence of Evil," in which he indulges the weak imagination that Evil, or, rather, what puny human intelligence presumptuously adjudges to be Evil, may eventually be effaced entirely from the human character and the human condition, he distinctly recognizes the vast differences which actually exist between the African, Mongolian, and Caucasian, as well as between the less distinctly different Races of mankind. But, in reference to these differences, he uses this highly exceptionable language—"Whence all this divergence from the one common original stock? If adaptation of constitution to conditions is not the cause, what is the cause?"*

Here we find manifestation again of the Anglo-Saxon *mud on the brain*. This great Anglo-Saxon thinker here shows himself, like nearly all of his race, incapable of discerning the *unfathomable depth* of the mystery of causation. He presumes to account for everything, to explain everything. It is enough for him, that he cannot discern any other explanation of the origin of Ethnological diversities than that which refers it to different external conditions. Hence he concludes, triumphantly to his own understanding, that such is the origin and explanation of this vast mystery, which is but one ramification of the vast unfathomable mystery of Universal Being. He does not discern—it does not belong to his Race very readily to discern—that, as the most fundamental and important laws by which human society is governed are precisely those which are never written, which men voluntarily and unconsciously yield obedience to, without inquiring into their authority, so the most fundamental and important influences by which human destiny, in every respect, is controlled or directed, are precisely those which can never be explained or accounted for—are precisely those which lie beyond the reach of human view, precisely those which appertain to the OCCULT FORCES of creation, which, like all the silent and unseen forces of nature, are ever the greatest.

It seems that Mr. Spencer requires to be reminded of the profound remark of Mr. Carlyle, one of the few Anglo-Saxon thinkers whose mind has been thoroughly baptized in the deep waters of German thought—"Science has done much for us, but it is a poor science that would hide from us the great deep sacred infinitude of Nescience, which we can never penetrate, on which all science swims as a mere superficial film."†

Were we disposed to be satirical, indeed, we might deliver over Mr. Spencer to the terrible invective of Mr. Carlyle, in his Sartor

---

* Social Statics, Part I., ch. 2.
† See Carlyle's Heroes and Hero Worship, Lecture I., p. 7.

Resartus, against those who, like him and the whole race of Anglo-Saxon philosophers, with scarcely an exception, undertake to explain everything, to account for everything, or else to reject everything. We might quote upon him the notable passage—"Doth not thy cow calve, doth not thy bull gender? Thou thyself, wert thou not born, wilt thou not die? 'Explain' me all this, or do one of two things," &c.*

But we need not inflict on Mr. Spencer, or his disciples, these abstruse problems, suggested by Carlyle. We may simply ask him to explain, by his theory, or any other that he can conjecture, the notorious fact, which is of repeated occurrence, and within the observation of every one, that the different children of the same common parentage, raised under the same roof, educated in the same school, subjected, from infancy to manhood, to the very same external conditions, in every appreciable respect, are yet so widely different in their characters. "Whence all this divergence from the one common original stock?" If influences that lie beyond the reach of human ken be not the cause, what is the cause? Whence comes it that one of these children is a villain, another a virtuoso—one a coward, another a hero—one a dunce, another a demigod? Explain all these, and then, but not till then, will have been explained the origin of diversities of Race, which are simply the diversities of individual character expanded into diversities of national character, or yet more comprehensive diversities.

§ 10. The SIXTH proposition is compounded of several distinct and separable ideas, which are, nevertheless, so intimately related, that they, naturally appertain to, and ought all to be comprehended in one and the same category; and yet so partial and imperfect has been the scope of thought hitherto in the philosophy of society, that no one mind appears as yet to have so comprehended them. On this account the proposition cannot be attributed, entirely, to any one of the many illustrious thinkers who have shed their brilliant, though scattering lights, over this wide domain of thought and research. It is only a part of this proposition that

---

* Sartor Resartus, Chapter XI.

can be attributed to any one of those authorities. So much more does the entire mind of humanity embrace than any one individual mind.

This main proposition is evidently compounded of three distinguishable and separable ideas—*first*, that the most fundamental laws which govern human society, and determine its destiny, are precisely those which are never written; *second*, that those laws are not less fixed, necessary, and inevitable than those which govern the material universe; *third*, that the science of Sociology is to be regarded as one of the natural sciences, to be studied in connection with all other sciences, physical as well as moral, and that it is the apex or crowning point of all other sciences, resting, for its support, on the pedestal of all anterior science.

The first of these three ideas has been most distinctly, emphatically, and forcibly expressed by an author who has totally ignored the other two, if not directly rejected them—Joseph De Maistre, an author whose eminent merits will force him upon our more particular attention in a subsequent chapter. By no writer has this great and eminently important idea been so clearly or forcibly expressed as by him, although from the stand-point of the mere Theologian, rather than from that of the Philosopher in the largest sense, and that too a theologian of the most essentially contracted views—of all Christian theologians at least—a theologian of the Romish church.

In his brief and brilliant Essay on the Generative Principle of Political Constitutions, in the very first words of that valuable Essay, after the Preface, which is scarcely less replete with rare and valuable thoughts than the main body of the discourse, this writer says: "One of the grand errors of an age, which professed them all, was to believe that a political constitution could be written and created *à priori;* whilst reason and experience unite in establishing that a constitution is a Divine work, and that that which is most fundamental, and most essentially constitutional, in the laws of a nation, is precisely what cannot be written."*

To the same point, and in illustration of the same idea, he sub-

---

* See Boston Edition, 1847, of this work, as translated from the orginal French, p. 25.

sequently uses these immortal words concerning the English constitution, which, as we shall presently show, more distinctly, put to shame the superficial idea of Hallam, and his brother Anglo-Saxons in general, in regard to that constitution: "The true *English Constitution* is that admirable, unique, and infallible public spirit, beyond all praise, which guides everything, preserves everything, saves everything. That which is written is nothing."[*]

After so brilliant a recognition of the great truth that the most fundamental laws of human society are precisely those which are not written, and are not of human design—those which, in other words, appertain to the silent and unseen forces of nature, which are ever the greatest—it might reasonably be expected that this brilliant thinker would advance onward, to the discovery, that those laws are as fixed and inevitable as any of the laws of nature, and form a part of those immutable laws. But he does not do so. On the contrary, we find him, in the spirit of the most contracted theologian, referring those laws to the arbitrary decrees of a personal Deity—thus shutting the door to all further human inquiry, altogether too soon, and, instead of attempting "to look through nature up to nature's God," vainly and presumptuously attempting to look through God, in order to discover what nature is—a method which must ever put a stop to scientific advancement and progress in knowledge. How little, alas, is any one human mind permitted to discover! How little is any one intellect, by the flashes of its own intuitions, however brilliant, able to light up the vast surrounding darkness of THE UNKNOWN.

The second of the three ideas involved in our Sixth main proposition, has been expressed, more or less distinctly, by various authorities, but by none so emphatically, appreciatively, and forcibly, as by those who have, also, not less emphatically expressed the third of these ideas—Auguste Comte, and Herbert Spencer. Whatever differences may exist between these two transcendent thinkers—differences which the latter, not very creditably to his judgment, has sought unduly to exaggerate—[†]

---

[*] Same, p. 37.
[†] See Preface to American edition of his "Illustrations of Universal Progress," Edition of 1865, and his letters therein quoted.

in this, as well as in other important respects, they agree, to the great praise of both, in asserting that the laws which govern human society are but more diversified and complex ramifications of the universal laws of nature to be studied in connection with all other natural laws, and that the science of Sociology rests, for its pedestal and support, on all anterior science. Not so clearly, as yet, has Mr. Spencer expressed himself, to this effect, as has done Mr. Comte, who no longer lives, to correct, amend, or enlarge his observations. But this is manifestly the drift and tendency of all his reasonings, as we may expect to find more clearly manifested in the writings which he has promised to the world, in the prosecution of his vast scheme of Universal Philosophy. But as both of these great thinkers will presently come under more particular consideration, in another chapter, it would be superfluous to consider their peculiar views more particularly here.

§ 11. The SEVENTH, and last of our seven main propositions, although compounded of several more particular ideas, is, nevertheless, so homogeneous in all its parts, so manifestly all-adhering and logically inseparable, that it would be of little advantage to sever those more particular ideas from the general form of the more comprehensive truth to which they appertain, as the natural members of one common body. This comprehensive proposition, indeed, cannot properly be regarded as the expression, so much of any one mind that has hitherto rendered its thoughts, as of the general drift, and essential tendency, of many minds, if not indeed of all minds since the world began, unconsciously to themselves, as the great waves of human destiny roll onward—sweeping all things, that on them float, to the end which none can resist, none can very clearly foresee.

It is in regard to the great truth, or truths, embodied in this last proposition, that the march of mind may be, most appositely compared to the march of the separate divisions of the grand army of Napoleon, in the ever-memorable Russian campaign, to which we have before had occasion to refer.* How many bold

---

* See Chap. IV., § 5.

and brilliant thinkers have been marching on unconsciously, through centuries past, to deliver their thoughts, in concentration upon this little village of Beszenkiewiczi, so to speak, in this vast domain of human science, which they have been attempting, hitherto unsuccessfully, to subjugate to their dominion!

How little do the greatest thinkers often appreciate the full significance of their own thoughts, and words! How often may the critical philosopher apply to the significant words of his fellow-men the exclamation of Othello to Iago, in the play, although under very different circumstances from those to which the remark of unhappy deluded Othello had application, "There is meaning in thy words!" Aye, he might often add, more meaning than thou art perhaps aware of—a meaning, a significance, of which thou dost not dream.

How little did many of the greatest thinkers that ever lived, dream—how little did Adam Smith, Sismondi, John Stuart Mill, Buckle, Spencer, Comte, the great orator of Britain, Chatham, the great statesmen of America, Jefferson, Calhoun, and many of their illustrious disciples in political creed, imagine—how greatly would they be astonished, at being told, that the essential drift and tendency of their doctrines, and of all real progress in society, is TOWARDS THE EVENTUAL TRIUMPH OF THE INDIVIDUAL OVER SOCIETY!

One transcendent intellect alone, appears as yet, to have towered high enough to look forward to this discovery. One mind alone seems to have been highly enough inspired to make this oracular announcement. One human brain alone seems to have been so touched with the genuine fire of an exalted poetry and philosophy as to be rendered capable of emitting this brilliant and dazzling light, which throws itself far, very far in advance of all anterior lights. The highly favored prophet, who has been endowed to make this great announcement so far in advance of prevailing ideas as to be utterly incomprehensible, except to a very few, is Henry James, an American thinker of a highly inspired metaphysical order, and by profession a *theologian*, though of the highest and most advanced school of theology—or of Christian theology, at least—the rationalistic Christian. In his collection of rare and valuable essays on Moralism and Christianity, Henry James utters these oracular words—"This is the last great triumph of humanity, the signal for the complete inauguration of God's kingdom on earth—the triumph of the individual over society."*

This triumph, of course, mankind will never actualize, or fully attain. He who even hopes it is but a philosophical dreamer and star-gazer. But it may be approximated, and with reference to the nearest possible approximation to this grand attainment, should all speculations and endeavors in Social Philosophy be shaped. It helps materially, therefore, to furnish us a chart and compass by which we may steer our course, if, indeed, it may not be regarded as the veritable POLE of social geography, by which we are to calculate our direction and bearings, in our scientific explorations for human advancement.

The mariner does not expect to reach the North Pole. But it is of inestimable value to him, nevertheless, to have a North Pole to steer by, and take his latitude and direction in stormy weather. Nor is it any less true that the brilliant idea in question, although it can never be attained or actualized, may, nevertheless, be of inestimable value, as a kind of intellectual Pole, or Polar Star, by which we may safely take direction, and steer our course, through the uncertain and often troubled sea of human endeavor.

It may be worthy of a passing notice, as not a little remarkable, that the three ideas, of the many involved in our seven main propositions, which are the most valuable, the most suggestive, and the most in advance of commonly received opinions, are all the contributions of theologians, or of those who have spoken from the stand-point of theologians. These are the idea of Chalmers, as to the Collective Will of Society, as expressed in our *second* main proposition; that of De Maistre, as to the most fundamental laws of society, expressed in our *sixth* proposition, and that of Henry James, now under consideration, and which may be regarded as the essential rendition, in brief, of our whole *seventh* proposition. It is true that De Maistre was not

---

* Moralism and Christianity, p. 154.

avowedly, or by profession, a theologian. But he has evidently thought and written as a theologian, in the work from which we have quoted, and the evident aim of that work was to vindicate many of the tenets and bold assumptions of the Romish Church.

It is remarkable, too, that, while the author of the present work has found it advisable to shape the thoughts, as well as the words, of all the other authors whom he has undertaken to interpret, in order to condense their thoughts into their most essential expression, these thoughts of these three illustrious authors have not needed any shaping of his, but have rather shaped, controlled, and powerfully modified his own. It is furthermore remarkable, that, while the thoughts of all the other authors whom it has been attempted here to represent, as particularly noteworthy, have been also the thoughts of the present author himself, and mere repetitions, to his mind, for the most part, of ideas previously entertained and arrived at, through his own spontaneous intuitions, these three grand ideas of these three preëminent thinkers have alone struck him, as before unknown and unrecognized truths—have alone flashed upon his mind, as new and startling revelations, throwing light upon the pathway of inquiry, far in advance of the light of his own understanding, and of all anterior thought.* For this great service, which has been rendered to his own understanding, as well as to the cause of Science, with profound respect and gratification, he here acknowledges his obligations to these illustrious names.

Nor is it, perhaps, any less remarkable, or worthy of note, that these three preëminent thinkers have represented, respectively, the three different schools of Christian theology, as, indeed, of all theology—which, in its applications to every religion, naturally divides itself, like everything else, into three main parts, which

---

* From this remark, it is perhaps due to the author to except the idea of De Maistre. For that is essentially one of his own most fundamental ideas, revealed to his view unaided by the suggestions of any other mind—the idea as to the fixity and necessity of the laws of mind, not less than matter. But the particular expression which De Maistre has given to the general idea, has been to his thought eminently suggestive.

are substantially the same in all religions—namely, the Papistical or formalistic, the Puritanical or doctrinalistic, and the truly Orthodox, or rationalistic and practical—De Maistre, of course, representing the first, Chalmers the second, and Henry James the third of those schools.

Should not these notable facts tend, in some degree, to rescue THEOLOGIANS from the philosophical, or rather, unphilosophical contempt, which too many philosophers of late have been disposed to throw upon theology, and theologians? Or shall we, in respect to these three great ones, paraphrase the famous language of Pyrrhus, concerning the Romans, "These barbarians are by no means barbarous," and say that these theologians are by no means theological? But no such subterfuge can rescue this class of philosophers from the merited criticism to which they render themselves liable, although, prominent among the class, stand such illustrious names as Comte and Buckle—a fact by no means creditable to their sagacity, preëminent as it has proved itself in many important respects.

Philosophers of this class, it appears—nay, Comte has openly avowed it—would ignore Theology altogether, would ignore all idea as to GOD, or the great primary and fundamental CAUSE, from which all other causes spring. Would they, indeed? And pray, what sort of Philosophy would that be, which should have no Theological system to stand upon—neither theistical, atheistical, nor pantheistical? But enough of this digression.

§ 12. That the grand utterance of Henry James, here brought into prominent view, is truly expressive of the essential tendencies of the highest Civilization, and the highest Thought, will be readily apparent to the higher order of thinkers, who will dwell, but for a few moments, upon the idea. Much more apparent will it become to such, on a more thorough consideration.

It must be apparent, to a very little reflection, that this is the essential significance of many of the most extensively received popular ideas, and most universally admired popular sentiments, that have currency among the most advanced races and nations of mankind.

Consider, for example, the latest and most advanced popular idea, now universally accepted, professedly at least, among the American division of the great Anglican or Anglo-Saxon family, that "every man is a sovereign." What is this, but a general, if not universal, popular recognition of the great truth in question, which, if stated, in its true import and full significance, in a scientific point of view, men start back from, and disclaim? So true it is, as we have repeatedly before had occasion to remark, that mankind are constantly in the habit of receiving and asserting truths, the full import and essential significance of which they do not comprehend, and cannot, without great difficulty, be made to comprehend.

What is this doctrine, however, but an implied avowal of the essential tendency toward the triumph of the individual over society? Nay, may it not be regarded as an avowal that the individual has already triumphed over society—to a certain extent, in legal contemplation, and in the eye of essential justice and fundamental right?

If the INDIVIDUAL is the true SOVEREIGN, then evidently the society or its legal representative, the state, or collective authority of the society, is the true *subject*, whose proper function or business is to see that every one of the many individual sovereigns, who have concurred in appointing it, is not, in any respect, molested or disturbed in his sovereignty—in order to insure which end alone, most essentially considered, the true *subject*, or state, has any right to interfere with the sovereignty of any one individual. The state has no right to interfere with the sovereignty of any individual, except in so far as may be necessary to vindicate the co-equal and independent sovereignty of other individuals. In other words, every man has the right to do just what he pleases, provided he do not interfere with the rights of other men, and will pay his fair proportion of the taxes necessary to maintain that collective force of the society, which may be necessary, to protect individual sovereignty from outrage, violence, or wrong of any kind.

This is the LAW, as it is even now received, throughout the mighty domain of Anglo-Saxondom—shamefully as it has been violated of late in America, as we have seen in the audacious and heretofore unparalleled assumption of power by the state or government, to compel individual sovereigns to commit murder and other flagrant crimes, against their will, in the prosecution of *aggressive* war, against their fellow-men of coterminous states.*

It is very manifest that the doctrine of the inviolability of the person of every man, universally received in Britain, as well as America, is but another manifestation of the same tendency. The so-much extolled writ of Habeas Corpus, for vindicating the sacred right of personal security, with all that has been said in its eulogy, is but a recognition, in logical *embryo*, of the tendency toward the eventual triumph of the individual over society. So is, evidently, the idea that "every man's house is his castle," which has long ago passed into an Anglo-Saxon proverb. And who is so obtuse as not to read the same assertion in the immortal words of Lord Chatham—"The poorest man in his cottage may bid defiance to all the forces of the crown. It may be frail; its roof may shake; the wind may blow through it; the storm may enter; the rain may enter; but the King of England cannot enter. All his power dares not cross the threshold of that ruined tenement."

The late great war in America, the real nature of which is so little understood by the superficialists to whom its consideration has been hitherto mainly consigned on both sides of the Atlantic,

---

* This assumption of power is almost unparalleled in Anglo-Saxondom, though not, of course, in despotic Russia, Austria, or France, nor among the ancient semi-barbarous nations, mis-called civilized. It is to be remembered that the British government has never dared to assert the right to compel her sovereign citizens, or *subjects*, as they are mis-called, to enlist for foreign wars, except in the now exploded method of "impressment." It is to be remembered, also, that the Constitution of the United States, impliedly, if not expressly, denies the right of the general government to employ the militia of the several states, except " to repel invasion." Or rather it expressly delegates the right to use them only for this purpose. And all "powers not expressly delegated are reserved to the states respectively, or the people." It was a great oversight, however, in the framers of the Constitution not to provide that the militia of no state shall be compelled to march into another state, except on the request of the regularly constituted authorities of that state. Such a provision was necessary to assert distinctly the true Anglo-Saxon idea of liberty.

most essentially considered, was a great practical manifestation, though, thus far, and to the outer view, unsuccessful, of the same tendency. It was by far the most decided and emphatic movement in that direction on any large scale that has ever occurred in human history. This is its most marked characteristic feature, to the philosophical and truly discerning mind, though not its only marked feature.

Taken altogether, that war affords, beyond all doubt, the most remarkable, the most instructive and suggestive chapter of equal length, in human history. Never before in the known history of the world were men fighting at cross purposes, on so large a scale. Never before were the upper and under currents of human affairs running in opposite directions with so great intensity and force. Never before were the apparent and real condition of things so widely different. Avowedly, and apparently too, to a certain extent, fighting for liberty, the successful party were in reality inflicting a most disastrous blow on that divine principle, a blow calculated indeed to be fatal, but not likely to prove so—because inflicted on a RACE that does not easily die, and does not readily part with its liberty, while it lives. Avowedly, to some extent, and not less apparently, fighting for slavery, the other and unsuccessful party were in reality fighting for liberty, and that, too, in the most marked, emphatic, and distinctly defined manner, that liberty has ever been contended for on so large a scale.

The first great revolutionary war in America, most essentially considered, was an assertion of the idea that sovereignty does not reside in the government, or concentrated collective force of the society, but in the society itself, or the people composing it. The second or last war, most essentially considered, was an assertion, or attempted assertion, thus far unsuccessful, of the more important idea, which it is much more difficult to vindicate, or render theoretically or scientifically intelligible, even to those who have long ago practically accepted it, and adopted it into their common proverbs—the idea that sovereignty does not reside in A BARE MAJORITY of the society or people, as vulgarly imagined, but in at least something more than a bare majority, in something approximating A UNANIMITY, if not alone in A UNANIMITY of the society, or, in other words, in the whole society, and in each individual member of it.

This was not, of course, the avowed significance or object of the war on the part of those who in reality represented this idea in the contest. Nor was its real significance thus understood generally, if indeed by any who participated in it. How seldom do men understand the real significance of their own acts or words! It requires the very highest effort of Philosophy to do that. The real significance of men's acts is nearly always far, very far, in advance of their existing ideas, or capabilities of comprehension.

It should, however, be highly gratifying to the philosophic mind, to know how much of the real significance of this war was comprehended by many of those noble spirits who covered themselves and the human race with immortal glory by their heroic efforts to vindicate the principle for which they fought. They did not know, indeed, that they were fighting to vindicate the great idea that sovereignty resides in the INDIVIDUAL, and to advance mankind toward the ultimate triumph of the INDIVIDUAL over society. But they knew that they were fighting to vindicate the rights of MINORITIES, as guaranteed by State Sovereignties — to vindicate the idea that minorities have their rights as well as majorities — that the rights of the FEW are as sacred and inviolable as the rights of the MANY — that the *weak* should be respected as well as the *strong*. This was a great and noble advance toward the ultimate and most radical idea toward which all true human progress is tending.

This idea of state sovereignty, most essentially considered — this idea that a considerable minority of any entire political organism, having of itself an integral political existence, like the separate states of the American confederacy, has the right to arrest the action of the larger organism of which it forms a component part, so far as that action may apply to itself, despite its liability to great abuse, like everything else, it will readily be discerned by the true Social Philosopher, has a very important tendency in the right direction. It tends to block the wheels of government, which have a constant tendency to run when they have no business. It tends to tie up the hands of legislation, which are constantly busying themselves with matters that would much better be let alone. It tends to the denial of all government by the collective force or political authority of society, which all experience has demonstrated to be but a "necessary evil," of which the more we can dispense with the better. It tends to transfer the motive principle of government from the public or collective force of society to the individual. It tends, in short, towards "the eventual triumph of the individual over society."

This tendency, however, does not appear to have been discerned even by the illustrious Statesman, who has been the most prominent apostle of this idea of State Sovereignty, the late John Caldwell Calhoun. Still less has it been discerned by his disciples. By him and them it has been too much regarded as a mere question of pure constitutional right, of dry abstract constitutional law. It should, much more prominently, have been regarded as a question of policy, of practical expediency, of fundamental propriety and right. Instead of disputing with their superficial opponents upon the question whether the idea exists in the Federal constitution, as they have mainly done, they should rather have demonstrated that it ought to be there, if it is not, and that a revolution ought to be attempted, even at the cannon's mouth, if necessary, in order to put it there. They should rather have demonstrated that the idea exists in the constitution of Nature and ought to exist in the Constitution of the United States.

The principle of State Sovereignty in American politics, is to the rights of minorities what the writ of Habeas Corpus is to individual rights. It is the great bulwark of liberty. It is the great breakwater to despotism. It is the only bulwark, the only breakwater, that can prevent American liberty, under the great confederacy now existing, from being, within a comparatively short time, swallowed up in a vast consolidated despotism.

A critical analysis will not less clearly show that the essential tendency of many of the most eminent formal disquisitions on government and society, that have ever been written, is also in the direction indicated by the bold aphorism of Henry James under consideration. Such is evidently the tendency of Rousseau's Social Contract, and of Calhoun's masterly disquisition on Government. They both tend to the denial of all government that is not approved by something more than bare majorities, as *by concurring majorities*, or the like, which tends to secure something like unanimity of consent to all binding political action, the further tendency of which, it should be manifest, is towards the vindication of individual sovereignty, inasmuch as it tends to tie up the hands of government except as to those acts to which every individual gives his consent.

Such is also the tendency of the work of Henry James on "Democracy and its Issues," one of the most valuable contributions to Social Philosophy, in its purely political bearings, that has appeared in the English language. Such, too, is the tendency of Mill's recent work on Liberty, of Buckle's social philosophy, as developed in his great work on the History of Civilization, and not less, also, of the whole philosophy of Herbert Spencer, so far as it has been as yet developed, in respect to its bearings on the Philosophy of Society. Nowhere, indeed, has the ultimate tendency of the highest civilization, in respect to the relations between the individual and society, been better expressed than it has been by the last-named author, in his work on "The First Principles of a New System of Philosophy."

In the sixteenth chapter of this work, the chapter on Equilibration, Mr. Spencer thus expresses himself on this head: "The conflicts between Conservatism, which stands for the restraints of society over the individual, and Reform, which stands for the liberty of the individual against society, fall within slowly approximating limits; so that the temporary predominance of either produces a less marked deviation from the medium state. This process, now so far advanced among ourselves that the oscillations are comparatively unobtrusive, must go on till the balance between the antagonist forces approaches indefinitely near perfection. For, as we have already seen, the adaptation of man's nature to the conditions of his existence cannot cease, until the internal forces which we know as feelings are in equilibrium with the external forces they encounter. And the establishment of this equilibrium is the arrival at a state of human nature and social organization, such that the individual has no desires but those which may be satisfied without exceeding his proper sphere of action, while society maintains no restraints but those which the individual voluntarily respects. The progressive extension of the liberty of citizens, and reciprocal removal of political restrictions, are the steps by which we advance towards this state. And the ultimate abolition of all limits to the freedom of each, save those imposed by the like freedom of all, must result from the complete equilibration between man's desires and the conduct necessitated by surrounding circumstances."*

It will readily be perceived, by the critically discerning mind, that in the foregoing passage Herbert Spencer has expressed substantially the idea of Henry James under consideration. But he has expressed it with more critical accuracy, with its proper qualifications or limitations, and therefore with less striking sententiousness and epigrammatical piquancy. The expression which Henry James has given to the idea is that of the highly inspired poetical philosopher. The expression of Herbert Spencer is that of the calm unimpassioned critical philosopher.

It will readily be perceived, from the discriminating and admirably just expression which the latter author has given to the idea, that "the triumph of the individual over society," as the highly wrought inspiration of Henry James has so strikingly expressed it, does not consist, as to superficial readers might appear, in the unbridled license of the individual to do whatever he may please, regardless of the rights of society, or other individuals, but in that happy harmonizing of his desires with the rights of all other men which dispenses with the necessity of restraints, or coercive measures, on the part of society.

That the essential tendency of the highest civilization, or, in other words, of the most complete development of man's nature, is in this direction, no profound and justly discerning thinker can fail to see. Whether such a condition can ever be attained, in

---

* See Spencer's First Principles of a New System of Philosophy, Ch. XVI., pp. 470, 471. New York Edition, 1865.

other words, whether man can ever become so highly civilized, or his nature can ever become so completely and generally developed, is very much to be doubted, nay, we should rather say, is hardly to be hoped.

But, even if this condition should ever be attained, and however nearly it may ever be approximated, it is to be distinctly understood that man, as a member of human society, in which society alone he can ever attain his proper development, must ever be, to some extent, and to a large extent, under the influence of the society to which he is attached, under the powerfully reactive influence of the whole upon its parts, and that from this influence he can never be emancipated, either in point of fact, or in reference to a due regard for his welfare and the essential laws of his being.

Human society, like the society of the planets, must ever be, not only in the aggregate, but in all its parts, under the dominion of two great and constantly active forces, the one CENTRIPETAL, and the other CENTRIFUGAL, the one conservative of ORDER, the other of LIBERTY, the one tending to COMMUNISM, and the complete merger of the individual in the society, the other to INDIVIDUALISM, and the complete triumph of the individual over society. It is in the happy equipoise, or, as Herbert Spencer has expressed it, "equilibration," between these two forces or principles alone that a harmonious state of human society can ever be realized. Neither of these forces can ever be abrogated. Among rude, imperfectly developed, or but partially civilized men, the centripetal or central force of society must be powerfully exerted. Among highly developed, highly civilized men, the exertion of this force may be to a great extent dispensed with.

It is remotely possible that conditions of society might exist, among the most superior races of mankind, on a somewhat considerable scale, in which this central force of society, or its outward manifestation, might be dispensed with altogether; as we see illustrated, on a small scale, and for short periods, at the dinner-table of gentlemen, which affords us a practical illustration, on a small scale, of the triumph of the individual over society. In the capability of dispensing with this central force of society altogether would manifestly consist the triumph of the individual over society.

But this triumph does not consist in the abrogation of the influence of society on the individual, of the whole on its parts, but in the absorption of that influence into the individual. It consists in that development and expansion of the individual which enables him to wield and to direct both the momentum of his own proper individuality and that of the society, and so accurately to describe the orbit of his own personality, as not to interfere with those of other personalities—which enable him to comprehend, within himself, and to control both of the two great antagonistic or counterbalancing forces which pervade all organic existences, and to become a sort of living universe within himself. It consists, in short, in that high development of man which exalts him, in some degree, to the character of a God.

Quite evidently there is not much ground for hope that such development of man will ever become very general or extensively prevalent. Nevertheless, it is in this direction that we must look for indication of the real tendencies of the highest human development and attainment. God can only be, to the apprehension of mankind, the highest type of MAN. Of this truth, indeed, we find at once both recognition and happy illustration in the character we have been, perhaps wisely, taught to attribute to the most august and beneficent of all human reformers, HIM whom we have been taught to regard as the incarnate manifestation of both God and man—the GOD-MAN.

§ 13. Thus have we completed, though imperfectly, a work of great labor and responsibility, that of condensing, into a few words, the essential significance of the latest, the largest and most developed thought of the human understanding, in regard to the Philosophy of Society. Thus have we condensed, into a single chapter, the essential significance of many volumes.

In the chapters that are to follow we shall but find the ideas of this chapter more particularly developed, as they have been exhibited to view by the various writers whom it is proposed more particularly to consider. On most points we shall find the ideas announced in this chapter somewhat enlarged, and brought more distinctly into view, as more particular views have a natural tendency to do. On others, perhaps, we shall find that the announcements of this chapter are somewhat larger, more distinct and more emphatic, than is fully justified by the actual announcements of any other authority, that we shall therein consider, or may be able to cite.

On some points, doubtlessly, the essential significance of the most developed thought has been represented, in the present chapter, as somewhat larger than is actually warranted by any anterior thought, that has, at least, rendered itself audible. But all that has been herein laid down is, so manifestly, the true and proximate logical sequence of what has been actually expressed by anterior thinkers, that the author may be excused—even while playing the part of the mere critical historian of the world of thought—for thus anticipating, somewhat, the actual manifestations of the human understanding.

In former parts of the main work to which this appertains, in the *third*, *fourth*, and *fifth* parts, which treat respectively of the Political, Politico-Economical, and Malthusian systems of thought, all, of essential significance or value, that has been contributed to the Philosophy of Society, by those three schools of thought, has been amply considered. In the present work, all the later, and more advanced thought, whether anterior or posterior in mere chronological order, in its most essential rendition, is now offered to the world. When the three other works, which have not as yet been published in the book form, nor otherwise than in disjointed fragments, shall have been formally published—if this should ever be rendered possible—the whole combined result of all anterior thought and research, in the Philosophy of Society, will be laid before the view of the scientific world. They will then be able to judge, more clearly and distinctly, what has been done and what remains to be done, in order to reduce this vast department of general knowledge into order and proper system. They will then be able the better to appreciate the more particular contributions which the author of the present work proposes to make, and which, he ventures to hope, will harmonize and systematize all anterior thought of essential value, and leave the Philosophy of Society, for all practical purposes, somewhat in the condition in which the labors of Newton left Siderial Philosophy.

CHAPTER VII.

A BRIEF RETROSPECT INTO THE WISDOM OF ANTIQUITY—AS MANIFESTED IN CONFUCIUS AND SOLON.

§ 1. It has been well, said, by Rosseau, that, " the body politic as well as the physical, begins to die at the moment of its birth, and bears in itself the cause of its destruction."* Nor is this observation any less true of systems of thought, than of corporeal systems.

Of this truth we find striking illustration in the history of the Political system of thought in Social Philosophy, which, though it still lives and maintains its pernicious hold on the human understanding, may be clearly ascertained to have begun to die more than two thousand years ago, and at the very moment it first assumed a well-defined shape, and may be said to have begun vigorously to live, both among the Mongolian and Caucasian branches of the human family. The germs of its death, or, as we should rather say, the germs of a higher life, involving its death, may be distinctly discovered in the masterly brains of two of the greatest lawgivers that the world ever saw—Confucius and Solon. These great ones may be said to have given the first well-defined organic development to the Political system of thought in Social Philosophy among their respective races. Yet, at the same time, we may discover, from the very fundamental ideas of the one, and from one of the profound general remarks of the other, which has been transmitted to our times, that they both had the sagacity to perceive, in some degree, at least, how superficial and imperfect was that system of thought—how vain was the attempt to control the destinies of human society by the mere political authority of states, and that, in short, it is rather the MAN that forms and gives character to the state, than the STATE that forms or gives character to the man.

---

* Social Compact, Book III., Ch. XI.

§ 2. Of the Four Books which constitute the main body of Chinese classics, a part of the first only is actually ascribed to Confucius, although nearly the whole of those four books is commonly regarded as the result of his teachings, as the embodiment of his ideas, subsequently written out by some of his disciples, as were the teachings of Socrates and Christ. "It is the business of the first of the four books," says Mr. Davis, in his valuable History of China, "to inculcate, that from the knowledge and government of one's self must proceed the proper economy and government of a family, and from the government of a family that of a province and of a kingdom."*

It may readily be perceived that this fundamental idea of Confucius is the germ of a higher system of Social Philosophy, than that false and puerile one which regards the government of a state as the cause of the condition of its people, and in accordance with which we so often witness pernicious attempts to subvert the existing governments of the world in the vain hope of thereby improving the condition of the people. Nay, it is very manifest that it is the germ of the very opposite system, of the system which asserts that it is the people who are the cause of the condition and character of their government, and that it is vain and futile to attempt to change the mere government of a people, unless you can first, or at the same time, change the character of the people.

How does this wise and profoundly just idea of this ancient sage, so little known or considered among European nations, put to shame the school-boy philosophy of those pestiferous agitators of modern society who are constantly distracting the nations of Europe with their pitiful endeavors to reform society by merely changing the form of its government, and the nations of America by their not less pitiful attempts to make white men out of negroes, Caucasians out of Ethiopians, by merely changing their *legal status* in society, their mere political conditions.

This highly valuable idea of Confucius has also this great merit, which so few reasonings on the philosophy of society pos-

---

* Davis's History of China, Chap. IV. See, also, Martin's China, on same point.

sess, that it directs attention directly to THE INDIVIDUAL. It is here, as we shall hereafter more clearly see, that the *key* to the solution of nearly all the great problems of Social Philosophy is to be found. As the microscope reveals to us far more valuable and essential knowledge than the telescope, and as it is in the infinitesimal, after all, that we must look for comprehension of the infinite, so it is, much more indisputably, true, that it is in THE INDIVIDUAL that we must look for clear understanding of the phenomena of society, or reliable calculation of its destiny. The great obstacle to the progress of knowledge in Social Philosophy, hitherto, has been that vague generalities alone, or, for the most part, have been dealt in, instead of coming down to the particular, simple, and familiar illustrations afforded by the consideration of the individual. If social philosophers had taken instruction more from this first great teacher in Sociology, they would not have persisted in this unwise course. They have been altogether too lofty in their speculations. Had they condescended to an humbler and simpler view of the great problems of society, they would have been much more likely to find their solution.

Confucius has afforded *the key* to the solution of the whole business, in the simple yet grand idea under consideration. If you would truly and effectually control the destinies of human society, he virtually tells you, look well to the INDIVIDUALS composing it. Would you improve society, improve the individual man. Can you not improve the man? Then you cannot improve the society. This is point number ONE, in the Philosophy of Society. It may be regarded also as point number TWO, and a great many more besides. Nay, the Alpha and Omega of the whole business is pretty nearly all comprised in this simple formula, deducible from this simple yet grand doctrine, inculcated more than two thousand years ago, yet how little heeded, especially by nations who consider themselves the wisest under the sun.

As the well-read comparative anatomist is able, from a single bone or two of the extinct *mastodon*, to reconstruct the entire skeleton, so the well-read and thorough Sociologist might, from the single idea of Confucius, construct, what, however, has never yet been constructed, the outlines of the entire Philosophy of Society.

Remarkable it is that so great should be the significance of the doctrine of one of the very earliest teachers in Social Philosophy. Not very favorable is the fact to Comte's favorite and greatly overwrought idea of the steadily advancing progress of the human mind.

Nor is it unworthy of note that Confucius, who treated extensively of both morals and politics, made morals the basis of politics, in which he approved himself a far more profound Sociologist than the over-estimated Aristotle, who, like a great many others of less note, preposterously made politics the basis of morals, as if men were to be *legislated into virtue*. It is very evident that this subordination of politics to ethics is entirely in harmony with the idea already attributed to Confucius, though not directly asserted by him, THAT IT IS THE MAN THAT MAKES THE GOVERNMENT, NOT THE GOVERNMENT THAT MAKES THE MAN*— an idea which, despite the boasted wisdom of the present age, mankind in general have not yet come to understand, nay, not even many of the self-esteemed most enlightened of mankind.†

§ 3. Not less conspicuously in the mind of Solon, than in that of Confucius, may be detected the germ of death to the Political system of Social Philosophy; or, perhaps we should rather say, the germ of life to a higher system, destined eventually to root out and supplant that superficial, false, and pernicious system. It is clearly revealed in the famous remark of that great lawgiver, in reply to the question whether he had given the Athenians the best possible system of laws—" The best of which they are capable."

How full of significance is this pregnant remark of the Grecian sage! How does it, like that of the great Chinese sage, just now considered, put to shame much of the folly of the present age— that folly which is so constantly manifesting itself in vain, futile,

---

* See pages 133-134 of this Chapter.

† For a more thorough criticism of the views of the great Chinese sage, see Chapter First, Part Second, of the main work to which this appertains, in which the contribution of the Mongolian mind in general to the Philosophy of Society is particularly considered.

and pernicious endeavors to give to all men the same kind of government, the same kind of laws.

In this pregnant remark of Solon we find clear recognition of the important truth, that laws and governments must have reference to the capacity of the people, for whom they are intended, to receive them, to use without abusing them—of the truth that all men are not fitted for the best possible laws, or system of government—that, in short, and most essentially expressed, it is the man that must determine the character of his government, rather than the government that must or can determine the character of the man. Other sages of Greece have also recognized this important truth, as we find illustrated in the remark of Aristotle, in his elaborate though disjointed treatise on Politics, "Every legislator ought to establish such a form of government as, from the present state and disposition of the people who are to receive it, they will most readily submit to and persuade the community to partake of."* But by none has the idea been at once so tersely, briefly, and pointedly expressed, or in such immediate reference to its practical applications, as by Solon, in the remark here cited.

For how many grave questions that have divided opinion, and convulsed society in modern times, for how many that still divide opinion and threaten to convulse society, does this wise remark of Solon furnish a just response! If this great lawgiver of antiquity had arisen from the dead, and were consulted upon any one of many such questions, it is hardly to be doubted, by any sound and intelligent thinker, that he would make substantially, if not identically, the same response that he is reported to have made concerning the laws of the Athenians.

If Solon were asked, for example, whether the present government of France, which so many crack-brained republicans, as they style themselves, are seeking to undermine and subvert, is the best government for the French people, he would doubtlessly reply—" the best of which they are capable." If he were asked whether

---

* Aristotle's Politics, as translated by Walford, Book IV., Ch. I. For a more particular notice of the views of Aristotle, and other Grecian sages, see Chapter II. of Part II. of this series, or the Chapter on Grecian Sociology.

the present constitution of England, which so many superficial reasoners are seeking to change, at least to the extent of rendering the right of suffrage universal, regardlessly of the existing condition of a large part of the population—is really the best possible government for the English people, he would undoubtedly reply—"the best of which they are capable." If he were asked whether the existing *status* of the *negro* in American society, which has always been, ever since American society began, in some form or other, one of *subordination* to the white man, but which distempered ignorance has been disastrously attempting, of late, to revolutionize, is really a just or right condition—is, in other words, the best possible condition for the negro, as well as for all others concerned, if he should respond worthily of the Solon of antiquity, he would, beyond all doubt, reply—"the best of which they are capable."

§ 4. It may be objected to the remark of Solon under consideration, as here interpreted, that it discourages if it does not positively condemn all effort, by the intentional agency of man, to modify or improve his condition, or that of his fellow-man—that it proposes to leave all human affairs to the natural drifting of events, to the *involuntary* action of nature, so to speak, and, in the largest and most philosophical sense, most correctly to speak, rather than attempt to control them by the action of man, or the *voluntary* action of nature, as manifested in the intentional and rational efforts of man. Undoubtedly the remark, as here interpreted, is liable to this criticism, to some extent, and to a very great extent. But it is not unqualifiedly liable to the criticism.

The interpretation here given of this celebrated remark of Solon, and the right interpretation, does indeed disparage, and hold in light esteem, the efforts of man to modify the fundamental laws of society, or the laws of nature as manifested in human society, but it does not assert that they can be of no avail whatever. The remark and the interpretation will alike stand the test of any criticism which they may provoke. They are simply expressive of a truth, that will become more manifest the more it is controverted, a truth none the less important because it is so little recognized or understood.

It is truth, which no flippant sophistry nor intolerable stupidity need attempt to assail, that all the efforts of man are insignificant, when opposed to the natural current of events, the inevitable drift of destiny. It is a truth, that as all that man can ever know is as nothing, compared with what he cannot know, so all that he can ever do is as nothing compared with what he cannot do. It is a truth, that it is but very little that man can do, at the best, by his own concerted and voluntary action, and that that little can only be done by attempting to aid or shape the course of nature, not by vainly and presumptuously attempting to oppose it.

It is true, and so the philosophy, which finds a partial expression in the remark of Solon under consideration, inculcates, that man, by his voluntary and intentional activity, can do but little, if anything at all, except by co-operating with the natural course of events—that his efforts are only of any real avail, when they conform themselves to the laws of nature, whether as manifested in external nature, or in man himself.

The remark of Solon, rightly interpreted, does not inculcate the idea, that the efforts of man are totally insignificant, or incapable of avail, but only that they are totally insignificant and unavailing when they oppose themselves to the inevitable laws or facts of nature. It teaches, indeed, that when man attempts to dam up Niagara, or turn back the Mississippi in its onward course to the main, his efforts are totally vain and futile. But it does not deny that they may be of some avail in turning the waters of those mighty rivers to some account, or even in giving some new direction to their courses, to a very limited extent. It does not deny that his efforts may be of some avail when they merely attempt to raise *levees* against the inundations of the Mississippi, or to give some new direction, here and there, to its resistless current.

This philosophy teaches, indeed, that when human ingenuity attempts to convert an ass or a zebra into a horse, or a Negro or Mongol into a Caucasian, its efforts are futile, and ridiculously absurd. But it does not teach that all efforts to improve the *equine* genus, according to their respective species or varieties—

whether horse, donkey, zebra, or quagga, which last appears to be but a modification of the zebra—are futile or unavailing. Neither does it teach that all efforts to improve the human genus, according to their respective species or varieties, are futile or un-unavailing—whether those efforts be applied to the Caucasian, the Negro, the Mongol, or the Indian, particularly so called, who is evidently but a modification of the Mongol, and related to him as the quagga to the zebra, or *vice versa*, rather, as the zebra to the quagga. For the Indian, as he is commonly called, in America, is evidently the true ZEBRA of the human genus, wild and untamable.

The remark of Solon under review, and the philosophy which finds partial expression in this profound remark, condemns the folly of attempting to cut the FOOT to fit the SHOE, like the stupid Chinaman, or, in other words, to shape the MAN to suit the LAW, and recommends that we should rather strive to cut the SHOE to fit the FOOT, or frame the LAW to suit the MAN. It inculcates that the FOOT OF HUMANITY has been shaped by the unerring hand of Nature, while the SHOE OF HUMAN INVENTION, whether political or purely mechanical, has been shaped by the erring hand of man, who is at best but a SECOND RATE MECHANIC.

The philosophy in question, condemns, moreover, the schoolboy folly of attempting to pluck the FRUIT before it is ripe—a folly of which so many juveniles in Social Philosophy are habitually guilty. It recommends, on the other hand, that man should rather wait until, in the natural course of events, the FRUIT has ripened, or at least is on the eve of ripening, and that he should then step forward, and gently assist the work of nature, or very slightly anticipate the natural course of events. It inculcates that this much at least may be done by the voluntary and intentional agency of man, and perhaps some little more.

CHAPTER VIII.

A CRITICAL REVIEW OF GUIZOT AND HALLAM.

§ 1. The transit of more than two thousand years, which we make in passing from the highest thought of antiquity in regard to the Philosophy of Society, as manifested in Confucius and Solon, to the highest thought of the modern age, reveals manifestation of some advance unquestionably in human ideas, but not of so much advance as might reasonably have been anticipated. Very slight manifestations, indeed, of any such advance, in respect, at least, to essential or fundamental ideas, shall we be able to detect in the two illustrious savans who are to be particularly considered in the present chapter—Guizot and Hallam.

As general disquisitions on Society, as expositions of the philosophy of history, in so far as exhibited in those portions of human society and history to which they relate, the History of Civilization in Europe, though more particularly in France, by Francis Pierre William Guizot, and the History of the Middle Ages, by Henry Hallam, are undoubtedly deserving of a very high rank among the efforts of the human intellect. They far exceed any production of the kind that antiquity has transmitted to our times, not excepting the work of Aristotle on Politics, nor the far greater work of Polybius on General History.

The great merit of these valuable works of Guizot and Hallam consists, mainly, indeed, in their method of dealing with history— in their distinguished advance towards what history should really be—in their subordination of facts to principles, of events to the ideas which they represent—in their tendency to portray the world of THOUGHT rather than that of ACTION, to which last-named superficial and vulgar view of human history, attention has been hitherto almost exclusively directed. Their great merit, in short, mainly consists in the fact that they are essentially, and to a very great extent, illustrations of the Philosophy of History, without, however, claiming to be such—in the fact that they are really more successful efforts of this kind than many of those that have been avowedly and expressly shaped with reference to this idea—that they are really far more practical, and, upon the whole, more valuable contributions to the Philosophy of History, than the undoubtedly more profound works of Cousin, among the French, or Brucker, Tidemann or Tennemann among the Germans. In this respect they indicate a very decided advance of the human mind, and mark an epoch in human history, although, in point of happy and brilliant execution, their works very far fall short of the more recent and transcendent effort of Buckle, to be hereafter more particularly noticed.

It is by reason of the marked resemblance, in these respects, between the works of Guizot and Hallam, of the essential similarity in their methods of dealing with human history, as well as of the avowed similarity of their subjects of discussion, that they are here associated for consideration in the same chapter.

§ 2. Much, however, as we must extol these excellent works of Guizot and Hallam, in respect to their method of dealing with human history, in respect to the kind of facts, as well as ideas, to which they give main prominence, and in other less noteworthy respects, we cannot award to them the merit of having given any very distinct, bold, or emphatic prominence to any particularly valuable fundamental idea in Social Philosophy, or any such idea that has not been hitherto commonly received. The only idea of this character, indeed, that we can detect in their writings, is that which we have already attributed to Confucius and Solon. Not much to their credit must we adjudge, that they have added very little to the force and effect with which the idea has been asserted by those renowned sages of antiquity.

The idea is that which we may as well, at once, and once for all, designate as the TRUE COPERNICAN IDEA in Social Philosophy —the idea that it is the MAN that makes the government, not the GOVERNMENT that makes the man—the idea, that it is MAN, and not his institutions, or, as some profound superficialists are pleased to assert, his *conditions*, that is the prime cause of his social condition and general destiny—the idea, in short, and most comprehensively expressed, that MAN is the true CENTRE of the social universe, around which all his institutions revolve, and that as in human history, and in universal history, facts should everywhere be subordinated to IDEAS, so in Social Philosophy, more particularly, all institutions, all laws, all ideas should be subordinated to the great paramount idea of MAN, and the congeries of IDEAS which he embodies and represents.

This idea has not indeed been anywhere, as yet, clearly, distinctly, and emphatically expressed, much less, so clearly, distinctly, or emphatically, as it is here asserted. No writer or speaker appears hitherto to have had the boldness to make this assertion, if any one has had the discernment to recognize so fully its truth. Many approximations to the assertion may indeed be readily discovered. We have already seen this manifested in the sages of antiquity, in Confucius, Solon, and Aristotle. Still more decided manifestations of it shall we find in modern times. Nearly all the great thinkers of the present age evince, more or less distinctly, some appreciation of the truth. In every direction, indeed, we find manifestations of the general approach of the human mind to the recognition of this grand and extensively revolutionary idea. As the various worlds composing the solar system, in their grand march through space, if they should, perchance, approach very near some other great world, or group of worlds, would, by the laws of Siderial Philosophy, give manifestations of their approach, by certain irregular movements and disturbances of the ordinary forces of gravity; so the various leading and controlling minds, that compose the world of thought, by the extensively prevalent manifestations which they have lately given of a strong gravitation in this direction, clearly indicate that the human mind is nearly approaching this great truth, and will soon attain to its clear and distinct general recognition.

The author of the present work, therefore, feels assured that he is but slightly anticipating the general movement of the human mind, when he steps forward, as he aims to do, in this leading enterprise of his life, to announce this great truth, in common with some others, somewhat more boldly, distinctly, and comprehensively, than any anterior thinker appears to have done. In the present work, however he is merely reviewing the thoughts of others, rather than attempting the communication of his own. Having drawn on his own thoughts, nevertheless, so far as to express the idea in question, in its most essential and comprehensive significance, we shall be the better able to appreciate the actual testimonials to its truth, or recognitions of it, that have been hitherto afforded.

In the preceding chapter, having briefly glanced at some noteworthy recognitions of the idea in ancient times, we come now to consider the testimonials to it which the modern age has afforded, and, more particularly, in the present chapter, as it has rendered itself through two of its most eminent thinkers, the Frenchman Guizot, and the Anglo-Saxon Hallam. Very feeble indeed, timid, indirect, indistinct, hesitating, and equivocal, has been the rendition of the idea by both of these savans, even by Guizot, in whose writings the idea very often crops out, though never very boldly, and still more so by Hallam, who, only once, very timidly asserts the idea, and afterwards shamefully abandons it, falling, most palpably and grossly, into the vulgar habit of regarding the institutions of a people as the real cause of their condition and character.

§ 3. The most valuable thoughts of the great French statesman, François Pierre Guillaume Guizot, or as we should render it in English, Francis Peter William Guizot, are doubtless to be found in his lectures on History, delivered at Paris, during the years 1828, 1829, and 1830, and subsequently published in the book form, under the title of " The History of Civilization from the fall of the Roman Empire to the French Revolution." It is of this work that we have already spoken, when extolling his merits in respect to his method of dealing with the facts of history; and it is in this work that we find the expressions of the great fundamental idea in Social Philosophy, which it is here sought to bring into prominent view.

Somewhere in this work, Guizot has clearly, tersely, and forcibly enough expressed this idea, where he says, " Saving a powerful reaction, governments are what the people make them." But where precisely, or in what connection, he uses this language, the author is not able now to ascertain. Remembered from a reading of some years past, it has been of late diligently sought for in vain, and is here cited generally without any special reference.* Other expressions of the idea abound throughout the work, but none so terse or strong as this.

In his fifth lecture, which treats mainly of the religious element in European society, Guizot justly says: "In addressing itself to the understanding, in determining the will, in acting by purely intellectual means, the government, instead of reducing, extends and elevates itself. It is then that it accomplishes the most and the greatest things. On the contrary, when it is obliged incessantly to employ coercion, it contracts and lessens itself, and effects very little, and that little very ill."† Here, it may readily be perceived, is a faint and very imperfect recognition of the idea. It is but an argumentative recognition, however, at the most, not a positive or direct one, and even as such, it is but a faint and feeble recognition. It wisely enough asserts that government acts most effectively by addressing itself to the WILL of the men to be governed. But it does not penetrate deeply enough into causes, to discern and declare, that it must be that WILL, on which it should seek to operate, that has primarily operated upon itself —has moulded, determined, and created itself—that, in short, the government of a Society, in acting upon the Society, is in reality, for the most part, Society acting upon itself, or rather reacting upon itself, through the intervention of the government.

This more profound and equally just idea is implied, nay, indeed, plainly enough expressed, in the idea of Guizot, first quoted, "Saving a powerful reaction, governments are what the people make them"—the idea which the author of this work is not able precisely to locate in the writings of Guizot, which has,

---

* The author would be much indebted to the editor of "Notes and Queries," if he would ascertain and inform where precisely in this work of Guizot, or any other of his translated works, this passage occurs—not the substance of the passage merely, but the identical passage.

† History of Civilization in Europe, as translated by William Hazlett, Vol. I., Lec. V., p. 91   London Ed. of 1846.

to a certain extent become lost to his view, and which, like the *lost pleiad*, is more to be prized than all the rest. But how feebly and imperfectly must an author have apprehended and appreciated such an idea, to have asserted it distinctly, only once, among the many occasions for asserting it, which Guizot had, in the great work from which we quote.

In his Sixth lecture, while speaking of the great influence which the people of France exerted on their government, at a period when they had the least legal influence, by means of political institutions, namely, under the reigns of Louis XIV. and Louis XV., he speaks somewhat more clearly and forcibly to the point under review. In explanation of this phenomenon, he very justly remarks: "It is because there is a force which cannot be enclosed by laws, which, when there is need, can dispense with institutions. It is the force of ideas, of the public mind and opinion. In France, in the seventeenth and eighteenth centuries, there was a public opinion, which was much more powerful than at any other epoch. Although deprived of the means of acting legally upon the government, it acted indirectly by the empire of ideas, which are common alike to the governing and the governed, and by the impossibility which the governing felt of taking no note of the opinion of the governed."[*]

In the Ninth lecture of his History of Civilization, Guizot again expresses the idea quite as forcibly and distinctly as in the Sixth. In this lecture, which treats mainly of Royalty, he argues, very rightly, that the extensive prevalence, if not universality, of this form of government, proves its accordance with the laws of human nature, and the demands of human society, under many, if not most, of the conditions to which it is subjected. In the course of this argument he uses this eminently correct and noteworthy language: "Force plays a great part, and an incessant one, in human affairs; but it is not their principle, their *primum mobile*. Above force and the part which it plays, there hovers a moral cause which decides the totality of things. It is with force in the history of societies, as with the body in the history of man.

---

[*] Same work, p. 107.

The body surely holds a high place in the life of man, but still it is not the principle of life. Life circulates within it, but it does not emanate from it. So it is with human societies; whatever part force takes therein, it is not force which governs them and which presides supremely over their destinies; it is ideas and moral influences, which conceal themselves under the accidents of force, and regulate the course of the Society. It is a cause of this kind, and not force, which gave success to royalty."* Admirably just language.

In other words, the people are themselves the cause of that monarchical form of government, sometimes called despotism, and sometimes rightly, of which they so often complain. It is their follies that render such government necessary. Does not the whole history of the world prove this? Does not the late war in America demonstrate it? Why complain of kings? It is the people that create them. Why give mankind the best and freest government in the world—if the freest be indeed the best? By their own folly and madness they will recklessly throw it away. Man is the architect of his own destiny. Let him, then, blame himself, not his neighbor, for his misfortunes. Let him lay the fault on the truly responsible party, in so far as there is any responsibility in the case, on himself—not on his rulers, on his ill lot, on his *stars*. "The fault, dear Brutus, is not in our stars, but in ourselves that we are underlings."†

§ 4. In the Fourth of his lectures on the History of Civilization in France, more particularly, which immediately succeed those on the History of Civilization in Europe, in the volume here quoted from, Guizot again expresses the same idea, with some degree of commendable clearness and force. He speaks, in this lecture, directly of the reciprocal influences of the moral and social states of society on each other, which, it may readily be perceived, is but speaking, in other words, and in more accurate, more philosophical parlance, of the reciprocal influences of MAN, and his social ORGANISM, on each other.

---

* Same work, p. 163.

† Cassius to Brutus in the play of Julius Cæsar.

On this point, he says: "The moral state, then, must be acknowledged to be not only distinct from, but, to a certain point, independent of the social state. It should be seen that situations, institutions are not all, nor do they decide all in the life of nations; that other causes may modify, contend with, even surmount these; and that if the external world acts upon man, man, in his turn, acts upon the world. I would not, that it should be thought I reject the idea which I combat—far from it; its share of legitimacy is great. No doubt but that the social state exercised a powerful influence upon the moral state. I do not so much as wish that this doctrine should be exclusive; the influence is shared and reciprocal; if it be correct to say that governments make nations, it is no less true that nations make governments."*

Here, too, Guizot speaks well, but not so well altogether as truth warrants and demands. In the necessary action and re-action of man and his government upon each other, this superior thinker is evidently inclined to give the order of priority and paramount influence to the MAN, but he does not do this so emphatically and boldly as truth justifies, and the present exigencies of society, as well as the requirements of true social science, imperatively demand. Very true it is that, to a certain extent, "governments make nations." But it is far more indisputably true, and to a far greater extent, that "nations make governments." This latter, it should be constantly borne in mind, is the primary and paramount idea. For, most essentially and correctly speaking, even in those instances and those respects, in which we may say that "governments make nations," it is the nation acting on itself through the agency of its government, —through the activity of the most superior portions of itself, of its most superior minds—that effects the end accomplished. The principal exception to this general remark is afforded by the instances of FOREIGN INTERVENTION, which has, doubtless, ever been one of the potent instrumentalities in the civilization and advancement of nations.

Subject to this qualification, except in so far as the rulers of a

---

* History of Civilization, before cited, pp. 318-9.

nation may be of foreign origin, the observation here made will hold good, that the action of government on the society or nation is but the secondary action, or reaction, of the society or nation upon itself. In such cases it is but the action of the more superior portion of the society upon the more inferior, just as we see that the higher and nobler qualities of our individual nature often dominate over, and control, our lower and more ignoble qualities.

Peter the Great civilized the Russians, as we commonly say. But Peter the Great was himself a Russian; and the so called civilization of Russia by him was, in reality, but the Russian nation civilizing itself, through the highest energies with which it was endowed. Whether a nation can be civilized so rapidly, or to so great an extent, as were the Russians in this case, therefore depends materially upon the question whether it is capable of producing a Peter the Great—whether there is that much of intellectuality and moral force inherent in itself. We shall not be likely to hear of any Negro nation, for example, nor Mongolian either, ever becoming so signally civilized as were these Russians, or in so short a time. The negro race has, indeed, produced its Toussaint L'Ouverte, a man of great merit, of whom his race may well be proud. But he was no Peter the Great. Every nation or race has its great men. But it is not every nation or race that has, or can have, a Peter the Great.

§ 5. The same great truth has been also recognized, and partially or impliedly asserted, by this eminent authority, in his remarks on the Feudal System, which it has been the common habit hitherto, in accordance with the superficial system of thought hitherto prevalent in Social Philosophy, to regard as the CAUSE of the distracted and unsettled condition of society then prevalent in Europe, but which he has had the sagacity to discern, was rather the EFFECT of that condition of society—the EFFECT which was truly referable to the existing condition of society in Europe, at that time, as its proper CAUSE—the natural outgrowth of the prevailing habits and ideas of the MEN at that time composing European society.

Thus, in commenting on the futile attempt of Charlemagne, in the *ninth* century, to consolidate society under an extensive political system, by combining the principles of the extinct Roman government with those of the warrior bands and free tribes of Germany, he says: "He succeeded for a moment, and on his own account. But this was, as it were, a galvanic resurrection. Applied to a great society, the principles of the imperial administration, those of the warrior band, and those of the free tribes of Germany, were equally impracticable. No great society could be maintained. It is necessary to find its elements, on the one hand, in the minds of men—on the other, in social relations. Now, the moral and the social state of the people at this epoch equally resisted all association, all government of a single and extended character. Mankind had few ideas, and did not look far around. Social relations were rare and restricted. The horizon of thought and of life was exceedingly limited. Under such conditions, a great society is impossible."* Further on, in the same paragraph, he adds: "Small societies, local governments, cut, as it were, to the measure of existing ideas and relations, were alone possible, and these alone succeeded in establishing themselves."†

Still more explicitly does Guizot express the same idea, in the commencement of his next lecture to that from which the foregoing extracts are taken, where, in recapitulating the views of the preceding lecture, as to the causes of the dismemberment of the empire of Charlemange, he says: "It seemed to me that the impossibility of a sole and extensive society, in the state in which social relations and minds then were, alone fully explains this great and so rapid metamorphosis; that the formation of a multitude of small societies, that is to say, the establishment of the feudal system, was the necessary consequence—the natural course of events."‡

In view of the foregoing observations of the eminent savan under review, what judgment are we to pass upon the superficial

---

* History of Civilization in France, Lect. XXIV; or Vol. II., p. 291, of Edition before quoted.
† Same work and page.
‡ Same work, Vol. II., p. 293.

idea, which has hitherto mainly controlled thought in Social Philosophy, that it is to the political institutions of a people we are to look for the causes which mainly determine their wellbeing, and which, in its practical manifestations, is so often found attempting to turn the world upside down, in order to force the FOOT of humanity into one common SHOE, politically, regardless of the form of national character, its natural environment, and the age of the society, as well as of the world, at the time such society finds itself developed on the stage of national existence?

§ 6. In passing from a review of the thoughts of Guizot, to a review of those of Hallam, we must be more than usually impressed with the tameness, if not positive timidity, which distinguishes the ordinary style of Anglican thought from the Frankish. Cautious and even timid SCEPTICISM is the leading characteristic of Anglican thought in general; bold, daring, and presumptuous DOGMATISM is that of the Frankish. Perhaps Anglo-American thought may be destined to strike the happy mean between the two, and present to the world a model style of thought.

It is rather probable, however, that nature understands her business, in this respect, as in most others, and that, by deliberate and wise design, she has assigned to different nations and races of men, different styles of thought, and different orders of mind, as well as different general functions to perform in the general life of humanity, and the grand economy of universal being. It is rather probable that the DIVISION OF LABOR, which we find to operate so advantageously in the ordinary industrial economy of society, is equally as beneficial in the grand economy of universal human life. It is rather probable that the ends of that grand economy are best subserved by assigning to different nations different orders of mind and character, which blatant ignoramuses are so constantly striving to ignore, and even to contradict with their petty twaddle about making all men alike by educating them alike.

It is doubtless by wise design, that the great nationalities, or demi-races, of the Caucasian family, who now compose the WORLD OF THOUGHT, the Teutonic, Frankish, and Anglo-Saxon, or more properly Anglo-Teutonic, have been endowed each with its own peculiar and distinguishing style of thought, and order of mind. Germany is metaphysical, France mathematical, Anglo-Saxondom practical. Germany is profound, France exact, Anglo-Saxondom efficient. Germany cogitates, France experiments, Anglo-Saxondom executes. Great, earnest, deep-thinking, oracular Germany utters her grand ORACLES, like voices from the unfathomable depths; subtle, ingenious, skilful France analyzes and dissects them; grave, thoughtful, cautious Anglo-Saxondom passes judgment upon them, and decides how far they may be relied upon, or turned to useful account, either in the speculative or practical sciences.

§ 7. Let us not, then, presume to despise or to disparage any one of these different styles of thought, which respectively distinguish these three great nationalities or demi-races of men, the greatest, beyond all doubt, that have ever yet illustrated the human family, not excepting the Hellenic or Romanic. Let us not—we might almost venture to say—least of all, presume to despise the Anglican style of thought, because of its tameness, its timidity, its cautious and many-sided scepticism. These are its distinguishing virtues, not its faults. What, indeed, to the truly philosophical mind, are *faults*, at most, but the extremes of virtue?

Assuredly, at any rate, these plain and home-spun qualities of the Anglo-Saxon mind, rightly interpreted, are rare and eminent virtues. They are the virtues that will yet enable THE RACE to bear off the honors of pre-eminence from all the rest. Its knowledge indeed generally comes last, but when it comes, it is generally turned to good account. If it is slow to learn, even that which is good and true, it is also slow to depart from it, when it has been once learned. It is, after all, to the true philosopher and philanthropist, the most hopeful of the nationalities. It is the great hope-field of humanity. It is the race "that tries all things, proves all things, and holds fast to that which is good."

§ 8. It is the more remarkable, however, that the thoughts of Hallam should appear tame, in contrast with those of Guizot, because Guizot himself is by no means one of the particularly bold, or daringly dogmatical thinkers of France. On the contrary, he is one of the most conservative, cautious, subdued, and least dogmatical, of all the philosophical thinkers of that country. Nay, he may be considered rather timid as a reasoner. In boldness of thought, as we shall presently see, he falls far behind the Anglo-Saxon, Buckle.

How happens it, then, that Hallam is to appear so tame in contrast with Guizot in our review? Is it that he is a particularly tame or timid thinker, even for an Anglo-Saxon; or is it that the general merit of his work is far inferior to that of Guizot? Neither of these suggestions is correct. In vigor, independence, and even originality of thought Hallam rises decidedly above the average of Anglican thinkers, rather than falls below it; and in general merit, his work under review is superior to the corresponding one of Guizot. It is a more elaborate work, and one of superior artistic execution. In what, then, consists the greater tameness of the thought of Hallam in question? It consists only in what relates to the particular idea under consideration—THE COPERNICAN IDEA IN SOCIAL PHILOSOPHY, as we have already designated it.

True to its instincts, and its legitimate functions in the grand economy of the world of thought, the Anglo-Saxon mind, as it renders itself through the grave, dignified, cautious, and sagacious Hallam, approaches this grave and extensively revolutionary idea, with great caution and timidity. Looking through his large and sagacious brain it catches a broad glimpse of the great idea, gravely and cautiously announces its observation, and then, as if alarmed at its own announcement, flatly contradicts it, and falls into the old habit of reasoning upon the Philosophy of Society—the old and vulgar habit of regarding the phenomena of the Social Universe from the stand-point of the INSTITUTIONS, as the true CENTRE of social gravitation, and the fundamental regulator of all social revolutions.

§ 9. In the Second chapter of his admirable work on the Middle Age, while making many just and excellent observations on the Feudal System, he makes this eminently just one: " If the view that I have taken of those dark ages is correct, the state of anarchy which we usually term feudal, was the natural result of a vast and barbarous empire feebly administered, and the cause rather than the effect of the general establishment of feudal tenures."*

Here we find a clear enough recognition of the true Copernican idea of Social Philosopy—the idea that it is the SOCIETY, or the MEN composing the society, that make the INSTITUTIONS, not the INSTITUTIONS that make the MEN, except, indeed, to a very limited extent, as the earth reflects back upon the sun the light which it directly derives from him.

In the Eighth chapter of the same work, however, which treats of English History, Hallam palpably departs from and contradicts the sound doctrine thus laid down in his second chapter. In speaking of the great advantages which the English people have long enjoyed, he says: "These advantages are surely not owing to the soil of the island, nor to the latitude in which it is placed; but to the spirit of its laws, from which, through various means, the characteristic independence and industriousness of our nation have been derived."† What a melancholy failure of thought does our author here betray! How shamefully does he retreat from the valid position which, but a little while before, he had so handsomely and creditably taken! To have been consistent with himself, very manifestly he should have said the advantages enjoyed by the English were owing to the spirit of the ENGLISH PEOPLE, from which, through various means, their excellent laws, as well as the characteristic independence and industriousness of the nation, have been derived. What a pitiful perversion of indisputable truth—which should have been the more obvious to Hallam, after his former partial recognition of it —thus to attribute the spirit of a PEOPLE to the spirit of their laws, instead of attributing the spirit of the laws to that of the PEOPLE!"

We have before had occasion,‡ and shall again, in the follow-

---

* Middle Age, Chap. II., Part II., or page 123, New York Edition of 1857.

† Middle Age, Chap. VIII., first page of chapter.

‡ Chap. VI. of this work.

ing chapter, to notice the admirably just and forcibly expressed counter idea of De Maistre, which is so admirably responsive to this weak observation of Hallam, that it is difficult to cite the one without citing the other also, as its legitimate antipode. "The true English constitution," says that profound thinker, " is that admirable, unique, and infallible public spirit, beyond all praise, which guides everything, preserves everything, saves everything. That which is written is nothing."

§ 10. These two observations of Hallam are all that can be regarded as particularly noteworthy in this part of our general work.* How tame and inconsiderable must we regard this little self-contradictory contribution to the Philosophy of Society, afforded by the Anglo-Saxon mind, compared with that contributed by the Frankish, as represented by Guizot! The first of the two observations is, indeed, highly creditable, but the last materially detracts from its merit by showing how imperfectly the idea was appreciated. Certainly the Anglo-Saxon mind has not acquitted itself very creditably in this instance.

Speaking in military metaphor, we may say, the Anglo-Saxon mind, as it has rendered itself through the brain of Hallam, marched up bravely to take THE HEIGHT, which commands the whole field of thought in Social Philosophy, and, when it had barely reached the summit, became suddenly panic-stricken, and beat a hasty retreat. Our disappointment, as well as the general interest with which we contemplate the movement, may be compared to that which the military chieftain is destined often to experience. As a Peter the Great may be supposed to have contemplated the movements of his awkward Russians, when he was training them to compete with the Swedes of Charles XII., and as a Washington must have regarded his raw militia, when he was vainly striving to educate them to stand up against the admirably disciplined British troops, so the philosopher who hopes on the Anglo-Saxon race, and calculates on their eventual development into the highest type of humanity, must regard this movement of the Anglo-Saxon mind.

---

* For other noteworthy ideas of Hallam, of a less high order, see Part II., Chap. VI., of our general work.

But, whatever disappointment or chagrin he may experience at the contemplation, let him not despair. Those awkward Russians, after severe suffering and much rigorous discipline, at last vanquished the Swedes. Those raw militia of Washington, aided by the *mathematically* disciplined French, were, after all, enabled to triumph over the British. And so, it is little to be doubted, the Anglo-Saxon race, slow as it is to apprehend, and rightly to apply, the most fundamental ideas, will attain them eventually; and after much discipline, much severe training in the rigid school of experience, will come out triumphant. Learning from every other race whatever real truth it has to impart, borrowing from every other, whatever really useful expedient it may have discovered, and combining with these the suggestions of its own inherent and excellent common sense, it will eventually, no doubt, take the lead of all other races or nationalities, and carry forward the human race to a much higher degree of development than it has ever yet attained.

CHAPTER IX.

THE VALUABLE CONTRIBUTIONS OF DE MAISTRE AND CHALMERS TO THE PHILOSOPHY OF SOCIETY CRITICALLY CONSIDERED.

§ 1. DESPITE the obvious points of difference between the two eminent savans who are associated in this chapter for joint consideration, it is by reason of their affinities of resemblance, rather than of contrast, that they are so conjoined. The points of resemblance between them are much more marked and essential than their points of dissimilarity.

De Maistre, it is true, was of Romanic nationality—a sort of half Italian half Frenchman, by parentage and nativity an Italian, but writing, and *thinking*, as we may say, in French—while Chalmers was an Anglo-Saxon. De Maistre was thoroughly a papist in his theological views—Chalmers as thoroughly a puritan. De Maistre wrote avowedly on the principles of Government, in the work which it is here proposed to review—Chalmers, avowedly on Political Economy. But they were both theologians, and intensely theological—using those terms in their narrow or more restricted sense—both religious enthusiasts, though of different styles of religion, both remarkable for their energy and power of thought, and both distinguished by the singular clearness and force with which they have respectively expressed two of the most essentially valuable ideas in the Philosophy of Society, that have been as yet formally announced.

In pronouncing De Maistre a theologian, however, it should be understood that we speak essentially, and not literally. So speaking we are fully justified in so designating him. For although he was not by profession a theologian, but rather a politician and diplomat, yet in the work which brings him under review in these pages, he has evinced the most intensely theological spirit, in so far indeed as such a spirit is essentially displayed in an overweening disposition to advocate a Theocracy founded on the arrogant pretensions of the Romish Church. A Hildebrand or Loyola could hardly have approved himself a more enthusiastic and bigoted advocate of those pretensions than De Maistre has done in the work in question. The Reverend Thomas Chalmers is so extensively known as a clergyman of the Established Church of Scotland, or of the ultra puritanical school of Christianity, that no particular remarks concerning his peculiar vocation in life are here requisite.

How little soever so contracted a system of theology, so purely THEISTICAL a theology, as that advocated by either of these eminent thinkers, may commend itself to the judgment of a true Philosophy, no true philosopher will despise the valuable truths which they have inculcated, merely because he may be compelled to reject their contracted views as to "the great first cause least understood." The true philosopher is ever ready to receive new truth from whatever quarter it may come, and it has been well said, that "a philosopher will learn something even from a fool, while a fool will not learn anything, even from a philosopher." The kingdom of Science is like the kingdom of Heaven, "to be received as a little child," with an humble and teachable spirit, ready to receive knowledge from whatever direction it may come. Too little perhaps has this truth been considered by many philosophers. Let us bear it ever in mind, and proceed to inquire what are the valuable truths in regard to the Philosophy of Society which have been presented to us by the two eminent authorities who form the subject of the present chapter.

§ 2. The Essay on the Generative Principle of Political Constitutions, published in the French language in 1814, by Count Joseph De Maistre, and translated into English by an anonymous author,* is one of the most remarkable productions of the human intellect. The work is distinguished alike for its exceeding brevity of language, and its vast voluminousness of thought. It comprises, with the Preface, only *a hundred and seventy-three pages*, duodecimo, in largely displayed type, nearly half of the gross

---

* See Boston Edition, or that of Little & Brown, of 1847, for the English translation.

amount of those few pages, moreover, being occupied with notes, mostly by the translator. Within this exceedingly small compass are compressed some of the rarest, most suggestive, and most comprehensive thoughts on the Philosophy of Society that have ever been submitted to the human understanding. The voluminousness of thought, which we thus attribute to this work, does not consist in the number of its thoughts, but in their weight and compass. It is indeed a work of very few ideas, as well as words, but those are weighty ideas, and expressed with a clearness and force eminently calculated to arrest attention and carry conviction. But the yet greater value of the ideas consists in their rarity, their originality, their opposition to common opinions that are erroneous, and their tendency to exert a powerful influence in turning attention from an erroneous view of highly important subjects to a more just view.

The great leading and fundamental idea of the work is that which we have already expressed, in the SIXTH MAIN PROPOSITION, laid down in our Sixth chapter, and there credited to De Maistre, that the most important and fundamental laws by which human society is governed are precisely those that are never written, except indeed in the minds of men. Around this great fundamental or central idea all the other ideas of the work are grouped—all other ideas, not purely incidental, which it contains, are but diversified or more particular statements of this grand controlling idea.

This important idea, so much opposed to commonly received opinions, must commend itself at once to the acceptance of every rightly discerning Social Philosopher. The immediate application which De Maistre makes of this, the most fundamental, general, and comprehensive idea of his work, or, as we should rather say perhaps, its next most fundamental, general, and comprehensive idea, or proposition, may or may not be accepted by the Social Philosopher; but the more remote application which he makes of it, or his third general proposition, and evidently intended as the conclusory proposition, or grand practical conclusion of the work, must be rejected by every true philosopher.

The immediate application which De Maistre makes of his main fundamental idea takes a THEOLOGICAL turn, and his second main idea, or somewhat less general one, is, accordingly, that the most fundamental laws which govern human society are of Divine enactment; and his design in publishing the work may be correctly stated, doubtlessly, in the words of the American translator, expressive of his own design, or hope in translating it, "that it may lead to a more just recognition of the Hand of God in the History of the World."*

The more remote and ultimate application which he makes of his main idea takes a SECTARIAN turn, and his third main idea, or still less general proposition, is, accordingly—to speak in accordance with the most comprehensive significance of his reasoning, in its most condensed form of expression—that the Divine enactments by which human society is most essentially governed, and by which alone it can be safely governed, are rendered through the religious establishments of the society or age, and, in the present age, consequently, through that artificially contrived ecclesiastical establishment known in history as the Church of Rome. He does not, indeed, so formally state this general aim of his reasonings, much less the more particular application of it to the Romish Church. He was too skilful and judicious an advocate for that. But this is evidently the essential drift and tendency of all his reasonings. To his eye the Divine Presence is only manifest in the world, under the form of the august ceremonies of that venerable Church. His mind was evidently not expanded enough in its theological conceptions to comprehend that the Divine Presence is most probably manifest in every work of nature, or, in other words, in every work of the "Hand of God," and that every human soul is a living temple of God, whose "holy presence" is constantly manifest therein.

This last application of his main idea, or more correctly to speak, this third form of his most fundamental proposition, every true philosopher, whether sociologist, physiologist, or philosopher of whatever kind, must respectfully reject. The first application,

---

* See Boston Edition of the work of 1847, Notice by the Translator, page 5.

or the second form of the most fundamental proposition, the social philosopher may or may not accept, indifferently.

It is obviously of no practical consequence to the social philosopher, whether the most fundamental laws that control the destiny of human society are to be regarded as of Divine enactment, or of some other kind, so long as it is conceded that those laws are beyond human control, and are referable to some higher power than that of man. It is obviously of no practical, or, at least, immediately practical, consequence to his reasonings, whether we call those most fundamental laws of human society Divine laws, or simply laws of Nature—whether, in short, we adopt the Theistic, Pantheistic, or the Atheistic view of nature and its eternal laws.

The Theist simply, and, as commonly understood, recognizes the *Theos*, or God, only in some particular things, whether developments in external nature, or in man; the Pantheist recognizes Him in everything; the Atheist, in nothing. To the contracted view of the simple Theist, only a part of universal nature and of man, the most important part of nature, is really animated by the Deity. To the enlarged view of the Pantheist the whole universe is alive with God. To the dull and leaden view of the Atheist, there is no God anywhere discernible, and to him universal nature is without a soul.

In reference to the science of Sociology, it matters not which of these theological views we may adopt. In so far as the reasonings of the Social Philosopher are concerned, it is a matter of indifference what may be our theology or idea as to the true fundamental and original cause or principle of motion. It is enough for him to know that the part which man plays, as a controller or modifier of events, even in the economy of society and of his own individual life, is very small, as compared with that which is performed by the great unseen cause least understood; nay, that even the part which he does play, or seems to play, or may be said—by way of contradistinction only—so to play, is not in reality his own, but that of the true original and fundamental cause, acting through him as an instrumentality—acting through him by *secondary* and more complex laws, as contradistinguished from those *primary* and more simple laws, which are commonly regarded as laws of nature; that, in short, man, in all the utterances of his speech or reason, is but a noisy TONGUE, speaking out of the mouth of UNIVERSAL REASON, and, in all the achievements of his industry and art, is but a little HAND, dangling beside the body of UNIVERSAL NATURE.

This is the great idea, the grand truth, which the reasonings of De Maistre, in the work under consideration, tend to bring distinctly into view. He does not, indeed, by any means, so fully present this great idea, but he marches forward bravely and nobly towards it. He lifts, to a great extent, the veil of vulgar error and dull common opinion, which has hitherto obscured it and kept it out of sight. It is the expression, or approximative expression, which he has given to this great truth, and the valuable contribution which he has thus made—unconsciously made—towards the great revolution that is to come in human thoughts, alike in Ethics and Sociology, that constitutes the great merit of his work under review. Let us see how he has acquitted himself in this respect, and what have been the actual testimonials of his superior intellect to this great and extensively revolutionary doctrine.

§ 3. In the preface of his work, De Maistre lays down twelve propositions, of which some are liable to some important exceptions, but which are, for the most part, unexceptionable and eminently just. They are as follows, omitting the interpolations, by way of amplification, in some places, of the American translator:

" 1. No constitution results from deliberation; the rights of the people are never written, or never except as simple declarations of pre-existing rights not written, of which nothing more can be said than that they exist because they exist.

" 2. Human action, in such cases, is so far circumscribed, that the men who act are only circumstances.

" 3. The rights of the *people*, properly so called, proceed almost always from the concessions of sovereigns, and then it is possible to trace them historically; but the rights of the sovereign and of the aristocracy have neither date nor known authors.

"4. These concessions themselves have always been preceded by a state of things which rendered them necessary, and which did not depend upon the sovereign.

"5. Although written laws are only the declarations of pre-existing rights, yet it does not follow that all these rights can be written.

"6. The more is written, the weaker the constitution.

"7. No nation can give liberty to itself, if it has it not. Human influence does not extend beyond the development of existing rights.

"8. Lawgivers, strictly speaking, are extraordinary men, belonging, perhaps, only to the ancient world and to the youth of nations.

"9. These lawgivers even, notwithstanding their wonderful power, have only collected the pre-existing elements, and have always acted in the name of the Divinity.

"10. Liberty, in a sense, is the gift of kings; for all nations were constituted free by kings.

"11. There never has existed a free nation which had not, in its natural constitution, germs of liberty as old as itself; and no nation has ever successfully attempted to develop, by its fundamental written laws, other rights than those which existed in its natural constitution.

"12. No assembly of men can give existence to a nation. An attempt of this kind ought even to be ranked among the most memorable acts of folly."*

It will readily be seen that the ideas expressed in the foregoing propositions are too strongly and unqualifiedly laid down. This fact, however, does not at all militate against their substantial

---

* Preface to work under review, pp. 11-17.

truth, while it tends more forcibly to press them upon the view. This is the merit of very energetic and intensely dogmatical writers, that they are impressive at the expense of accuracy and strict conformity to truth. This is eminently the merit of the writer under review.

In the main body of his Essay, and in its first paragraph, he says, to the same point, and with less exceptionable accuracy: "One of the grand errors of an age which professed them all, was to believe that a political constitution could be written and created *à priori;* whilst reason and experience unite in establishing that a constitution is a Divine work, and that that which is most fundamental and most essentially constitutional, in the laws of a nation, is precisely what cannot be written."*

It is in illustration only of the same idea, that he makes the observation on the English Constitution, so often before quoted: "The true English Constitution is that admirable, unique, and infallible public spirit, beyond all praise, which guides everything, preserves everything, saves everything. That which is written is nothing."†

Further on, in the same work, he expresses the same idea, in yet different language somewhat, but with so much clearness and emphasis as to merit quotation with all its imperfections, and despite the overdrawn intensity of expression which characterizes all the remarks of this energetic, though evidently embittered writer.

In Section 9 of his Essay, he says: "The more we examine the influence of human agency in the formation of political institutions, the greater will be our conviction that it enters there only in a manner infinitely subordinate, or as a simple instrument; and I do not believe there remains the least doubt of the incontestable truth of the following propositions:

"1. That the fundamental principles of political constitutions exist before all written law.

"2. That a constitutional law is, and can only be, the development or sanction of an unwritten preëxisting right.

---

* See same work, paragraph 1. † Same work, Section 7, p. 37.

"3. That that which is most essential, most intrinsically constitutional, and truly fundamental, is never written, and could not be, without endangering the state.

"4. That the weakness and fragility of a constitution are actually in direct proportion to the multiplicity of written constitutional articles."*

The foregoing quotation, like those already made, and more clearly perhaps than any of the others, brings clearly into view, at once, the merit and demerit of the author under review. For, while it shows him thoroughly animated with the great truth, that HUMAN AGENCY—even in so far as it can be regarded as anything more than the mere agency of UNIVERSAL NATURE, acting by secondary laws, and through human instrumentality—enters, only to a very limited extent, into human institutions, and that all written laws are, for the most part, only affirmations, or more formal distinct and explicit assertions of preëxisting unwritten ones—while it shows all this, very clearly and emphatically, it shows also that he is animated with an unnecessary and unwise hostility to written laws

This is certainly a very great error, or a very unjust prejudice. While it is certainly true, that written laws avail but little, and are of real efficacy only in so far as they are but affirmations, or more emphatic and explicit assertions, of preëxisting unwritten ones, it is as certainly true that the written laws cannot do any harm, may indeed do some good, and are, in short, of some little advantage. But this hostility of De Maistre to written laws, his evidently bitter prejudice against them, only betrays, in part, his intense Romish Catholic sympathies. The Romish Church can find no security except in uncompromising hostility to that which is written. This hostility, De Maistre, one of its great *profane* apostles, if we may so speak, manifestly betrays throughout his whole work under review. But this error we may well excuse, in our admiration for the great utterances of real truth which he has given forth.

---

* Same work, pp. 41-2.

With one quotation more we must take leave of this brilliant writer, and may well afford to do so, for there is nothing more of much value in his little book, than what is contained in that, and in those already made. In Section 28 of the book, he says: "Everything brings us back to the general rule—*man cannot create a constitution; and no legitimate constitution can be written.* The collection of fundamental laws, which most essentially constitutes a civil or religious society, never has been written, and never will be, *à priori*. It is only when society finds itself already constituted, without being able to say how, that it is possible to make known, or explain, in writing, certain special articles; but, in almost every case, these declarations or explanations are the effect or cause of very great evils, and always cost the people more than they are worth."*

§ 4. The most essentially valuable contribution which the Reverend Thomas Chalmers has made, to the Philosophy of Society, is comprised in what constitutes the essential contribution to that Philosopy which Malthusianism has made, and as such has already been noticed in a former Part of this general work.† Malthusianism, indeed, is mainly indebted to Dr. Chalmers and to John Stuart Mill for the valuable contribution which it has thus made; or, rather, that contribution has been made mainly through them. That contribution, which we have heretofore designated as the grand conclusory idea of Malthusianism, and which may indeed be regarded as constituting the grand conclusory idea of all Social Philosophy, and certainly the highest practical attainment that it has yet made, consists in the momentous assertion, variously made by both those two eminent authors, and reiterated, in many different forms, by Dr. Chalmers, THAT, IN ORDER TO EFFECT ANY PERMANENT AMELIORATION OF HUMAN SOCIETY, IT IS NECESSARY TO ELEVATE THE MORAL STATUS OF MANKIND.

---

* Same work, pp. 89-93. How heavily loaded with notes is the little book under review, may be seen in the fact that the brief quotation here made occupies, in part, four pages of it, the remainder of the pages being occupied with notes.

† Part V., which treats of Malthusianism.

It would be useless repetition to dwell upon this great idea here, or the various noteworthy and emphatic assertions of it which Dr. Chalmers has made. They have been amply set forth in Part V., Chapter V., of this general review, which it is hoped will shortly be before the public, although not comprised in the present publication. Brief reference was there made, moreover, to another idea of Dr. Chalmers, intimately related to that just announced, but having more immediate relation to the DIAGNOSIS OF CAUSES, which, it was there stated, appertained rather to a higher and more advanced system of Social Philosophy than Malthusianism constituted, of which Dr. Chalmers was one of the most distinguished apostles, and which would be more particularly considered in a subsequent Part of the work.* It is to the consideration of this idea that we now come. Nor is it proposed to notice again, in this place, any of the valuable reflections of Dr. Chalmers, except those which have immediate reference to this idea.

This idea, which has been already developed, to a considerable extent, in the Sixth chapter of the present publication, is expressed in the assertion there made, THAT IT IS THE COLLECTIVE WILL OF SOCIETY, AND OF EACH PARTICULAR CLASS IN SOCIETY, THAT DETERMINES ITS CONDITION. This idea, which, very manifestly, must be received with very important qualifications, is, nevertheless, and despite its qualifications, one of immense value, and, rightly understood, of indisputable truth.

§ 5. On the very threshhold of the idea, or rather of the consideration which we propose to give it, we have, however, to encounter a very great apparent contradiction between this idea, so highly estimated, of Dr. Chalmers, and that of De Maistre, which we have just now, and in this very chapter, so much lauded and esteemed. After having represented man as a mere part of the general frame-work of nature, we come now to represent him as invested with the attributes of God. After having regarded him as essentially nothing, we come now to regard him as virtually

---

* Part V., Chap. V., § 23.

everything—so far, at least, as his own immediate destiny is concerned.

This startling paradox need not, however, in the least degree, disconcert us. Truth everywhere presents, to the vulgar view, a tissue of paradoxes. Hence a great deal of the world's controversy. Hence we so often find contracted reasoners disputing and disagreeing, by putting one idea in opposition to another, both of which the comprehensive reasoner or true philosopher accepts and harmonizes. Hence, again, the chief mission of the true philosopher is to harmonize discords. For to his view it is manifest that all opinions, however contradictory, are, to a certain extent, true.

There is no great difficulty in explaining the paradox which we here encounter, and which De Maistre himself has incidentally expressed, with his characteristic brevity and sententious dogmatism, when, in alluding to the beautiful reflections of Plutarch, in his Banquet of the Seven Sages, he says that they "could not be more justly applied, than to the formation of political constitutions, where it may be said, with equal truth, that man does everything, and does nothing."* The words of De Maistre would have been less intensely epigrammatical, indeed, but much more explicit and correct, had he said—*where it may be said, with equal truth, that man* SEEMS *to do everything, and,* IN REALITY, *does nothing.*

The paradox presented by the counter ideas of De Maistre and Chalmers, or the assertion that man is essentially nothing, and yet ostensibly and virtually everything, in so far as relates to his own immediate destiny in this world, is readily enough explained by remarking that both the ideas are true, though only in a certain sense, or when viewed from a certain stand-point. Regarded in a *physical* sense, the idea of Chalmers is true, regarded in a *metaphysical* sense, that of De Maistre is true. Viewed from a human stand-point, in the ordinary acceptation of that phrase, the former idea is correct, viewed from a higher or superhuman stand-point, the latter idea is correct. Looking at human affairs from the

---

* See work before quoted, Sec. 10, p. 45.

plane occupied by men, meaning thereby ordinary men, and the generality of men, the idea of Dr. Chalmers is substantially just, that man is virtually everything—that his apparently creative WILL determines his destiny in this life. Looking at them from the *plane* occupied by Gods, or the higher order of beings, celestial intelligences, if we may assume that such exist, the idea of De Maistre is as indisputably true that man is virtually nothing—that his body is but a part of the body of universal nature, and his mind but a part of the universal intelligence—that HIS WILL, so called, is but an extenuation of the UNIVERSAL WILL, and that what he seems to do of himself is, in reality, but the action of the great vital forces of universal being, which find their highest known expression in the activities of his own rational existence.

§ 6. The paradox is thus obviously enough explained. The fact that the collective will of society determines its social condition, or that the individual will of every one determines his condition and destiny in life, is not at all inconsistent with the yet more fundamental idea that man himself, with all the power of HIS WILL, so called, with all his desires and activities, moral and intellectual, as well as physical, is a mere PUPPET, moved with and by the grand machinery of the universe. The indisputable power of the human will, in its own pitifully contracted sphere of action, does not imply any such absurdity as FREE-WILL. Nothing is free. Everything is under the dominion of law. The will governs the act, indeed, as we may say in common parlance, but God governs the will, or some power higher than that of man, and of which man is but the agent.*

Man is undoubtedly the immediate architect of his own for-

---

* Were we authorized to deal with sectarian ideas here, we might quote the highest Christian authority in support of our text. St. Paul, one of the most eminent of all the sacred writers, perhaps the most eminent, somewhere says, " It is God that works in us to will and to do of his own good pleasure." It is true that this same great teacher, feeling the difficulties involved in this, his own great assertion, somewhere else says, "Shall we make God the author of evil? God forbid." Very good. But who shall presumptuously undertake to say that there is any evil, except in a relative sense, except in relation to the limited and contracted views, aims, and desires of man?

tunes in this life, subject, however, to some important qualifications, and his fortunes may be said, in accordance with the idea of Dr. Chalmers, to be creatively implied in his WILL. But in thus achieving his own fortunes he is but an *agent*—a mere instrument. God, or Nature, if we prefer so to speak with the atheists, "the great first cause least understood," by whatever name we may elect to call Him, is the PRINCIPAL. Man, through the creative and quasi-divine energies of his WILL, is, indeed, the *immediate* cause of his social welfare and general destiny in this life; but a power higher and greater than that of man, and of which man, himself, is the mere instrumentality, is the *original* and *fundamental* cause of his action and destiny.

Man is, indeed, to a certain extent, and in his own little contracted circle of activity, a CREATOR; but he acts only by delegated power. He is no absolute originator, or essential self-creator. Yet he would be, if the partially creative energies of his will were, as commonly understood, free, or self-created. Absolute free-agency, or absolute free-will, and self-creation, are convertible terms. If man were capable of creating his own will, then he would be, to that extent, and to a very momentous extent, a SELF-CREATOR. But this is absurd and impossible. God himself cannot be a self-creator, or therefore a free agent—much less man. The human mind cannot affirm of God, or the genesis of God, any other postulate than that which is generally accepted—that he is a self-existent being. To say that He is self-created would be to assert the self-evidently absurd proposition, that He either acted when He had as yet no existence, or that He created Himself when He was already created. God himself is not, therefore, a self-creator, or, what amounts to the same thing, a FREE AGENT.

Leibnitz seems to have been one of the very few who have had the discernment to detect this great truth, to deny the free agency of God, and assert its impossibility.

The more deeply one thinks, the further he penetrates the mystery of universal being, the more will this delusion as to free-agency, or free-will, on the part of either men or Gods, vanish before his view, and the universe appear to him, in the realm of mind as well as matter, everywhere to be under the dominion of law. This is undoubtedly the true view. There is no free-agency, no free-will, anywhere to be discovered. Everything is under subjection to law. Every event, in the moral or material universe, is the necessary consequence of all its antecedents. Should the true secret of the universe ever be disclosed to human view, it will, beyond all reasonable doubt, be found to rest upon a series of mathematical propositions. Should the grand mystery of universal being ever be fully explained to us, we shall, doubtlessly, find that God and nature, or mind and matter, and MAN, who is but the blended extenuation of both, could not be otherwise than precisely what they are, or ever may be, under all the circumstances surrounding them—that they could no more be otherwise than could the square described upon the hypothenuse of a right-angled triangle be otherwise than precisely equivalent to the sum of the squares described upon the other two sides. The integral and differential calculus of this mathematics, however, as manifested in the complex activities of the human mind, must ever prove too abstruse to be comprehended by any but the highest intellects.

§ 7. Having thus sufficiently explained the paradox, presented by the apparent antagonism between the two great ideas of De Maistre and Chalmers, let us proceed to consider, more minutely and particularly, what is the precise significance of the idea of the latter, and what is the expression which he has given to the idea. Bearing in mind the more fundamental, and far more general, more comprehensive idea of the former, we shall be the better able clearly to appreciate that of the latter. The two ideas, like all other mutually qualifying, or intimately related ideas, are most advantageously considered together.

Bearing in mind, then, that the most fundamental laws by which human society is governed, in the aggregate, as well as in the individual indeed, are precisely those which are never written; are precisely those with the enactment of which, by their own voluntary and intentional activity, men have nothing to do; are precisely those, in short, which they find written in their hearts or minds, without knowing how they got there, and of which they take cognizance by a sort of blind instinct—bearing in mind, moreover, that even in those laws which men do, by their own voluntary and intentional activity, enact, or seem so to enact, they are, in reality, but the instrumentalities through which the more fundamental laws of Nature, or of nature's God, act and assert themselves, let us proceed to consider how this more fundamental, and, perhaps we may say, most fundamental idea, is qualified, by the more particular and more immediately practical one announced by Dr. Chalmers.

Readily enough may we discern that the qualification is not at all in antagonism with the fundamental idea. Readily enough may we discern that the latter, and more particular idea, is entirely in harmony with the former and more general one, as are the various branches of every general truth in harmony with each other, and with the main truth. The assertion of Dr. Chalmers, that the collective will of society determines its condition, is but another mode of asserting that the condition of society is determined by the character of the society, by the general disposition, or, in other words, the general will, which it finds itself to possess—which it finds itself to have derived from its inherent natural propensities, and the force of all its anterior and surrounding circumstances. For the general character of society determines its collective or general WILL—finds its expression in that WILL, or, in other words, in those habits, tastes, and dispositions, which are but the diversified and manifold manifestations of its COLLECTIVE WILL.

To say, therefore, that the collective will of society determines its condition and destiny, is but to assert, in different words, that the manifestation which universal nature, or universal being, makes of itself in man, and in the different races and societies of men, is such as we find expressed in the collective wills of the different races and societies of men.

The diversities of human character, will, or mind, are precisely analogous to the diversities of soil, climate, and other natural conditions; and, in fact, to a very great extent, vary in accordance with the variations in those natural conditions. As, in different parts of the globe, we find those natural conditions to be different, so, in different parts or divisions of the human family, we find different general characters, habits, or WILLS. But those different natural conditions do not create themselves; neither do these different general characters, habits, or WILLS of men. The former are but the manifestations of Universal Nature in its purely physical aspects. The latter are but the manifestations of the same Universal Nature in its psychological aspects. The different soils and climates of the globe, it is true, yield their diverse and appropriate fruits. So do the different national characters of men. "By their fruits ye shall know them," was wisely spoken of both the material and spiritual world. But there is no free agency in either case.

It would be about as wise to say that the soil and climate of a country are free agents, and self-created, merely because they creatively determine the character of its *flora*, as it would be to say that the WILL of man, or the COLLECTIVE WILL of any society of men, is free, or self-created, merely because it creatively determines, as indisputably it does, the condition and destiny of men in this life.

There is, therefore, no essential conflict between the idea of De Maistre that man is essentially nothing, and that of Chalmers that he is virtually everything, in respect to his agency, or the part he plays, in determining his fortunes and destiny in this life. It is his WILL—not indeed his merely momentary, or capricious will, desiring this or that, without any regard to reason, and without any fixed or definite purpose, but his settled and deliberate will and purpose—that WILL to which the whole conduct of his life is, in the main, conformed—it is this WILL that immediately determines his condition and destiny in life. But this will is not properly his own—not any more so, at least, than is any other part of his being, than is the shape of his body, the color of his hair, or the complexion of his skin. It is but a manifestation of Universal Nature, or of nature's God, in him, with which he has nothing to do, except to recognize the fact that such is his will, and to move forward, as he naturally and instinctively does, to act out the suggestions of this will. What he emphatically resolves to do, even as an individual, but much more by far, what he emphatically resolves to do, as a mass, as any entire society, or any large class of any society, that he will assuredly do, in the main, and in the long run, provided, of course, it be conformable to reason, and within the ordinary bounds of human possibility. But this resolve is no other than that which the laws of his being, under all the circumstances which surround and have surrounded him, constrain him to make—is no other, indeed, than the condensed result of all those laws. With the quasi-attributes of a god, in the little sphere of his own activity, HE WILLS AND IT IS DONE. But the true God, that impels him, who governs and directs his will, is unseen, is enshrouded in a mystery not to be penetrated by mortal vision, sits enthroned, amid the grandeur of universal nature, incomprehensible to man, and describable to him, only as "the great first cause least understood."

The collective will of society does, indeed, determine its destiny. But that collective will is but another name for the combined result of all the laws of nature, in so far as they relate to man, and to that particular society of men. As the different races and nations of men do not give themselves their different colors or physical configurations, neither do they give themselves their different characters, dispositions, or collective wills, although these characters, dispositions, and wills are, in some respects, more modifiable by circumstances than the purely physical characteristics, whence mainly springs the delusion as to *free agency*, in respect to those moral characteristics.

Men do not create the complexion of their skins. Neither do they create the complexion of their characters. The complexion of the three great divisions of the human family, the white, yellow, and black races, in respect to the color of their skins, is not more dissimilar than is the complexion of their respective characters. The collective wills of these different races, corresponding with their different general characters and dispositions, are different, and so is the general condition of society among them. Whatever that collective will may be, that WILL determines the destiny of the society, and, to a great extent also, of the individual. This is all that the idea of Dr. Chalmers asserts. It does not, indeed, fully assert so much, at least not distinctly or avowedly. But we are asserting his idea here, in its full and most enlarged logical import, and to an extent to which he does not appear to have discerned its applications, and perhaps would hardly have dared to apply it if he had. But he is a poor philosopher who cannot safely carry forward the idea of an illustrious predecessor beyond the narrow confines within which it was first timidly asserted.

§ 8. The assertion of the idea which Dr. Chalmers has made is restricted, in its application, to the two main classes of society, the laborers and capitalists. It is not so enlarged as to embrace the *whole* of society, on the one hand, or as minute a portion of it as the *individual*, on the other. Very obviously, however, the idea admits of both applications, although it may be, and undoubtedly is, with diminished force, in so far, at least, as its applications to the individual are concerned. Dr. Chalmers considers the idea only in respect to its effects upon the *wages* of labor, and the *profits* of capital. It is the collective will of the labor class, he very justly maintains, that determines the wages of labor, and it is the collective will of the capitalist class, that determines the rate of profit—the former by its agency in regulating the supply of labor, through its greater or less restraints on population, and the latter by its agency in determining the supply of capital, by its greater or less restraints on expenditure, or unproductive consumption.

If a people have such low ideas as to the dignity of life, such a low standard of comfort, such a despicable collective will in respect to their style of living, as to be willing to live on a few handfuls of rice per day, as in Hindostan, then they will multiply their numbers in accordance with such low ideas, and the consequence will be that men will be worth, for the purposes of raw labor, only *three pence* per day; such will be the rate of wages for raw labor, and the laborers will have only a few handfuls of rice per day to subsist on. If their collective will be such as we find it in Ireland, such that they are content to live on a few potatoes, then they will multiply their numbers accordingly, and the rate of wages will be so low that the common laborers will be only able to procure a few potatoes for their subsistence. If, on the other hand, the collective will of the great body of the people be such as we find it in England, such that they will not live on anything less than beef and potatoes with a mug of ale per day, then the numbers of the population will be multiplied, or rather restrained, accordingly, and the wages of labor will be so high as to enable the laborers to have their beef and potatoes with their mug of ale per day.

Such is the reasoning, and the very just reasoning, of Dr. Chalmers, somewhat more explicitly stated than he has stated it himself, in regard to the most important point for the welfare of society, the wages of labor. His reasoning is similar, though not so obvious and readily intelligible, in regard to the profits of capital. But it is time that we should consider this eminent author more particularly, on this important point, and hear from him in his own energetic words.

§ 9. The valuable work of Dr. Thomas Chalmers, "On Political Economy, in connection with the Moral State and Moral Prospects of Society,"* in which are embodied his valuable contributions to the Philosophy of Society, and which has been before critically and somewhat thoroughly examined, as before stated, is most essentially a disquisition on Malthusianism, rather than on Political Economy. It may be most correctly, as well as most essentially described, as a masterly demonstration of the futility of all expedients for the improvement of the condition of society, or rather of the poorer classes of society, which look merely to an enlargement of wealth, or the means of subsistence.

It may be defined, in other words, to the same purport, as a triumphant refutation of the Politico-Economical school of Social Philosophy. In opposition to the superficial, sensuous, and grossly material views of this superficial and contracted school of Philosophy, he nobly asserts the great idea, which has been already so repeatedly set forth in the pages of the present work, that it is to AN ELEVATION OF THE MORAL STATUS of the people

---

* See Part V., Chap. V.

alone, that we can safely look for any permanent or reliable improvement even on their mere material condition, or, as John Stuart Mill has expressed the same idea, it is only to remedies that "operate on and through the minds and habits of the people."

It is while asserting that great idea, in various forms, in the course of his great work under consideration, that he incidentally, rather than directly, asserts the kindred idea now under particular consideration, and which is, in truth, but the most fundamental idea, or the same idea most fundamentally and essentially expressed. It is the collective will of society, and of each particular class of society, that determines its condition and destiny. Therefore, and consequently, it is only by elevating that collective will, or the ideas from which it results and which compose it—it is only by remedies addressed to that collective will—that we can accomplish anything permanently efficacious towards improving the social condition of mankind.

This latter idea, in strict logical significance, is but a resultant, or corollary, from the former. Yet it is the latter idea which Dr. Chalmers has more clearly discerned and most emphatically asserted, while he seems to have only faintly discerned the former or more fundamental one, and has only feebly and somewhat timidly asserted it. Thus do we find again verified the observation which we have so often before had occasion to make, in the present pages, that mankind, in their progress towards the truth, in their advance in knowledge, always attain first the more superficial ideas, and afterwards advance, step by step, to the more fundamental.

§ 10. The first distinct trace of the great fundamental idea in question, which may, indeed, be regarded as the great TAP-ROOT of the true Philosophy of Society, Dr. Chalmers presents to our view, in his Thirteenth Chapter, which treats of emigration, that fruitful topic of speculation and declamation, on the part of superficialists, as to the possibility of evading the indisputable truth of Malthusianism, or the inevitable laws of population. In remarking upon the futility of this expedient, and after having conclusively demonstrated it, he says: "So utterly powerless, or rather so positively mischievous, is every expedient for the amelioration of the people, that it but adds, through the medium of their own improvidence, to the excess of their numbers. The high road to their collective comfort and independence, and there is no other, is their collective virtue, and intelligence, and worth. Off from this, both they and the patriots, or philanthropists who care for them, will find themselves alike helpless and bewildered. They may institute a thousand devices, schemes of benignant promise, smiling charities of goodly pretension and gracious aspect. They will terminate in nothing, or worse than nothing. They smile but to betray."*

The most explicit, and, at the same time, copious expression of the idea that we derive from Dr. Chalmers, is to be found in the appendix to his work under consideration, in the article on Profit. He there says: "Should there then be a high standard of enjoyment among laborers, they will not marry so as to overstock the country with population; and so, just because their taste is high, their wages would be high; thus landing us in the important and delightful conclusion, that the people, collectively speaking, have their circumstances in their own hands; it being at the bidding of their collective will, whether the remuneration for their work shall be a scanty or a sufficient one. The same principle has not been extended to profit, though it be as strictly applicable to the one element as to the other. It is for each capitalist to determine how much of his profits he shall expend on personal or family indulgences, or how much of them he shall reserve for additional outlays upon his business. Should there be a general and voluntary descent among capitalists in respect of expenditure, this of itself, by adding to the investitures in trade, would produce a general fall of profit. Whereas, by means of expenditure in this class of society, profits might be sustained at any given level; a level as much determined by the standard of enjoyment, or collective will of capitalists, as wages are by the collective will of laborers. However simple and obvious this consideration may

---

* Chalmers' Political Economy, p. 304. Columbus, Ohio, edition of 1833.

be, yet the most important, and as yet unnoticed conclusions are deducible therefrom."*

Farther on in his appendix, and in presenting a summary, or synoptical view, of the reasonings of his work, he lays down this, as the *fifth* proposition of that summary : " That high wages are not necessarily confined to the period when the wealth of society is in a state of progressive increase ; and neither does it follow, that, when this wealth has attained its maximum, and become stationary, the wages of labor must be low. That it remains in the collective power of laborers to sustain their wages at as high a level in the ultimate, as in the progressive stages of the wealth of a country. That the moral preventive check on population can achieve and perpetuate this result; but nothing else will do it."†

Farther on still in his appendix, he lays down, as the *fifteenth* proposition of his synoptical view, the following: "That the rate of profit is determined by the collective will of capitalists, just as the rate of wages is, by the collective will of laborers—the former, by the command which they have, through their greater or less expenditure, over the amount of capital ; the latter, by the command which they have, through their later or earlier marriages, over the amount of population. That by raising or lowering, therefore, the standard of enjoyment among capitalists profit is raised or lowered ; that, in this way, both classes may encroach on the rent of land, and share its produce more equally with the landlords."‡

These profound and momentous utterances of Dr. Chalmers serve to carry the mind forward considerably in advance of commonly received ideas, and they point more distinctly and appreciatively than any anterior known utterances, to one of the main grand conclusions of all Social Philosophy, and ultimately to be adopted as one of its main fundamental propositions. They are but approximative utterances of the great truth, to which they do not quite fully attain, that mankind are, in all respects, the real agents, or *immediate* agents of their own destiny, and are

---

* Same work, pp. 403-4.   † Same, p. 435.   ‡ Same work, pp. 438-9.

themselves responsible for their own condition—that they do not only, by their collective will, determine the rate of their wages and their profits, but determine, also, the form and nature of their government, and whatsoever else most essentially concerns them, excepting, of course, what appertains strictly to their NATURAL ENVIRONMENT.

These oracular utterances of Dr. Chalmers are but approximative expressions of the great truth, that mankind are, in a physical, though not in a metaphysical, or most essential sense, and for all immediate and practical purposes, the true originators or creators of their own fortunes, both collectively and individually—that it is not the government, not the politicians, not the kings, not the demagogues, against whom the demagogue flatterers of the people are so much addicted to railing, that are responsible for the sufferings of the people, but the people themselves—that it is not so much the government that is responsible for the wrongs suffered by the people, as it is the people that are responsible for the wrongs inflicted by the government—that the faults of the government are, in reality, the faults of the people themselves, cropping out in their faithful representatives and true natural exponents—that the crimes of politicians, kings, and demagogues, so constantly clamored against by superficial declaimers, are but a certain mode and manifestation of the crimes of the people, are but natural elevations, rising somewhat above the average summit level of the depravity of the people themselves.

These eminently just observations of Dr. Chalmers are but approximative advances toward the great truth which asserts that the people have despots, faithless politicians, and corrupt demagogues, to rule over and afflict them, because it is of such stuff that they are themselves made, and because they would do no better themselves if they were placed in like situations—that they have such rulers because they deserve them, are not worthy of any better, are not qualified to appreciate any better, will not, because they are not qualified to appreciate any better, choose any better to rule over them, because they will not, and cannot, for lack of appreciation, elect the wise and good, that are always to be found in every community, for their rulers, but on the contrary, either directly or indirectly, by their errors either of commission or omission, elect rather those unwise or corrupt men, and those unwise or corrupt principles that eventually bring down destruction on their own heads, of their own choice, and through their own folly. They are but philosophical recognitions and expressions of the great truth which has found its poetical rendition in the memorable words of Cassius in the play of Julius Cæsar,

> "The fault, dear Brutus, is not in our stars,
> But in ourselves that we are underlings."

They are but philosophical recognitions and expressions of the great truth which speaks to all nations, and to all men, whether individually or collectively considered, who are complaining of the faults of their government, or of their untoward fortunes, or hard lot in life, and admonish them, in the oracular words of Holy Writ—"PHYSICIAN, HEAL THYSELF."

CHAPTER X.

SISMONDI AND MILL—THEIR MOST ESSENTIAL CONTRIBUTION TO THE PHILOSOPHY OF SOCIETY BROUGHT PROMINENTLY INTO VIEW.

§ 1. AMONG the eminent contributors to the Philosophy of Society, whom the present century has produced, the two authors whose names comprise in part the caption of the present chapter, hold a deservedly prominent place. It is true that they have both written avowedly on Political Economy only, in those works in which their most essentially valuable contributions to that Philosophy have been rendered. But they have both risen above the low and contracted views of the mere Political Economist, and have both evinced a disposition—indeed, in some respects amenable to censure—to exalt the mere science of Wealth, or Political Economy, as it has been commonly called, into the science of SOCIOLOGY, or the science of Society in its largest and most comprehensive import.*

Mill, in his work on Political Economy, has risen to the dignity of a Malthusian, of which he has approved himself one of the most meritorious exponents, nay, has risen even above that higher school of thought; and Sismondi has not less risen above the views of both the Malthusian and Political Economist, although, upon the whole, not so valuable a thinker as his illustrious compeer. Mill has, indeed, entitled himself to give, and has prepared us to expect, something more than a mere treatise on Political Economy, in the valuable work which he has presented to the world on that science, by the very title which he has prefixed to his work—"Principles of Political Economy, with some of their Applications to Social Philosophy,"—and most creditably has he answered the expectations inspired by that title. Sismondi, while avowedly

---

* For a criticism on both Sismondi and Mill, for this censurable disposition which they have manifested, see Part IV. of the series of which the present work is but the SIXTH part, or that which treats of the Politico-Economical System.

writing on Political Economy only, has attacked that school of Social Philosophy—in so far as the Political Economists may be said to constitute a school of Social Philosophy—in its most vulnerable point. He has exposed the main fundamental error of that school of thought, and has, in short, completely subverted it, at the same time that he supposed he was advancing and promoting it. In this he has rendered a valuable service to the Philosophy of Society, and has, at the same time, inflicted a most disastrous, though well-merited blow, upon the pretensions of Political Economy, as affording the basis for a true system of Social Philosophy. In this double fact is exhibited, at once, the merit and demerit of Sismondi, the points in which he is entitled to commendation and liable to censure.

§ 2. Sismondi has clearly discerned, and emphatically announced the great fundamental error of fixing attention on Wealth, rather than on Man, as do the Political Economists—in making Wealth the primary object of consideration, and Man only a secondary object—in thus attaching more importance to the mere incident than to the principal, to a mere abstraction than to the true reality. This is the great merit of his writings on Political Economy, which, most correctly defined and entitled, indeed, should be regarded as Disquisitions against Political Economy, or, at least, criticisms upon it. But he has committed the error of supposing that he was thus reforming Political Economy, instead of actually subverting it, in reference at least to the ends which he proposed, and to which he far more wisely directed his attention. He has not evinced the discrimination to discern that he was thus essentially directing his attention to the far more comprehensive science of Sociology, or to the Philosophy of Society, in its largest sense, to which the science of Political Economy is but an appendage, having, however, its own proper and important, though subordinate and restricted province.

Sismondi does not seem to have discerned that Political Economy properly concerns itself only with the laws of wealth, and that the practical application of those laws to their true end—the promotion of the welfare and happiness of man—appertain to a higher science, to the science of politics or statesmanship, in its largest sense, and to the yet higher science of Sociology, of which politics is itself but a subordinate science, although of a higher grade, in subordination, than mere Political Economy. He does not seem to have discerned that the Political Economist who undertakes to concern himself with the proper applications of the laws of Wealth to the best interests of Men, although, indeed, undertaking a noble concern, and the true ultimate end, with reference to which all Political Economy should be prosecuted, transgresses, nevertheless, the proper province of his own peculiar science, as would the chemist who should undertake to make the laws of mechanical motion an appurtenance of his appropriate science, or the physiologist who should unnecessarily concern himself with the laws of pathology, and even of therapeutics. And this is the demerit of Sismondi or the aspect in which he is liable to censurable criticism in his writings on Political Economy.

Sismondi, therefore, was wrong in censuring Political Economists for fixing their attention on Wealth, rather than on Man; for that is precisely their very business—the very province of their science. But he was right, very right, and in a high degree commendable in asserting that they were censurable for supposing, as they seem generally to have supposed, that they were thus accomplishing the great end to be aimed at by Social Philosophy, or even by mere statesmanship, when they were bestowing their attention merely on the abstraction called Wealth, and were learnedly expounding, in the abstract, the laws which regulate its production, distribution and consumption—for supposing, in short, that any very important progress toward the true ends of Social Philosophy could ever be made by a system of thought that fixes its attention primarily on Wealth, rather than on Man himself, in reference to whom, alone, Wealth has any utility or essential significance.

Sismondi does not, indeed, so clearly or broadly assert this idea. But he so nearly approximates it, that, for most practical purposes, he may be regarded as having asserted it. In dealing with Sismondi, in this respect, as in dealing with Dr. Chalmers, De Maistre, and other illustrious authorities, we take the liberty of rendering his thoughts according to their most enlarged significance, and full logical import. In doing so, the author respectfully submits, that he is less liable to censurable criticism than those authors—by far the greater number, if he mistakes not—who are for ever seeking to restrict, contract, or contort the views of others, in order to afford themselves a broader margin for cavillings, exceptions, and criticisms, and in order, as it would seem, that they may appear the more original, and all the more wise than their predecessors.

Entertaining a very different disposition—setting out in his scientific and philosophical labors, from the very commencement, with the diametrically opposite policy—ambitious to coincide with anterior reasoners, as far as reason will allow, rather than to excite controversy with them—aiming at the abnegation of self, and the exaltation of humanity—fully impressed with the idea that what we most want in Science, and especially in this, the highest and most complex of all the Sciences, THE SCIENCE OF SOCIOLOGY, is a grand combination of efforts, a grand grouping of many ideas into one consistent and harmonious system—the author is rejoiced to find other and eminent thinkers coinciding with his main fundamental views, or even approximating coincidence.

Animated with this spirit and this purpose, he may be excused, it is hoped, for enlarging, rather than restricting, the views of his illustrious predecessors in this realm of thought—especially when he takes the pains, by ample quotations from those predecessors, of their own thoughts in their own words, to afford opportunity, for every inquirer into these pages, to judge for himself how far, if at all, he has so enlarged the import of the ideas of those eminent authorities whom he quotes, and on whom he relies, in part, for the maintenance of that, at once, more enlarged and more consistent system of thought, which he proposes to introduce.

It is to Sismondi that the author appeals, or rather refers, in vindication of his Third main proposition, as laid down in the Sixth Chapter, which asserts, substantially, that it is MAN HIMSELF, and not his Government, nor any institution that he has devised, not his Wealth, nor any creation that is the work of his hand, that forms the true main object of scientific contemplation and regard, in every plan for the improvement of human society, or of the social condition of mankind.* While the reasonings of many eminent thinkers all point in this direction, all tend to this conclusion, Sismondi is the only one, that the author has encountered in his researches, so far at least as is now remembered, who has directly asserted this idea, or rather partially asserted it, with so much directness, and emphatic distinctness, as he has done.

It will readily be seen, however, from the quotations we are about to make from Sismondi, expressive of his most essential renditions of this idea, that he has asserted it from the standpoint of the mere Political Economist, and consequently, not, by any means, with sufficient breadth and compass of thought. Not having been elevated quite enough, in his views of Social Philosophy, to discern that Political Economy is but a subordinate science to that Philosophy, and to the higher Science which it cradles, and towards which his own reasonings unconsciously tended—THE SCIENCE OF SOCIOLOGY—not having discerned how very low and grovelling are the essential aims of the whole Politico-Economical school of thought, he has not been able to divest himself of that contracted view of the real interests of human Society, which seems to be fundamentally and radically ingrained in all the reasonings of that school. For, although strongly tending towards a higher system of thought, although unconsciously yearning for such a system, and although uttering truths that rose above the average level of the contracted views of the Politico-Economical system, he belonged, nevertheless, essentially, or at least fundamentally, to that system. The valuable idea which we here accredit to him was but a prominent and commanding elevation, rising above the average level of his views of the Philosophy of Society—a sort of isolated peak towering above the dead level plain of Political Economy, to which nearly all his reasonings are fundamentally conformed. But let us proceed to question him more closely, and to consider his views on the point under consideration, as presented in his own words.

---

* See Chapter VI., § 3.

§ 3. The principal writings of Sismondi—or of John Charles Leonard Simonde de Sismondi, as his biographers present his name to us in full—that have any direct relation to the Philosophy of Society are his "New Principles of Political Economy," first published in 1819, his "Disquisitions on the Constitutions of Free People," first published in 1836, and his "Disquisitions on Political Economy," first published, in the volume form at least, in 1837, all in the French language. It is with the last of these works, containing his latest and most mature thoughts, that it is proposed here to deal, although the ideas which it presents do not differ essentially from those of his former publications.

The most condensed and forcible expression of the essential idea which Sismondi constantly labors to illustrate in this work, and which it is here sought to bring into prominent view, is to be found, however, not in this work itself, but in a conversation which he had with Ricardo, the English Economist, at Geneva, in which he is reported to have exclaimed, "What, is Wealth, then, everything, and Man absolutely nothing!"*

In this exclamation Sismondi strikes to the very heart of the Politico-Economical mode of regarding the interests of human society. This is just their very mode of reasoning, their dominating aim, their radical idea, graphically sketched, and presented to the view, by one stroke of the philosophic pencil of Sismondi. With them Wealth is everything, and Man absolutely nothing. With them the great question is not, how shall men be enabled to enjoy wealth—how shall they be enabled to possess a just and proper measure of those material comforts which constitute wealth—but it is simply how shall wealth be increased, or how, at most, shall wealth be regulated, without any reference to the question how far such wealth is to be really conducive to human good. It is against this false view of Political Economists that Sismondi has very justly levelled the shafts of his invective, and directed the powers of his reasoning. But let us inquire how he

---

* See English work, entitled, Political Economy and Philosophy of Government, a Series of Essays from the works of Sismondi, p. 43. London Edition, 1847.

has expressed himself, in reference to this point, in the more formal disquisition above referred to.

In the Introduction to his Disquisitions on Political Economy, or Etudes sur L'Economie Politique, he says: " What, then, is the end of human society? Is it to dazzle the eyes by an immense production of useful and elegant commodities; to astonish the mind by the empire which man exercises over nature, and by the precision and rapidity with which inanimate machines execute human work? Is it to cover the sea with vessels and the land with railroads, distributing in every way the products of an industry forever increasing in activity? Is it to give to two or three individuals in a hundred thousand the power of disposing of an opulence which would give comfort to all those hundred thousand? In this case, we have, without doubt, made immense progress, in comparison with our ancestors. We are rich in invention, rich in activity, rich in scientific power, rich especially in merchandise; for every nation has not only enough for itself, but for all its neighbors.

" But if the end which society ought to propose to itself, in favoring labor, and securing its fruits, should rather be to secure the development of man, and of all men; to spread with a beneficent hand through the whole community, though in different proportions, the fruits of the labor of man, those fruits which we call wealth; if those fruits, which comprise moral and intellectual as well as material benefits, ought to be a means of improvement as well as of enjoyment, is it sure that we have approached our object? Is it sure that in searching after wealth, we have not forgotten the order and regulation of the house, and of the city, Political Economy?"*

This passage, one of the most suggestive, pregnant, and valuable of all that Sismondi has furnished us, illustrates well his merit and demerit as a contributor to Social Philosophy, the truth and the error which his writings present. Most justly does he question the propriety of making the mere multiplication of com-

---

* Etudes sur L'Economie Politique, Introduction, p. 19. Brussels Edition of 1837.

modities the main end of human society, and recommend that attention should rather be directed to MEN, and the improvement of MEN. But he commits an error—an error tending to the confusion of ideas, in regard to the proper functions of the various social sciences—in suggesting that it appertains to Political Economy to concern itself directly or otherwise than incidentally alone with the improvement of MEN.

Society ought, indeed, to propose to itself the noble end which Sismondi suggests, and that should be regarded in the largest sense, as its true end, or one of its true ends. But it should not seek to accomplish this end through the science of Political Economy; for such is not the proper function of that science. It matters not what may be the philological import or original meaning of that term, on which Sismondi lays too much stress. It has come to imply a different idea. It has come to imply the commonly received title of the Science of Wealth—of the science which treats of the laws of wealth, meaning thereby the natural laws of wealth—the natural laws in accordance with which wealth is produced, distributed, and consumed. This has come to be regarded, by the most approved thinkers, as the proper province of Political Economy, or of the science that has by common usage received that appellation; and there is a propriety or necessity in that understanding of its proper function being strictly adhered to.* To aim directly at the improvement of MEN, or to aim directly at rendering the natural laws of wealth subservient to that end, appertains to the THERAPEUTICS of Social Science, whereas Political Economy constitutes simply its PHYSIOLOGY.

§ 4. Another criticism on Sismondi may be important here, the more especially as it will serve to bring more fully into view the

---

* Of all the Economists, Nassau William Senior has most clearly and justly appreciated, and adhered to the true and proper function of Political Economy. He is the counterpart or antipode of Sismondi in this respect. Perhaps we should rather say he is the *antidote* to Sismondi—to his diseased or distempered propensity to regard Political Economy as the science of society. See the valuable work of Senior on Political Economy, in illustration.

whole truth which he has but partially expressed. For this is the great utility of criticism, that it tends more clearly and distinctly, by the contrast of views which it affords, to bring the real truth into view, and to impress it on the mind. In asserting the great truth, that the end which human society should propose to itself is the development of man and of all men, Sismondi does not appear to have fully apprehended, by any means, the utility of this end, its vast significance and importance. In short, he seems to have discerned its utility simply as an END, without discerning also that it is, furthermore, a MEANS to an end—a necessary MEANS to the very end which the Political Economists aim at, and with such an all-observing intensity of interest as to have provoked the just censure of Sismondi. He does not seem to have discerned the great truth, that, in developing MAN, as he recommends, we adopt the most sure MEANS of developing WEALTH—that it is to the moral or intellectual nature of man that we must look for the security of his merely material interests—that, in short, MAN himself is the true fountain of wealth, and that it is by digging deeply into HIM that we most surely and most abundantly augment the supplies of wealth.

This is the great truth which the author of the present work desires, here and elsewhere, to bring into clear, distinct, and prominent view, but which it may readily be perceived Sismondi has but partially and imperfectly expressed. This truth does not assert merely, as Sismondi has asserted, in the passage above cited, and as he merely asserts in all the other passages which it is proposed to quote, or nearly all, that wealth should be considered only with reference to the great end of promoting the good of MAN, but that MAN himself should be considered with reference to the mere end of promoting wealth, with reference to the mere preliminary object of providing his means of subsistence —thus making MAN, as we have before said, "the Alpha and Omega, the beginning and the end, the first and the last," of all that concerns his social well-being or destiny of this life.*

This great truth declares that if we would secure the very instru-

---

* See Ante., Chapter II., § 4.

mentalities which we propose to employ for the good of man, we must direct our attention primarily to MAN, not less than ultimately. Do we wish to secure wealth for man, in order thereby to improve his condition, to elevate his moral and intellectual status? Then we must look to MAN himself, aim from the beginning, by whatever means possible, moral or physical, to elevate his moral and intellectual status. Do we wish to secure good government for man, and that, too, in order to improve his condition, to elevate his moral and intellectual status, which, Sismondi very justly reasons, should be the great end of human society? Then we must look to MAN himself, and aim, from the beginning, by whatever means possible, moral or physical, to elevate his moral and intellectual status. For by such means only can we make good government possible for man.

Thus do we reason in a circle, and thus must we reason, in order to reason correctly. For all truth is circular—all motion is circular, moral as well as physical. The beginning and the end of all things is the same. Man is the end of all human improvement, and he is also the beginning of it all. He is the true source alike of his moral and material prosperity. Let this great truth be really received and fully appreciated. It is high time that it had been. Often enough has it been asserted vaguely and imperfectly—loosely and disconnectedly. But it has never as yet been asserted as formally, emphatically, and authoritatively, as it should have been. Often enough has it been poetically asserted, and in the language of sentimental philosophy. But it has never as yet been scientifically asserted, or in the language of a truly rational or critical philosophy. We may be the less surprised, therefore, that it has not as yet been scientifically recognized, or systematically acted upon—nay, even reasoned upon.

Nor is the great truth, thus incidentally expressed, inconsistent at all, as might appear, with the assertion just before made, that Political Economy, strictly speaking, has nothing to do, otherwise than indirectly, with the business of improving men, or with "the development of man, and of all men," as Sismondi has expressed it. Political Economy, rightly understood, is a passive science, not an active one. It properly concerns itself only with the explanation of phenomena, not with the production of phenomena. If it has aimed at PRODUCTION, even of wealth, as it has done, almost all absorbingly, it has so far transgressed its true function, which is simply to explain the phenomena of production, and not less, also, those of distribution and consumption. Its proper office is simply to explain laws, natural laws, the natural laws of Wealth. It has nothing to do with the creation of laws. It has nothing to do with endeavors outside the laws of nature—if indeed the endeavors of man can be so regarded—it has nothing to do, at any rate, with the endeavors of man, by his own voluntary action, by his own laws, which are properly, indeed, but *secondary* laws of nature, to influence the production of wealth, or its distribution, except simply to explain how such attempts will operate—what will be their probable effects—how far will they really tend to good, or to the end proposed.

Assigning to Political Economy this function alone, restricting it to this, we yet accord to it a vast and varied and eminently intricate field of thought. Even thus restricted, it will be found a highly useful and noble Science, one of vast importance, and indispensable to the labors of the true Social Philosopher. Without the knowledge which it is the office of Political Economy to impart, the Social Philosopher would not know how to advise on many important questions. Without such knowledge he might, under some circumstances, give eminently disastrous advice to mankind, who ought always to look to him for advice, instruction, and guidance. For the Social Philosopher is the true KING, to whom mankind should ever look for the guidance and direction of their political, and, in a yet larger sense to speak, their social interests.

Unhappily, it is too true, mankind are but little disposed to look in this direction for instruction or guidance, but little qualified, indeed, to do so, but little qualified to appreciate either the counsellor, or the counsel they would be likely to obtain from him. Much more prone are they to seek the advice of the shallow demagogue, the charlatan, the knave, or any one rather than the philosopher, or truly wise man. Occasionally, indeed, they take higher direction, as when they stumble upon the recognition of an Antonine, an Alfred, or a Washington. But this is not often. Nevertheless, such men have more to do with the government of the world than is commonly supposed. Although too often excluded from the world's august ceremonials, they may be compared, as Lord Bacon has beautifully done,* to the images of Brutus and Cassius at the funeral of Junia, of which, being excluded from the procession, Tacitus splendidly says, *eo ipso præfulgebant quod non visibantur*—for that very reason, because they were not seen, they shone with preëminent lustre.

The silent and unseen forces of nature are greater than is apparent to the sensuous view. They are, indeed, ever the greatest. Nor is this, perhaps, less true of the moral than of the material world. Although the knaves and fools ostensibly govern the world, for the most part, yet the counsels of the wise and good have really more to do with the world's government and destiny than may readily be believed or be apparent to superficial observation.

Let not the prosecution of knowledge or true wisdom, therefore, be neglected. The teachings of true wisdom are not wholly lost. "Nothing is lost," says Carlyle†—nor is the observation any less true than beautiful. But let us proceed with our endeavor to rescue from loss, to preserve, and make manifest, the valuable thoughts of Sismondi.

§ 5. In the Introduction to his Disquisitions on Political Economy, a few pages in advance of the passage just now criticised, he thus defines Political Economy, and thereby justifies the very same criticisms already pronounced upon his views: "That science has always had, and ought always to have, for its object, men collected together in society. Economy, according to the proper sense of the word, is the regulation of the house; Political Economy is the regulation of the house applied to the city. These

---

* See Advancement of Learning, Book I.

† See his Heroes and Hero-Worship. Lecture on the Hero as Poet, and particularly in reference to the father of Burns, of whom he beautifully says, that his life was not lost, "for Robert was the outcome of him."

are the two grand primitive associations that are the objects of the science. All proceeds from man, all should have relation to man, and to man united by some common tie."*

UNDOUBTEDLY ALL SHOULD HAVE RELATION TO MAN; and in so far as Political Economy may properly concern itself with anything more than the simple explanation of the laws of wealth, in so far as it may properly, or incidentally, concern itself with the ultimate tendencies or applications of those laws, it should conform its reasonings to the suggestion of Sismondi in this passage. To that extent, undoubtedly, it has hitherto been greatly in error, except in the instances afforded by Sismondi himself, Mill, and a few others, who have manifested the commendable and justly appreciative disposition which is here manifested by Sismondi.

The strong disposition of Sismondi to direct philosophical attention to MAN himself, rather than to the mere abstraction called WEALTH, is again manifested in the following passage, from the Second Essay of the work under review: "If, instead of considering abstractly wealth, production, consumption, exchange, we penetrate more deeply into the organization of society; if we carefully inquire what it is that produces, what it is that consumes; if we discriminate with a view to ascertain in whose hands the exchangeable commodities are to be found; if we seek to know whether they are always those who have need of commodities to exchange; if, in fine, we have constantly before our eyes men, in their diverse conditions, and not wealth, and still less the essence of wealth abstractly considered, we should not be embarrassed with the difficulties or contradictions which we have ourselves created, we should not see any impossibility in the fact that extreme abundance may exist by the side of extreme indigence, and we should not deny, against the evidence, that the encumbrance of the markets and the very excess of production may become a cause of general suffering."†

But it may readily be perceived that, in this passage, Sismondi proposes to consider MAN only in a politico-economical point of

---

* Introduction to Etudes sur L'Economie Politique, p. 3. Brussels Edition, 1837.
† Etudes sur L'Economie Politique, Essay II., pp. 79, 80.

view, or with reference to explaining certain abstruse problems in Political Economy, as "the possibility of a universal or general glut" of the markets of the world, which Say, and some other economists have denied. He does not, however, always take such a contracted view of this paramount object.

In his Fourth Essay, or that on the Expulsion of Cultivators, he speaks more nearly to the true point, where, in reference to the *saving upon labor*, as he terms it, by throwing men out of employment, in order to procure cheap products, which he notices in different countries, he says: "While the Chrematistic School* desires to save upon men in order to obtain wealth, we hesitate not to say that we ought rather to sacrifice wealth in order to have men. They will have a fine time in demonstrating to us that every one of the innovations which we have repudiated is more advantageous in that pecuniary point of view which we will again repeat; if it diminishes the number of happy individuals, of intellectual and moral individuals living on a given space, it is bad; and it is in this point of view that we have combated, that we shall always combat that industrial system which has put human life at a discount. Nor can we let escape this occasion for making manifest anew how false is that system in even admitting the barbarous supposition that we ought to calculate only profits and losses for nations, and not the life or happiness of men."†

In the very first sentence of the Essay last quoted from, he more explicitly defines his idea of Political Economy than in either of the passages already quoted, which definition, indeed, should more properly have preceded our last quotation. "We have endeavored," says Sismondi, "to make intelligible the opposition of the two doctrines, the one which we name Chrematistics, or the increase of wealth, the other Political Economy, or the regulation of the house and city. The first proposes for its

---

* This is the title by which he designates the school of Political Economy which he opposes, and whose leading idea, as he rightly asserts, is merely *the increase of wealth*.

† Same work, Essay IV., p. 141.

object to produce much for a good market, the second to distribute labor and its products in a manner to assure the utmost possible welfare."*

Neither one of these objects, it is again respectfully submitted, is the true object of Political Economy, rightly understood. Its object, we repeat, is, strictly speaking, simply to explain the natural laws by which these two objects are to be attained. In so far, however, as Political Economists may transgress this proper limit of their scientific investigations—in so far as they may misapprehend that proper limit, and so transgress it—in so far as they may excusably, as well as naturally, be impelled beyond the mere diagnosis of phenomena, the mere explanation of the modes or processes by which wealth is naturally produced, distributed, and consumed, and aim at ultimate ends, aim at the applications of those laws, with a view to the attainment of desirable ends—so far it is undoubtedly true that the aim of Sismondi is right, and that of Political Economists in general, or of the Chrematistic School, as he is pleased to designate it, is wrong, or at least ill directed, delusory, and of but little significance.

In his Fifth Essay, while descanting on the advantages of the British nation, and its deplorable destitution, in spite of its high civilization, its freedom, its religion, and its wealth, he thus deplores that false system of reasoning which he so justly attributes to the Political Economists, in their ultimate aims, which loses sight of men, and looks only at wealth; "Moreover, it is not the moral sentiments that are in default. It suffers from the effects of that mournful theory which it has adopted for the increase of wealth, that mournful theory which has caused it to forget men for the sake of commodities." †

Further on in the same Essay, and in the same strain, he thus bewails the same system, in regard to Ireland. "It is not, then, wealth that is wanting, nor knowledge, nor industry, nor example, nor the encouragement that can afford great proprietors, nor the highest civilization and the protection of laws. The traveller

---

* Same work, p. 140. † Same work, p. 169.

who regards only things is everywhere struck with admiration: he who concerns himself with the kind of men experiences altogether either indignation, or the most dolorous pity." *

In illustration of the same idea, the opening words of Sismondi's Eighth Essay may be also worthy of quotation, where he makes this eminently just observation: "We have said, and we shall not cease to repeat, the prosperity of a nation is to be estimated not by the mass of wealth accumulated on its territory, but only by the amount of happiness which that wealth distributes to all who compose the nation."—to which totally unexceptionable and eminently just observation, he adds this questionable one as already before shown—"The true aim of Political Economy is to assure such a distribution of wealth that all may profit by its advantages, although some may be more favored than others." † This is the true aim of SOCIOLOGY, or of the Philosophy of Society, or a part, and no trifling part, of its true aim, in which it should cheerfully accept any suggestions that the Political Economists may have to make, although, as before said, in making such suggestions they are assuming the office of something more than the mere Political Economist—that of the Social Philosopher.

Not less worthy of citation and special consideration is the following passage in the same essay: "We have endeavored in the preceding essays to make intelligible the fatal consequences of those systems, which, without depriving the poor man of his liberty, yet leave him to struggle with the rich, and do not assure him any guaranty against an adversary too strong. It behooves us not less to make known the consequences of the system of slavery, a system the most gross, barbarous, and mournful in its effects, but which is only the application of the same principle, 'that states are enriched by producing more and spending less; that they are enriched by all that they can save on the labor of the hand; that they are enriched by extracting from laborers the most work possible for the least pay possible;' that is to say, of

---

* Same, p. 181.   † Same work, p. 262.

the false doctrine that it is not man and the good of man that governments should aim to increase, but wealth."*

§ 6. The foregoing quotations are all, except the first, from Sismondi's "Etudes sur L'Economie Politique," and have been carefully translated from the original edition of 1837, by the author of the present work, which has appeared to him preferable to citing the original French, inasmuch as there are many English readers who do not read the French readily, or without some difficulty, if at all.† Two passages from another work, or article of Sismondi, on Landed Property, and translated by another writer, appear worthy of citation here, although substantially but repetitions of the same idea already so copiously illustrated.

But so important is this idea, so little has it been hitherto heeded in the reasonings of men, so difficult is it to induce men to take the really true view of things, that the author is unwilling to let slip the occasion of bringing to bear, in further illustration of his own ideas in part, the impressive and emphatic language of Sismondi, as contained in those passages.

Will not the nations hear and heed these impressive words of Sismondi? "The existence of civilization, the safety of the human race in this our ancient Europe, are closely bound to the triumph of this true Political Economy, both in public opinion and in legislation, to the development of that science which has for its object man, and not wealth, which asks how this wealth can be employed for the happiness and virtue of all, not how it can be indefinitely increased."‡ That is precisely, or almost pre-

---

* Same, p. 265.

† Mr. Mill, in his work on Political Economy, however, quotes largely from Sismondi, in his own original words, a method from which the author of this work respectfully dissents. Difficult enough it is to induce men to read the truth, especially valuable truth, even in their own language. To expect them to tug at a foreign language, in order to get hold of it, is altogether out of the question.

‡ See Revue Mensuelle d'Economie Politique, February, 1834, and translation of same, in Political Economy and Philosophy of Government, &c., of Sismondi, an English work published at London in 1847, p. 158.

cisely, the very science which the author of the present work proposes to inaugurate; although he would not term it Political Economy. But of that science, it is obvious to his mind, Sismondi takes too contracted and superficial a view—a view altogether too Politico-Economical merely.

To the same point, but a little further on, in the same article, Sismondi speaks very well and impressively. "To endeavor to understand what there is yet to be done," he says, " to enable us to form some clear and simple ideas on the economy of the social state, we will fix on that condition among men which the new science has caused to deviate least from its former organization, that of cultivation We will look at the chrematistic mode of considering it. We will afterwards ask what true Political Economy ought to do for it ; and though this be of all questions the most simple and the most clear in either form of this science, yet we shall soon see how different is their object, how opposite is the advice which they give; and in treating of agriculture, we shall have occasion to set before us all the difficulties of the social state, which are aggravated by making wealth the sole object of consideration, and which can only be removed by fixing our attention on men and not on things."*

In this last passage, Sismondi comes more nearly up to the precise point, or the full measure of the idea which the author of the present work is solicitous to engraft on the thought and mind of the world, than in any of the preceding passages. He here loudly asserts that the difficulties of the social state can only be removed by fixing our attention on MEN, and not on things. This is indisputably true. But little real progress will be made in Social Philosophy until we cease fixing our attention on the mere *outward covering* of man, in accordance with what Carlyle would doubtlessly term mere " Clothes Philosophy,"† and fix it on MAN himself—until we cease wasting our strength on such abstract questions as how is wealth to be increased, or even distributed or consumed? or how is good government to be secured for man-

---

* Same, pp. 158, 159.
† See Carlyle's Sartor Resartus.

kind, and direct it immediately to MAN himself?—until we so remodel our formulas of thought in Social Philosophy, that, instead of taking such shape as in those questions, they will rather be conformed to such questions as these—What kind of men have we to deal with here or there, and how far and in what way can they be improved?—how far are they calculated to acquire wealth, to actualize a just distribution of it, and to use without abusing it?—how far, moreover, are they calculated for good government, or rather for free government, so called, which seems to be the constant aspiration of the human soul?—how much liberty are they qualified to enjoy, or how much can they use without abusing, to their own disadvantage or that of their neighbors?

§ 7. It is in accordance with such questions as these that the idea in question suggests, in part, the remodelling of thought and investigation in Social Philosophy. This is, as before said,* what we may regard as the COPERNICAN IDEA of Social Philosophy; and until thought and investigation in that philosophy shall be conformed to this idea, we shall make about as little real progress in it, as was made in Siderial philosophy until the Copernican idea of Astronomy had been definitively established and adopted.

This, we again repeat, is the COPERNICAN IDEA of Social Philosophy. What is the NEWTONIAN IDEA, which the author of the present work is not less solicitous to engraft upon the thought and mind of the world, will be developed in a subsequent work, or the Seventh Part of the main work to which the present appertains.

It will thus be seen that the author does not and cannot claim entire originality for the idea thus heralded to the world as the Copernican idea of Social Philosophy, however exclusively original it may have been with him. He is glad that he cannot. He gladly accepts the approbation, though but partial approbation, of such high and justly approved authority as Sismondi. Nor is he by any means the only authority that might be cited in support,

---

* See Chapter VII.

but only the most emphatic one, and the one who has moreover spoken most explicitly to the point.

No real truth, no highly important truth, at least, is entirely or exclusively original with any one mind. The Copernican idea in Astronomy had been before distinctly conjectured by Pythagoras, and partially approximated by other astronomers. Sismondi is but the Pythagoras of the idea in question—nay, he is but one of many Pythagorases. But he has been the most plainly spoken, at least, of those who have fallen under the observation of the present inquirer. It has been made sufficiently manifest, however, that he has but imperfectly attained to the idea, and has not fully compassed it. More ample demonstrations will be necessary in order to establish it. These the present inquirer proposes hereafter to give.

The Egyptian astronomers knew that two of the planets, Mercury and Venus, revolved around the sun. But this discovery did not bring them to the full recognition of the great Copernican idea that they all revolved around the sun. Neither will the discoveries and demonstrations of Sismondi, valuable as they are, be sufficient to demonstrate the great truth, which he only partially approximates, that MAN IS THE TRUE CENTRE OF THE SOCIAL UNIVERSE, AND THAT AROUND HIM REVOLVES ALL HIS DESTINY.

II. OF JOHN STUART MILL.

§ 8. The most essentially valuable thought which this eminent philosopher has contributed to the Philosophy of Society, is that which has been already so often before quoted that it may almost appear useless tautology to repeat it here. It is that announced in his chapter on Popular Remedies for Low Wages, which asserts that "No remedies for low wages have the smallest chance of being efficacious, which do not operate on and through the minds and habits of the people."*

It requires but a little enlargement of this assertion to render it expressive, in the most comprehensive form, of one of the

---

* See Principles of Political Economy, Book II., Chap. XII., § 4, or Vol. I., p. 444, of Boston Ed., 1848.

most important fundamental truths in Social Philosophy. The circumscribed assertion of Mr Mill in the foregoing passage is not any more true than is the more extensive and comprehensive one, that NO REMEDIES FOR ANY OF THE ILLS OF HUMAN SOCIETY HAVE THE SMALLEST CHANCE OF BEING EFFICACIOUS WHICH DO NOT OPERATE ON AND THROUGH THE MINDS AND HABITS OF THE PEOPLE. The former is, indeed, but a partial and imperfect expression of the latter, and logically involves it.

It may readily be perceived that this assertion of Mill, either in his own restricted words, or in the more comprehensive ones in which we have rendered it, is not only entirely in harmony with that of Sismondi, which we have just now been considering, but that it is, in reality, only the assertion of the same idea in a more special form, and in more immediate reference to its practical applications. To assert, as Mill does, that remedies for social or economical ills should be addressed to "the minds and habits of the people," is evidently but to assert, in other words, and in a more definite, particular, and practical form, that they should be addressed to the people themselves, or yet in other words, to MAN.

Many similar assertions to this, in various forms, and in reference to different phases of the social condition, are to be found in Mill's valuable work on Political Economy. But as they have been extensively quoted and critically commented on in another work, which although not as yet before the public, it is hoped may yet before very long be enabled to make its appearance, it would be unnecessary repetition to reiterate them here, the more especially as that unpublished work forms but a part of the Series to which this appertains, and in logical order precedes it. In the author's elaborate work on Malthusianism, as yet unpublished, and forming the *Fifth Part* of the SERIES, of which this is but the Sixth Part, he has somewhat thoroughly considered and illustrated the valuable contributions of John Stuart Mill to the Philosophy of Society. For these contributions, as there and elsewhere asserted, are essentially Malthusian, and embrace what may be regarded as the most essential contribution of the Malthusian school of thought to that Philosophy—which contribution, as there and elsewhere repeatedly asserted, is among the most valuable that have ever been made. For, as there and elsewhere stated, although the *diagnosis* of causes which Malthusianism presents is very meagre and imperfect, its *therapeutics* is admirable and almost exhaustive.

As the alchemists, although aiming at a very vain and frivolous idea, the philosopher's stone, nevertheless incidentally made highly important discoveries in chemistry, so the Malthusians, although aiming at the comparatively small, if not trivial idea, of merely restraining population within proper bounds, have made some of the most important discoveries, or rather suggestions, in the Philosophy of Society. Of those discoveries, or suggestions, which may be all embraced in the grand aphorism, so often before asserted in these pages, in one form or other, THAT THE MORAL STATUS OF MANKIND MUST BE ELEVATED, John Stuart Mill has been one of the most distinguished and valuable exponents. This is the condensed essence alike of Malthusianism and of John Stuart Mill, most essentially expressed, in reference to their most essentially valuable contributions to Social Philosophy.

So highly important, so preëminently important, is this idea, that although it more properly appertains to the anterior work on Malthusianism than to this, which mainly aims at heralding only the more advanced ideas, than any which appertain to that school of thought, yet we cannot forbear here also repeating the idea. We should, indeed, present a very inadequate view of the Present Status of the Philosophy of Society, which the present work aims to give, if we did not present, if we did not bring prominently into view, this important idea. For this idea does not belong to the past only, but to the present, to the future, and to all time. It no longer appertains to Malthusianism alone, but to the Philosophy of Society. Into that august philosophy it is henceforth to be incorporated, and will endure so long as MAN endures, or until his career on this planet terminates.

Thanks to John Stuart Mill!—not less than to the Reverend Thomas Chalmers!—for the important part he has played in contributing to bring this great truth prominently into view! How difficult it is, alas! to effectuate this end—to bring the truth, more especially the most essential truth, the most important truth, before the human view!—in such a manner at least as to render it appreciable and rivet it in the human mind! Ably has Mill contributed to this end, as may be seen in the pregnant passage here cited, as well as in many others not deemed necessary to be cited. And yet it is evident, from the immediate context of this passage, that his views are essentially Malthusian, and that the idea is promulgated by him with reference only to the contracted aims of the mere Malthusian.

Thus, immediately following the passage quoted, in reference to "the minds and habits of the people," which he so justly says must be operated upon, in order to remedy low wages, he continues: "Whilst these are unaffected, any contrivance, even if successful, for temporarily improving the condition of the very poor, would but let slip the reins by which population was previously curbed; and could only, therefore, continue to produce its effect, if, by the whip and spur of taxation, capital were compelled to follow at an equally accelerated pace. But this process could not possibly continue for long together, and whenever it stopped it would leave the country with an increased number of the poorest class, and a diminished proportion of all except the poorest, or, if it continued long enough, with none at all. For 'to this complexion must come at last' all social arrangements which remove the natural checks to population without substituting any others."*

§ 9. In other respects also, as well as in respect to the idea above considered, the views of Mill bear a near resemblance to those of Sismondi. Like him, although not with the same degree of earnestness, he deprecates the undue importance generally attached by Political Economists to the increase of production, and recommends attention rather to improved distribution. Thus, he says, in the Seventh Chapter of his Fifth Book: "The observations in the preceding chapter had for their principal object to deprecate a false ideal of human society. Their applicability

---

* See work before cited. Same Book, Chapter and page.

to the practical purposes of present times, consists in moderating the inordinate importance attached to the mere increase of production, and fixing attention upon improved distribution, and a large remuneration of labor, as the true desiderata."*

In some other respects his views transcend in sagacity, or a just discernment, those of Sismondi. For while Sismondi, like nearly all French thinkers, belongs to the school of Social Philosophers, who, speaking at once most essentially and sententiously, aim at the complete merging of the individual in the society, Mill far more justly belongs to the school whose aim, most essentially expressed, is to secure the eventual triumph of the individual over society. This is manifest, not only from the whole scope of his reasonings in the work on Political Economy, but also, and still more so, from those of his later work on Liberty. Nevertheless, in the Fifth Book of his Political Economy, which treats "Of the Influence of Government," he lays down, with singular justness and perspicuity, some of the many important qualifications of this idea, or the *Laissez Faire* doctrine, as it is designated by Political Economists, to which their doctrine is subject.

§. 10. This disquisition on the most essential contribution of Mill to Social Philosophy should not, perhaps, be closed without noticing the somewhat more than faint trace, discoverable in his writings, of an eminently valuable idea, never as yet so prominently set forth as to warrant us in accrediting it to any authority, although more nearly approximated in full, as we shall hereafter show, by the great American statesman, Daniel Webster, than by any other. The idea is that THE MOST ESSENTIAL NATURE OF THE EVILS OF BAD GOVERNMENT IS UNCERTAINTY. Faint recognition of this idea, partial approximations to it, are indeed to be detected in very many reasoners. But the recognition of Mill is somewhat more explicit than the average of such recognitions. He says, in one of his chapters on Taxation: "Over-taxation, carried to a sufficient extent, is quite capable of ruining the most

---

* Same, Vol. II, p. 318.

industrious community, especially when it is in any degree arbitrary, so that the payer is never certain how much or how little he shall be allowed to keep."* In this passage, however, Mr. Mill does not show any more just perception of the essential mischief of UNCERTAINTY, in the action of government, than does Adam Smith, whom he quotes in the same chapter, and who says, "The certainty of what each individual ought to pay is, in taxation, a matter of so great importance, that a very considerable degree of inequality, it appears, I believe, from the experience of all nations, is not near so great an evil as a very small degree of uncertainty."†

Neither Adam Smith nor Mr. Mill has had the boldness to assert the truth which they have thus feebly expressed, so tersely as it may be expressed in the sententious aphorism :—It matters not what the tax may be, provided only it be certain and fixed, so that we may know what it is, and that it is not to be capriciously or suddenly raised. So stated, indeed the aphorism would not be strictly true, but would need one important qualification, namely, that the tax be not so great as to paralyze industry, by leaving it no margin for profit, and, consequently, no motive for exertion. But so stated, it would be more likely to arrest attention and awaken some more just ideas as to the true Philosophy of government and society in the stolid brain of the world.

The unqualified and exaggerated statement of principles has this utility, that it tends to bring them into recognition, when otherwise they would remain unrecognized. This has been the case, no doubt, with the important principles involved in Malthusianism. If Malthus had stated those principles with their proper qualifications—if, in other words, he had stated them with entire correctness, it is very questionable whether they would have been particularly noticed, or would have influenced materially the course of human thought. But, stated in the exaggerated and

---

* Same work, Book V., Ch. VII., § 7.
† Wealth of Nations. Book V., Ch. II.

highly overdrawn manner in which he has stated them, they have been forcibly impressed upon the attention of mankind, and, by the controversy, discussion, and investigation to which they have given rise, have vastly improved the thought of the world in regard to the Philosophy of Society.

CHAPTER XI.

OF COUSIN AND BUCKLE, AND THEIR MOST ESSENTIAL CONTRIBUTION TO SOCIAL PHILOSOPHY.

§ 1. IN coming to question these two great thinkers, we come to strike a higher and grander note in the vocalism of thought than any we have as yet sounded in our special examination of illustrious authorities. In these two transcendent geniuses, the human intellect towers into the majestic, the grand, and the pre-eminent. Not only is the particular thought presented to view by their reasonings more important, but it is associated altogether with a higher and grander system of thought—clearly and distinctly appertains to a higher and grander system. In communing with these transcendent thinkers, we almost forget, indeed, that we are communing with men, and feel as if we were holding converse with a higher order of beings.

As between Sismondi and Mill, and as between Guizot and Hallam, so, likewise, a near resemblance exists between Cousin and Buckle, both in respect to the character of their thoughts and the stand-point from which they are developed. Both have written essentially on the Philosophy of History, and both have evinced some misapprehension of the essential character of their own writings, by the titles which they have respectively bestowed on them. Cousin has entitled his work, here to be considered, " Introduction to the History of Philosophy," when it should rather have been entitled, Introduction to the Philosophy of History. Buckle has entitled his, " History of Civilization in England," when it should rather have been entitled, Philosophy of History, as illustrated more particularly in the Histories of England, Scotland, and Spain. Both have subordinated facts to ideas. Both have questioned history to ascertain what ideas it represents. Both have thereby rendered their works essentially disquisitions into the Philosophy of History, and have, moreover, rendered them splendid illustrations of what human history should be.

Both suggest, as do, indeed, Guizot and Hallam, already noticed, the propriety of throwing aside such windy, verbose, and inconsequential histories as those of Livy, Gibbon, and Macaulay, nay, as even Tacitus, Hume, and Prescott, and substituting in their stead Cousin and Buckle, and histories conformed to their mode of considering the phenomena of human development.

One important difference is noticeable and noteworthy, between Cousin and Buckle. Cousin is more purely philosophical in his mode of considering the development of humanity, or rather more exclusively absorbed with ideas. Buckle is more practical, and deals more with facts. The difference in this respect is, indeed, precisely what we might expect to find between a Frenchman and an Englishman, and illustrates well the characteristic differences between the two nationalities. Cousin is entirely carried away with the ideas—with his theory—presents but a meagre array of facts, in illustration of the ideas, and shows a constant disposition to shape the facts to suit the theory, rather than to shape the theory to suit the facts. Buckle, on the contrary, although far bolder in thought than is common with Anglican thinkers, displays a commendable caution in dealing with his theory, and, while he brings forward, prominently and often grandly, his ideas, he does not fail to sustain them with an ample array of facts. He thoroughly baptizes his ideas with facts. Nay, he pours forth a flood of facts delightfully refreshing to the thirsty mind, and all the more appreciable, impressive, and interesting, because exhibited to view in illustration of the idea or principle which they represent, or, at least, seem to represent.

Cousin is too metaphysical, deals too much with the higher ideas. Buckle confines himself far more to the realm of the physical, and deals almost exclusively with the more practical ideas. Upon the whole, his is a far more valuable, more laborious, and more meritorious work. Both are, however, eminently valuable works, the one for the higher order of minds, the other, only for the highest. The work of Cousin presents an eminently philosophical view of the Philosophy of History—that of Buckle an eminently practical view of that Philosophy.

§ 2. In bestowing such high praise on these two transcendent geniuses, we should not, perhaps, omit all reference to their obvious faults, although our object here is not so much to present a general criticism upon them as to note their specially valuable contributions to Social Philosophy.

Cousin, like nearly all Frenchmen, is altogether too dogmatical, and, what is scarcely less objectionable, altogether too mathematical. Like nearly all Frenchmen, he carries his mathematics into the domain of Ethics and Sociology, where it is utterly out of place, at least so far as human observation and human reasoning are concerned.

A striking exemplification of this mathematical exactness, as well as dogmatical audacity, Cousin affords us in many of his startling announcements, and particularly in that where he says, "The government of this world is perfectly just; prosperity and misfortune are distributed as they ought to be; prosperity is awarded only to virtue; misfortune is inflicted only on vice. I speak generally, and saving exceptions, if such there be."*

Doubtlessly, this observation of Cousin is true, in that enlarged and transcendental sense in which the poet sometimes speaks, in that sense in which Pope has spoken, where he says, "This much is sure—Whatever is, is right." But for all the practical purposes of human life how grossly false is the assertion! What a mockery of the truth does it present! How does it appear before the notorious truth, which finds its poetical expression in the famous line—"Man's inhumanity to man makes countless millions mourn," or that great truth which finds its expression in that other not less famous exclamation of the great poet—

"O that estates, degrees, and offices
Were not derived corruptly! And that clear honor
Were purchased by the merit of the wearer!"

Had Cousin merely asserted that there is a constant tendency in human affairs to the ultimate triumph of justice, despite innumerable violations of the principle—had he merely asserted,

---

* Introduction to History of Philosophy, as translated by Linberg. Lecture IX., p. 283. Boston Ed., 1832.

that, for the most part, on the general average, and in the long run, "prosperity is awarded only to virtue, misfortune is inflicted only on vice," he would doubtlessly have made an unexceptionable observation, and announced an important truth, not generally received, or, at least, duly estimated.

No such grave or vital error can be imputed to Buckle. He never outrages common sense. If not so transcendently great a thinker as Cousin, he does not even so far transcend the bounds of propriety. Although he is bold and dogmatical, far more so than might be expected of an Anglican mind, his dogmatism seldom if ever transcends the bounds of propriety any farther than a philosopher may excusably do, when strongly urging important truths not commonly received, or strenuously endeavoring to overthrow long established and widely prevalent errors.

The only error that it is proposed here to note in Buckle is of this kind. It consists in the disrespect, bordering on contempt, with which he generally, if not habitually, speaks of the clergy, or priestly order of society. While attacking the errors of which they may justly be regarded as, in a large degree, the shelter and refuge, if not, indeed, the school and nursery, he is altogether too unqualified in his censure and denunciation of that order. In his indignation for their errors, and the wrongs of which they have been guilty, he seems to lose sight of the great truths which they have represented, and the great benefits which they have conferred. The evils which the priestly order of society—of Christian society, as well as of every other—have inflicted, are obvious enough. The far greater evils from which they have saved us are not so obvious. Of these Buckle does not appear to have taken due estimate. Nay, had he even attentively scrutinized the list of distinguished contributors to Science, and the cause of human advancement, his attention must have been arrested by names that would have tended greatly to mitigate the severity of his censure against this order. For, among a multitude of others, he would have discerned, in conspicuous letters, the illustrious names of the Reverend Thomas Malthus, and the Reverend Thomas Chalmers.

§ 3. The resemblance between Cousin and Buckle does not consist alone in the general character of their works, here specially referred to, but also in the specific ideas, of essential value, which they have contributed to Social Philosophy. Both have given distinguished prominence to one and the same great fundamental idea in that Philosophy—the idea already often before announced in these pages, and which has been laid down in our Sixth Chapter, as the FOURTH of the SEVEN main fundamental propositions that have been heretofore, in one form or other, disconnectedly thrown out by eminent minds. This idea is that which substantially asserts that, "It is the NATURAL ENVIRONMENT of man, mainly in respect to climate, soil, and geographical configuration, that *primarily* determines, to a great extent, if not exclusively, or mainly, his real character, and therefore, *secondarily*, determines the character of his political institutions and social condition."

This is the only idea of vital importance in Social Philosophy to which Cousin has given prominence. Buckle, however, has given distinguished prominence not only to this idea, but to the not less important and intimately related one, already noticed in De Maistre,* as to the paramount importance and supremacy of NATURAL LAWS in human affairs, or, to speak with more definite meaning and philosophical accuracy, as to the paramount importance and supremacy of the PRIMARY LAWS of nature, in human affairs, as contradistinguished from the merely SECONDARY LAWS of nature, which the laws of man, so called, constitute in part, and to which so much undue importance is attached by superficialists and juvenile philosophers.

Nor is the resemblance between these two illustrious authors confined only to their agreement in giving distinguished prominence to the influence of natural environment on human destiny. It is observable also in their failure to recognize the importance, we might say, the still greater importance, at least the more fundamental importance, of Race, or that inherent predisposition with which a man or nation of men is born into the world.

---

* See Chapter IX.

§ 4. Victor Cousin, one of the most brilliant lights that has ever illuminated the world of thought, in his Lectures, entitled Introduction to the History of Philosophy, delivered at Paris in 1828, with his characteristic terseness, boldness, and dogmatical emphaticness of speech, says: "Yes, gentlemen, give me the map of any country, its configuration, its climate, its waters, its winds, and the whole of its physical geography; give me its natural productions, its flora, its zoology, and so on, and I pledge myself to tell you *à priori* what will be the quality of man in that country, and what part its inhabitants will act in history."*

Nowhere has the important truth in question been expressed with more emphasis, with less qualification, or in a manner more calculated to arrest and fix attention than in these emphatic words of Victor Cousin. The only criticism to which they are justly liable—except in regard to the somewhat arrogant assumption of the ability to predict, *à priori*, what the character of a people will be, from its complex natural surroundings, after the pretentious manner of the quacks in phrenology—is that they omit all reference to the more fundamental and paramount influence of Race, or Ethnological Influences. A philosopher makes a poor exhibition of his sagacity when he tells us that he is able to predict, *à priori*, nay, that he can even explain it, *à posteriori*, from the mere physical geography of the two countries, "what will be the quality of man," in such a country as sublimely mountainous Switzerland, or monotonously level Holland, without any regard to the primitive quality of the men settling in those countries—without any regard to the question whether they are of the white race, the yellow-skinned race, or the black race—without any regard, in short, to the question whether they belong to the *horse* type, the *zebra* type, or the *donkey* type of the human genus.

Cousin would have a lively task in attempting to demonstrate, that a colony of Guinea negroes, or North American Indians, cantoned among the Alps for a thousand years, or even two thousand, would exhibit the same state of society that we now find among

---

* Introduction to History of Philosophy, as translated by Linberg. Lecture VIII., p. 210. Boston Edition of 1832.

the hardy, intelligent, and virtuous Switzers—that they would have built the fine city of Geneva, and be making the finest chronometers of the world.

This oversight is the more remarkable in Cousin, even than in Buckle, in whom we have to note the same highly culpable omission. For Cousin was one of the very deepest of thinkers—a deeper thinker by far even than Buckle, although, and perhaps on that very account, in part, not uniformly expressing himself with so much circumspection and propriety. Cousin was highly metaphysical, and of the very highest school of metaphysics. He was of that school which subordinates matter to mind, which gives pre-eminence to mind in everything—nay, which has some faint recognition of the great idea of the homogeneousness, the sameness, the *oneness*, so to speak, of THE INTELLIGENT PRINCIPLE, of the identity of the Divine and human, of God and man. This idea is conspicuous in nearly all the writings of this transcendent genius, although more especially in his psychological writings. All his writings are, indeed, to some extent, psychological, although his Elements of Psychology are more especially so.

Cousin does not, indeed, fully assert the idea of the identity of the human and Divine, nor does he very boldly assert it in so far as he asserts it at all. For he is guilty of the common folly of imputing something to the personality of man, not recognizing fully the grand truth that man is but one of the manifold phases of Nature, or of Universal being—but a part of one and the same grand machinery. He merely asserts that our reason is not our own, and plainly intimates, although he does not so directly assert, that it is but an extension of THE UNIVERSAL REASON. Strange that he had not the sagacity to discern that our passions, our wills, not less than our bodies, are no more so. But perhaps he did not deem it prudent or wise to indicate all he saw. Perhaps, indeed, it would not have been wise or prudent to do so. He wrote and spoke in the earlier part of the NINETEENTH CENTURY. The philosopher may speak somewhat more plainly in the latter part of the century. The human mind has advanced a step or two within these few past years. Demigods have spoken in these latter days. Conspicuous among them stand Victor Cousin and Henry Thomas Buckle—pre-eminent Victor Cousin.

§ 5. Strange, it must appear, that impressed, even to a partial extent only, as Cousin evidently was, with the identity of the human and Divine, with the idea that man is in reality and not in mere name—not in mere sectarian cant—THE OFFSPRING OF DEITY—that his nature is the Divine nature, not indeed in its highest type, but only in one of its infinitely various types, all harmonized into one grand and consistent Unity—strange it must appear, that, discerning all this, he did not attach more importance to the influence of Ethnology, of Race, or of that Divine nature with which a man, or a nation of men, is born into the world.

If man does indeed come into the world animated with Deity, surely that which he thus brings with him into the world must play an important part in his action and destiny here. If, as Cousin everywhere intimates, and seems to believe, this Divine principle is paramount, then this influence which a man brings with him into life, this portion or type of Divinity which he has within him, must be of paramount importance, as it is undoubtedly of most fundamental importance, in moulding his destiny in life.

The superficial idea, which even some great philosophers still persist in adhering to—apparently even Cousin and Buckle—that Race, or natural inherent predisposition, is of but little influence on national destiny—that it is of subordinate influence to physical causes, as Buckle maintains—nay, that it is but the mere creation of external causes or conditions of some kind or other, as Herbert Spencer ridiculously asserts—this superficial idea is virtually but the idea that matter is paramount to mind. It is but the grossly sensuous idea that mind is a mere appendage of matter, rather than matter a mere appendage of mind—that mind is, forsooth, as some Frenchman has asserted, a mere "secretion of the brain," rather than the counter idea, which is much more philosophical, or at least philosophically plausible, though hardly less false, perhaps, that matter is a mere *effusion* of mind—the brain a mere *excrescence* of thought.

It belongs to the same low and vulgar school of thought. As

such it comports very well with the low and sensuous fundamental ideas which dominate, for the most part, in Anglican thought. But it is altogether out of place in that higher system of metaphysics and fundamental philosophy which dominates in German thought, and of which Cousin is one of the most brilliant exponents, and one of the very few that France, still more sensuous than England, though not so superficial, has ever produced.

II.—HENRY THOMAS BUCKLE.

§ 6. Of all the eminent thinkers who have attempted to educe order out of the chaos of human history, who have endeavored to subordinate facts and events to the ideas which they represent and from which they spring, who have undertaken closely and critically to question history, in order to ascertain, as far as possible, what it signifies, and to classify and systematize events according to the ideas which they signify, or appear to signify, Henry Thomas Buckle is, beyond all question, the most illustrious and eminently meritorious. Others may have been more learned, others have been more profound, but none have been, no one has proved himself, at once so learned, so profound, so just, and so practical.

He has struck the happy mean between the intensely philosophical, and altogether too condensed, too abstract view of human development, which Cousin presents, and that excessively diffuse, bewilderingly miscellaneous and almost totally inconclusive, if not meaningless view, which Macaulay, Gibbon, and historians of that old, and we may hope now antiquated, school present. He has presented to the human race, at one and the same time, one of the most splendid productions of the human intellect, and one of the most valuable works ever deposited in the archives of human science.

It is not, however, for the purpose of dilating on the general merits of this matchless production of genius and learning that we here bring it under brief review. Our object is merely to emphasize, and bring more distinctly and prominently into view the valuable ideas in Social Philosophy which it represents, with some incidental criticisms on its omissions, or imperfections of reasoning in regard to that philosophy.

§ 7. The most fundamental idea of Buckle's great work on the History of Civilization, its most general and comprehensive idea, is, that human actions, not less than the movements of the external or material world, are governed by fixed and regular laws. It is the idea, somewhat differently stated, of "moral necessity," so called, as contradistinguished from "free agency," as commonly understood. This momentous idea, so extensively revolutionary in Ethics and Criminal Jurisprudence, not less than in Theology and fundamental Sociology, is now cropping out in every direction, from the higher plane of thought into which the human mind has been uplifted by the slow upheaval of centuries, and is grandly conspicuous in the reasonings of Buckle. It is the same idea which we have already noticed in De Maistre, and shall have occasion presently to notice in Comte and Spencer. It is, in short, the COPERNICAN IDEA of universal Psychology, as we have already designated another and less general, less fundamental idea, the COPERNICAN IDEA of Sociology. It is the great revolutionary idea to which all reasonings will have to be ultimately conformed, alike in Theology, Ethics, fundamental Sociology, and Criminal Jurisprudence, before we shall be able to reason correctly on any of those extensive domains of thought—nay, before we shall be able to BEGIN aright with our scientific labors or investigations. Just as all investigations in Astronomy were inconclusive and barren of results, before the Copernican idea had been adopted, so have all investigations and reasonings, hitherto, in Theology, Sociology, and their subordinate domains of research, been inconclusive, unsatisfactory, and barren of results, because they have not been conformed to this great truth, which finds one of its most comprehensive, extensive, and practical illustrations in the reasonings of Buckle.

§ 8. Until this great idea of the fixity and uniformity of human actions, or rather of the laws of mind, as well as of matter, from the joint and complex union of which human actions solely originate, shall have been adopted, let it be repeated, no important results can be attained either in speculative or practical Sociology —nay, we shall not be able even to BEGIN aright our investigations. For here again we have to note the momentous truth—so often before coming into view in these pages, or rather in the series to which these appertain—that the most fundamental truths come last into view. Yet these are the very truths, without the knowledge of which we cannot even BEGIN aright our scientific reasonings or investigations. Hence it follows, startling as the paradox may appear, that the last thing we learn in any science is how to begin our studies. Hence also follows the yet larger truth, that we have to finish our work before we know rightly how to begin it—a truth, alas, of which we find but too melancholy an illustration in the conduct of life. For it is only when we have finished our earthly career, it is only at the end of the longest human life, that we come to learn, and forcibly to realize, how we ought to have begun it.

Paradoxical and startling as may be the assertion, this is the truth—subject, of course, to some important qualifications—the last thing that we learn in any science is how to begin our studies in relation to it. For when we have learned this, then do we learn that little or nothing remains for us to learn, or rather that we can ever learn. For, still more startling as the paradox may be, it is, nevertheless, true, in the main, that when we have learned how to begin our studies, then do we discover that they are at an end, or for the most part at an end; that is to say, in other words, then do we discover that we have gone as far as we can possibly go—that we have attained the utmost limit of our finite powers—that we have reached the ULTIMA THULE of the human understanding.

§ 9. Such is the paradoxical law of mental progression. When we have attained the most fundamental truths attainable by human intelligence, when we have thus learned, and for the first time, how to begin our investigations in any science, then do we learn that we have reached the utmost limit of human investigation, that we can go no further, that we can only go back, and recast, or more correctly systematize our views—oftentimes completely reversing our former ones. The last thing that we discover in any science is generally, if not universally, some fundamental truth which is an *ultimatum* of the human understanding, and which admonishes us that we can go no further in that direction. No science is ever duly organized or systematized until it has attained to some such ultimate truth, and has been constructed or reconstructed accordingly.

The attainment of these ultimate truths generally discloses, in clear view, the very limited extent of human intelligence, and, still more, of the powers of human achievement. They generally make manifest how little we can know, and how much less we can do. Hence it is that true philosophers, the really deep thinkers, who have attained these ultimate or most fundamental truths, are always distinguished by humility and moderation of purpose. They are too strongly impressed with the feebleness of human effort, either to know or to do, to admit of their being otherwise.

Hence it is that when we come to ascertain the most fundamental truths in Social Philosophy, we come to discern how little—how next to nothing—it is that human agency can do, of its concerted design, or voluntary effort, so called, towards controlling or modifying the course of human events. For then we come to learn that human affairs are governed by fixed and inevitable laws, not less than the affairs of the external world—by the fixed and inevitable laws of mind and matter, of psychology and physiology—by laws as fixed and inevitable, however much more complex and various, as those which wheel the planets in their spheres.

§ 10. It is only the mountebank, the charlatan, the quack, or, at best, the dreamy, visionary, and puerile philosopher, that aspires to accomplish anything, nay, that dares even hope to accomplish anything for human society, beyond that necessary influence, indeed, which the diffusion of knowledge, or correct opinions, gradually and in process of time produces, as seed cast upon the ground springs up and yields a vegetation that, in course of time, reacts upon and modifies, to some extent, the soil in which it grows.

Ask the mountebank, the superficial prattler about social reform, nay, even the amiable visionary, like Robert Owen, or the transcendental lunatic, like Fourier, what they propose to do for human society, and they will promptly display their superficial knowledge and reasoning, by telling you of the wonderful things they are going to accomplish, if society can only be prevailed upon to swallow a box or two of their wonderful pills, charged with the true *elixir* of social life.

Ask an Owenite what it is that he proposes to do, and he will tell you he proposes radically to reform human society and human nature itself, by a radically different system of education, by one conformed to "the ALL-GLORIOUS SCIENCE of the influence of circumstances over human character"—nay, so radically to reform human character, "that not an inferior human being shall be formed, at maturity, to walk the earth, or disturb the universal happiness of man, or his progeny, in whatever country or clime he may be found."*

Ask a Fourierite what it is that he proposes, and he will tell you he proposes to bundle up the whole human family into a multitude of small packages, not to exceed 810 each, all to be enclosed in one common workshop, of many and various different compartments, and that thus he will actualize for men on earth that harmonic state which has been long enjoyed by the "harmonized planets," but which, by some ill luck or other, has been hitherto denied to the denizens of this less favored orb.†

Ask the true Social Philosopher what it is that he proposes to do for human society, and he sorrowfully replies—Nothing—Nothing, at least, except to EXPLAIN LAWS—to explain laws, the understanding of which, once established in human minds, will indeed become new laws of themselves—necessary laws—laws having as necessary and inevitable an influence on human affairs, as

---

* See Robert Owen's Book of the New Moral World, Part II., Ch. IV., p. 59, First American Edition, 1845.

† See Fourier's Passions of the Soul, as translated by Morrell.

a new planet introduced into the solar system would exert upon the existing arrangements of that system.

§ 11. This is the idea, for the most comprehensive, enlarged, and extensively practical expression of which, hitherto, Social Philosophy is indebted to Henry Thomas Buckle—the idea of the fixity and regularity of the laws which govern human affairs. He does not, indeed, like Comte, deliver over human society entirely to Physiology, thus rendering Sociology but a convertible term with " Social Physics," but he justly delivers it over to laws not less fixed and regular, however much more complex and various—to the conjoint influence of the laws of Physiology and Psychology. This is the great merit of Buckle. It is his most fundamental idea, and his most valuable, most unexceptionable, and unqualifiedly correct idea. His somewhat less fundamental or more particular fundamental idea is not so unexceptionable, not so correct. It is that which we have just now observed so conspicuously manifest in Cousin, namely, that it is the NATURAL ENVIRONMENT of man alone which determines his action and destiny.

Buckle, like Cousin, thus takes notice only of the fundamental PHYSICAL influences that operate on man, but not of the fundamental PSYCHOLOGICAL ones. He does not notice the important influence, in truth, the paramount influence of Race, or those PSYCHOLOGICAL TENDENCIES with which a man, or nation of men, comes into being. In other words, he notices only the influence of the outward surroundings of man, and takes no notice of MAN himself—totally ignores MAN—as a fundamental cause, when he is, in truth, the most fundamental of causes. He forgets, as have all, or nearly all, who have hitherto reasoned on these momentous themes—nay, even those who have had the sagacity to recognize the important influence of Race—that MIND has its own inherent vitalities, forces, and tendencies, not less than MATTER,—and that the individualized as well as composite types of mind are as various as those of matter—differing from each other, so far as the utmost capacities of psychological analysis, of psychological *chemistry*, so to speak, have as yet gone, as do the various elementary physical substances—differing as widely as do the fundamental metals

—as widely as do iron, lead, platinum, mercury, silver, and gold. He forgets the great truth which finds its expression in the grand words of Milton, the full import of which the great poet himself perhaps did not fully recognize—

> "The mind is its own place, and in itself
> Can make a heaven of hell, a hell of heaven."

If the mind is thus ITS OWN PLACE, has it not also *its place* in the grand economy of causes or influences operating to determine the social destiny of man? If the different minds, or rather orders of mind, that appear in the world, are, in themselves, as different as are the fundamental metals of the material world, is it not a great error to omit all estimate of the fundamental differences between them? Is it not preposterous, nay, ridiculous, to suppose that the iron of the mind can be converted into silver, its lead into mercury, or its platinum into gold, by different material conditions? Is it not quite as preposterous and ridiculous as to suppose that the iron, lead, or platinum of the material world can be so changed or modified?

§ 12. The reasoning of Buckle on this point is not less illogical and inconsistent than it is essentially superficial and defective. It is illogical on its own face, and inconsistent with itself—thus showing, again, and as so often before shown, how slow and apparently reluctant is the human mind to march up to the whole truth, how it shirks and dodges before it will dare advance right on to the truth, and boldly clutch it. We find this propensity here illustrated in one of the boldest and greatest of thinkers.

Buckle virtually admits the influence of Race, or, most essentially to speak, of PSYCHOLOGICAL INFLUENCE, on human destiny, not less than physical influence—nay, he lays it down explicitly in his premises or fundamental propositions, and yet totally ignores it in his inferential reasonings, or practical applications of these fundamental propositions. Hear him, for example, in the very first chapter of his great work:

"And as all antecedents," he says, "are either in the mind or out of it, we clearly see that all the variations in the results—in other words, all the changes of which history is full, all the vicissitudes of the human race—their progress or their decay, their happiness or their misery—must be the fruit of a double action; an action of external phenomena upon the mind, and another action of the mind upon the phenomena.

"These are the materials out of which a philosophic history can alone be constructed. On the one hand, we have the human mind obeying the laws of its own existence, and, when uncontrolled by external agents, developing itself according to the conditions of its organization. On the other hand, we have what we call Nature, obeying likewise its laws; but incessantly coming into contact with the minds of men, exciting their passions, stimulating their intellect, and therefore giving to their actions a direction which they would not have taken without such disturbance. Thus we have man modifying nature, and nature modifying man; while out of this reciprocal modification all events must necessarily spring."*

Excellently well said. No one could have expressed it better. Thus has Buckle laid down, in brief outline, the two great fundamental ideas, that lie at the foundation of the whole Philosophy of Society—the ideas of MAN and his ENVIRONMENT. Had he strictly adhered to both of these two fundamental ideas, in all his subsequent reasonings, he would have presented a wholly unexceptionable view of the Philosophy of History, which is obviously but one phase, the *dynamical* phase, of the Philosophy of Society; or, perhaps we should rather say, one aspect of the *dynamical* phase. But he has not done so. Unconsciously to himself, very evidently, he has dropped out of view one of these ideas—the idea of MAN himself, or of those fundamental PSYCHOLOGICAL FORCES that are enveloped in MAN, which find their scientific designation in the term Race, or Ethnological Influence.

This omission is the great error of his work. It is this omission from the consequences of which he is constantly embarrassed in his endeavor to explain the phenomena of History. Thus we find him repeatedly emphasizing the fact that the English mind is

---

* History of Civilization, Vol. I., Chap. I., p. 15, New York Edition, 1863.

inductive, and the Scotch deductive,* which he feebly attempts to account for by the only modifying influences which he fundamentably recognizes, that of external agencies, but evidently without fully satisfying even himself. Thus we find him, too, as before noticed,† greatly embarrassed to explain the marked difference between the course of events in Spain and Scotland, notwithstanding the resemblance which he asserts in their physical surroundings, and in their mental proclivities in respect to "superstition," which he attributes to that resemblance in physical surroundings. Surely Mr. Buckle could not have experienced any difficulty in explaining these diverse phenomena, if he had only recognized the manifest truth, implicitly laid down in his own premises, that Scotchmen are, *by nature*, different from Englishmen, and Spaniards different from both—just as John is, by nature, different from William or Thomas—just as a horse is different from a zebra, or donkey, and as gold is different from lead, or iron.

Does not this mode of explaining the variations in question follow, indeed, from Buckle's own premises, as laid down in the passages just quoted? If, as he says, "we have the human mind obeying the laws of its own existence, and, when uncontrolled by external agents, developing itself according to the conditions of its organization," has not the mind of John or William, or Thomas, if you please, the laws of its own existence?—has not the mind of Scotchmen, Englishmen, and Spaniards, respectively, its own peculiar laws?—has not, in a yet wider import, the mind of Hindoos and Europeans respectively, nay of Ethiops, Mongols, and Caucasians? Can we expect that a horse, zebra, or donkey will be anything else than a horse, zebra, or donkey, no matter what may be the climate or other physical surroundings in which he may be placed? Wonderful, indeed, is the modifying influence of climate on some forms of animal life. Wonderful is the difference between the Arabian horse and the little Shetland pony. But that little Shetland pony is a horse, in spite of his diminu-

---

* See particularly Vol. I., Chap. V., pp. 177-8, New York Edition, 1863.
† See Chap. VI.

tive size, and nothing more nor less than a horse. You can make nothing else out of him but a horse, except indeed by crossing him with a donkey or zebra.

Do we expect to make gold out of lead? Or do we expect to make a philosopher out of a fool, or a fool out of one of Nature's own nobility? Has not Nature her nobility, and also her innate plebeianism? Is not one man as superior to another as gold to lead or iron? And does not this diversity extend itself to nationalities and groups of nationalities? What, indeed, is diversity of Race or nationality but individual diversity of character extended to nationalities and races?

What is a nation but an enlarged family; and what is a Race but a group of such families? Does any one doubt that distinctive peculiarities distinguish certain families, in every society, who have long intermarried within certain genealogical circles? And why should not such peculiarities extend themselves to a nation, or a group of nations, as the Teutonic, Celtic, or Sclavonic, which we designate as different races? What, indeed, is a nation, most essentially considered or defined, but a group of mankind, that has long intermarried within a certain circle of affinities? As smaller circles of affinities have their distinctive peculiarities and diversities, why should not also the larger ones?

§ 13. It would be superfluous to quote any of the many pregnant passages which Buckle affords, illustrative of the great influence which external circumstances, or Physical Geography in its largest sense, exerts on human character and destiny. It would be merely to repeat substantially what we have already cited from Cousin,* who has, in the passage so cited, expressed the idea as comprehensively and forcibly as it admits, only too much so indeed, or too unqualifiedly, as we have before remarked.

Some passages, from this brilliant author, expressive of the more general and more fundamental idea, of which this is but a more particular and less unexceptionable statement—the idea as to the regularity and fixedness of the laws which govern human

---

* See § 4 of this Chapter.

actions, we cannot, however, refrain from quoting here. It will be seen that they are entirely in harmony with the ideas of Confucius, Solon, Guizot, Hallam, and De Maistre, already noticed, and that they are only more emphatic, more copious, more enlarged, and, at the same time, more particular, more practical expressions of the same great ideas. It will readily be seen how the reasoning of this great philosopher, in common with that of those other illustrious sages, rebukes the folly and presumption of those little minds that aspire to regulate human affairs by merely human laws. It will readily be seen how it rebukes the restlessness of those pestiferous little busy-bodies—who, like the little waggle-tails that inhabit the mud-puddles are for ever switching and flirting around in the muddy pools of political legislation, thus stirring up the effluvia that too often tend to vitiate the health of society, and who vainly imagine that their petty little performances are seriously to affect the great movements of the world.

§ 14. In the opening words of his Sixth chapter, Buckle says: "I have now laid before the reader an examination of those conspicuous circumstances to which the progress of civilization is commonly ascribed; and I have proved that such circumstances, so far from being the cause of civilization, are at best only its effects, and that although religion, literature, and legislation do undoubtedly modify the condition of mankind, they are still more modified by it."* This, it may be seen, is identically the idea of Hallam, in almost identically the same words, as to the Feudal System, that it was the *effect* rather than the *cause*, as commonly supposed, of the distracted condition of European society, while it flourished. To the same point Buckle says, in the preceding chapter to that just quoted from, in reference to the rulers of states, who are commonly supposed to effect so much for society, "Such men are, at best, but the creatures of the age, not its creators."†

To the same point, he says, in his chapter on Spain, "To

---

* Vol. I., Ch. VI., p. 209, New York Edition, 1863.
† Same, p. 197.

seek to change opinions by laws, is worse than futile. It not only fails, but causes a reaction which leaves the opinions stronger than ever. First alter the opinion and then you may alter the law. As soon as you have convinced men that superstition is mischievous, you may with advantage take active steps against the classes who promote superstition and live by it. But however pernicious any interest or any great body may be, beware of using force against it, unless the progress of knowledge has previously sapped it at its base, and loosened its hold on the national mind."* What a lesson and rebuke does this passage administer to certain shallow politicians in America, who, by their reckless disregard of the wisdom it suggests, have deluged their country in blood, and overwhelmed it with debt!

It is to the same point precisely that he speaks, when he says, a little farther on in the same chapter: "No reform can produce real good unless it is the work of public opinion, and unless the people themselves take the initiative."† Eminently just and true is this assertion, and entirely in harmony with all that we have before laid down as worthy of acceptance in Social Philosophy. Entirely in accordance it is with the great idea so prominently dwelt upon by Sismondi, although only in a Politico-Economical point of view, and which we have designated as the Copernican Idea in Social Philosophy, that it is to MAN himself that we must look, primarily and fundamentally, in all our reasonings and endeavors in regard to the improvement of the social condition.

What a rebuke, too, does this passage read to many of the restless reformers or revolutionists of the world! If the people must themselves take the initiative in all reforms, why constantly seek to excite them to insubordination, or precipitate them into crises that may compel them to revolution, or violence of some kind, against the existing order of society? It is very seldom that any real good comes of such endeavors, or any good that fully compensates for what it costs. For all truly great reforms we

---

* Same, Vol. II., Ch. I., p. 91.   † Same, p. 103.

must await the gradual maturing of the harvest of those more correct ideas which the superior intellects of the world have sown in the popular mind. We must wait until the fruit is ripe before we shake the tree, in order to gather in the crop.

§ 15. The foregoing passages, it may readily be discerned, do not so directly or immediately illustrate the idea that human affairs are governed by uniform and fixed laws, as the idea that they are governed by deeper and more fundamental laws than those of positive human enactment. But indirectly they illustrate that idea. For it is precisely because those laws are uniform and fixed, or, in the same sense that the laws of nature, as commonly understood, are so—it is precisely because those laws are but ramifications of the fundamental Laws of Nature, that they lie beyond the reach of control by human legislation, and in reality determine that legislation, to a much greater extent than they are determined by it.

Nowhere has this important truth, so little understood, or generally entertained, been more clearly or admirably expressed than it has been by Buckle, not only in the passages already quoted, but more especially in this, where he says: "The truth is, that every institution, whether political or religious, represents, in its actual working, the form and pressure of the age. It may be old; it may have a venerated name; it may aim at the highest objects; but whoever carefully studies its history, will find that, in practice, it is successively modified by successive generations, and that, instead of controlling society, it is controlled by it."[*]

It is but in illustration of the same idea, from a practical standpoint, that our author says, in the very next page: "But the aristocracy of Scotland little knew the men with whom they had to deal, still less did they understand the character of their own age. They did not see that in the state of society in which they lived, superstition was inevitable, and that, therefore, the spiritual classes, though depressed for a moment, were sure speedily to rise

---

[*] Same, Vol. II., Ch. III., p. 183. N. Y. Edition of 1859.

again. The nobles had overturned the Church; but the principles on which Church authority is based remained intact. All that was done was to change the name and form. A new hierarchy was quickly organized, which succeeded the old one in the affections of the people."*

§ 16. This great idea, which the author of the present work is solicitous to *stereotype*, if we may so speak, in common with some others, upon the mind of the world, cannot surely need any further illustration or vindication than is afforded by the following passage, and the last that it is proposed here to quote from this preëminently great thinker, and admirably just delineator of truth. Speaking in reference to the undue expectations, which were entertained by many, from the downfall of Popery in Scotland, he says: "But what was forgotten then, and what is too often forgotten now, is, that in these affairs there is an order and a natural sequence, which can never be reversed. This is that every institution, as it actually exists, no matter what its name or pretence may be, is the effect of public opinion, far more than the cause, and that it can avail nothing to attack the institution unless you can change the opinion."†

Here again we find the great truth expressed by Hume coming into view, that "all governments are founded in opinion." So consistent is truth, so do many concurring witnesses testify unconsciously to the truth of some new system of thought, long before ideas have been sufficiently developed or matured to organize that system, or to comprehend it in all its bearings.

§ 17. Before taking leave of this great and eminently instructive reasoner, it may not be amiss to pass one other criticism upon his reasonings, somewhat more fundamental than either of those already pronounced—a criticism the more important because it must tend to bring into view a great truth, almost totally unrecognized as yet, even among our greatest thinkers, despite the frequent symptoms discernible of an unconscious *gravitation* towards

---

* The same, p. 181. † Same, p. 182.

it. That criticism is, that he does not appear to recognize the identity of the laws of Man and the laws of Nature. He adheres to the old notion of an antagonism, or, at least, essential difference, between man and nature, which is but a counterpart, or rather a mere extension of the stupid old idea in Theology of an antagonism, nay, a constant antagonism, between God and man.

Buckle has shown a great advance, indeed, beyond vulgar and commonly received ideas, in distinctly recognizing the truth that human actions are governed by laws not less fixed and regular than those which govern the external world; than those, in short, which he, in common with the superficial reasoners, styles, par excellence, *laws of Nature*. But he has not advanced quite far enough to discern that those laws—the laws which govern human actions—are themselves laws of nature, and that the true designation of the one class of laws, as contradistinguished from the other, is to be found in styling the one class, the PRIMARY laws of Nature, and the other, the SECONDARY laws of Nature. We shall presently see that Comte has come to the distinct recognition of this great fundamental truth, although he has not so distinctly or lucidly expressed it as might be desired. Herbert Spencer, too, as we shall presently see, has very nearly attained to the same idea, notwithstanding the weak and puerile views expressed in his Social Statics, which may appear inconsistent with that higher and grander system of reasoning to which this great truth leads, and specimens of which he has abundantly exhibited in other of his reasonings, on the Philosophy of Society.

§ 18. Not only is it true, as Buckle has so splendidly illustrated, that human actions are governed by laws not less fixed and regular, however much more complex and modifiable, than those which are commonly styled Laws of Nature, but those laws are themselves laws of nature, forming but one branch or division of those eternal laws. The movements of human society are but a part of the movements of the universe, of the movements of universal nature. Those movements are regulated partly, and to a very great extent, nay, to the greatest extent, by far, by the *primary* laws of nature, just as are the movements of all organic life, and partly by the *secondary* laws of nature, which the so-called voluntary or intentional activity of man, and the laws of man, commonly so called, constitute. All the legislation of man, and all the adjudications of man, taking the form of binding law in human society, are most essentially considered but *secondary* laws of nature.

And here we may detect one of the most fundamental distinctions, as it is the most truly philosophical one, between the Science of Political Economy and the Science of Politics, with the whole system of jurisprudence, which it comprehends. Political Economy is founded on the *primary* laws of nature, rightly concerns itself only with the *primary* laws of nature, while Politics, with its handmaid Jurisprudence, is founded on the secondary laws of nature, or the laws of nature as they manifest themselves through the reasonings and so-called voluntary activities of man.

And here again we discover renewed justification of our criticism on Sismondi, in respect to his misapprehension of the true province of Political Economy, and his disposition to consider it as a science which rightly concerns itself with the modifications which the legislation of man may produce on the natural laws of wealth, or with the voluntary endeavors of man to insure any particular distribution of wealth. For, in so doing, he was endeavoring to make Political Economy concern itself with the *secondary* laws of nature, when its true office is to concern itself only with the *primary* laws of nature—when it is, rightly considered, the mere physiology of Social Science, not, to any extent, its therapeutics.

§ 19. Great as is the advance which Buckle has made in reasoning on the Philosophy of Society, let it be again repeated, he has shown a serious lack of discernment in not advancing still farther, in not advancing to the discovery that the laws which govern human society, even the positive laws enacted by its formal legislation, are, in themselves, *laws of nature*. To this truth, with all its kindred and intimately affiliated truths, the human mind must advance, before it can organize a sound or true system of Social Philosophy, or Philosophy of any kind. To this truth, and to all those great kindred truths, it is evidently tending, and to them it must ultimately attain, and at no distant day.

The old idea as to an antagonism, or even any essential difference, between man and nature, nay, between God and man, will have to be abandoned, and we shall have to come to the clear and distinct recognition of the identity of all substance, except the two grand fundamental and elementary ones—MIND and MATTER. These are the only two essentially different substances, discernible to man at least, in universal nature. These are the two great principles, the male and female principles, from the mystic union between which has been born all organic life. The former of these principles finds its grandest expression in the name of God, to which all men, in one form or other, render homage. The other lies open to the view in every sensuous form. Man, like every other organic being, is but a product of the mystic union between these two principles. He is only the highest product, or highest known product, to which that union has ever yet given rise. In his intellectual or psychological nature he represents the one principle, in his physical he represents the other. His mind is but an extension, or rather extenuation, of the mind of God. His body is but an extension, or attenuation and refinement, of matter.

§ 20. We may exclaim against these ultimate fundamental postulates, and fancy that they are profane. We may call them Pantheism, Spinozaism, or, if we please, the doctrines, substantially, of the Sooffee philosophy of Persia, regarded as infidel, of course, by the Mahometan Doctors of Divinity. It will only show, perchance, that Pantheists, Spinozaists, and the Sooffee philosophers of Persia, have been hitherto deeper thinkers and more correct metaphysicians than ourselves. For to this complexion it must come at last, in spite of all our attempts to blindfold or to hoodwink our reason, and in spite of "all that saint, sage, or sophist ever writ," to the contrary. The human reason will eventually assert its divinity, by coming to the recognition of its divine origin and nature, to the recognition of its essential divinity, and the identity of the human and Divine, not less than the identity of man and all the other forms of nature. May we not indeed already detect in the grand and holy faith of Christianity a partial and imperfect recognition of this truth, and accept the character and life of Jesus, as a beautiful allegory, if not, indeed, an actual manifestation, of the substantial identity of the human and Divine?

We have said already, that, if the true secret of the universe should ever be disclosed to human view, it would probably be found to rest upon a series of mathematical propositions.* May we not carry forward the suggestion yet a little farther, and venture to assert that the universe may be illustrated, in its fundamental relations, BY THE RIGHT-ANGLED TRIANGLE, of which God represents the square described upon the HYPOTHENUSE, while man and nature respectively represent the squares described upon the other two sides? Thus, although the august form of God, if form we may venture to assign to Him, is totally unseen by human vision, yet his dimensions may be taken by the infallible calculations of mathematics. For we have the dimensions of man and nature, or rather of man and the remainder of nature, who comprise the two smaller squares of the right-angled triangle. The dimension of God we may know, therefore, for it is, by the hypothesis, precisely equivalent to the sum of these two squares—is precisely equivalent to the conjoint dimensions of man and nature.

§ 21. It would be both interesting and instructive, to draw more largely from the pages of Buckle than it has seemed accordant with the aims of the present work to do. Regretfully we take our leave of him, and still more regretfully at the thought that he has so soon taken leave of the world. His career was sorrowfully brief, though transcendently brilliant. Like a new and unexpected visitant of our Solar System, from the unknown realms whence come the comets, like a comet of extraordinary magnitude and splendor, he blazed upon the world, unannounced, in his transcendent work on the History of Civilization. But while the world looked on, with admiration and wonder, expect-

---

* See ante, Chap. IX.

ing to see him shine with yet greater splendor as he advanced to his *perihelion*, and hoping to enjoy long the brilliant light of his genius, as he should slowly, and in the ordinary course of nature, retire towards his *aphelion*, his career was suddenly arrested, and the light of his genius extinguished, leaving the world again to mourn the brevity of human existence, and admonishing it most impressively how insignificant is the part that any one mind is permitted to play in the grand economy of universal being.*

---

* Henry Thomas Buckle died at Damascus in May, 1862, aged only 40 years, and only some four or five years after the publication of his immortal work.

CHAPTER XII.

OF COMTE AND SPENCER, AND WHAT THEY HAVE DONE FOR THE PHILOSOPHY OF SOCIETY.

§ 1. AT the head of the column of most advanced thinkers, or, rather, of most enlarged thinkers, in Social Philosophy, stand undoubtedly Auguste Comte, and Herbert Spencer—the one a Gallican, the other an Anglican author, and each illustrating well, as do most of the authors already contrasted, the characteristic differences between the two orders of thought which respectively distinguish the two nationalities. These two are among the latest, as they are among the most advanced, or most enlarged thinkers, that have thrown light upon this, the highest and most diversified field of Philosophy.

Unlike the other writers who have been considered, Comte and Spencer have addressed their reasonings directly to the Philosophy of Society, while the others have only incidentally thrown out their valuable ideas. On this account their reasonings should be the more entitled to particular consideration. While the points of dissimilarity, nay the lines of demarcation, between these two eminent thinkers are obvious enough, those of resemblance are still more obvious and important, in respect, at least, to their mode of reasoning on the phenomena of human society.

§ 2. Both of these great thinkers have regarded the phenomena of society as merely a part, or branch, a higher branch only, of the phenomena of the universe. Both have regarded human society in connection with universal nature, and as governed by the same general and universal laws, slightly modified only, which govern all the lower forms of nature. Both have regarded the physiology of society as but an extension of the physiology of the individual—the body politic as organized upon the same type with the animal body. Both, in short, have regarded the science of human society as resting upon the pedestal of universal science, and have thus illustrated, to a greater extent than any other known authorities, the SIXTH of our seven main propositions,* in regard to the Philosophy of Society, that are as yet recognizable in the thought of the world.

§ 3. Both Comte and Spencer have subordinated Politics to Ethics, and have looked to a more improved system of morals for a more improved system of society, in which respect they have but reasserted the idea of Confucius, as already shown † For this is essentially the philosophy of Spencer, as shown by his work on Social Statics, although, in his order of classifying, or considering the sciences, as announced in the prospectus of his disquisition on universal science, now in progress of preparation, in separate parts, he places Sociology before Morality. Both have been guilty of the error of overestimating greatly the expectations that may reasonably be entertained from any such source. Both seem to have anticipated some radical improvement of society, " the regeneration of society," as Comte styles it, from this source. Comte avowedly aimed " to construct a system of morality under which the final regeneration of humanity will proceed."‡ Nor does Herbert Spencer appear to have aimed at anything less in his Social Statics, or rather his disquisition on the perfect standard of morality, misnamed " Social Statics."

Both these eminent reasoners seem to have forgotten how difficult it is to reform men, or to drill them into the true rules of morality. They both seem to have forgotten that there is no difficulty in teaching men morality—that the only difficulty is in prevailing on them to practise it. They both seem to have forgotten the truth announced by Cousin, that " the first man was as much in possession of them as the last comer into the human family"§—a remark manifestly applicable to the great moral truths which form the basis of a true system of morality. They both seem to have forgotten that Jesus of Nazareth, the greatest and most impressive of all moral teachers, attempted to improve

---

* See Chapter Sixth.
† See Chapter Seventh.
‡ See Comte's General View of Positivism, as translated by Bridges, London Edition, 1865, p. 48.
§ Cousin's Introduction to History of Philosophy, Lecture II., p. 33.

the morality of the world, by the most powerful inducements that can operate on men, the transporting hope of Heaven and the terrific fear of Hell, and that he has signally and lamentably failed—except indeed to a very partial and limited extent.

§ 4. Both Comte and Spencer have recognized the great truth that it is the man that makes the government, not the government that makes the man—that the government of a state is but the natural outgrowth of the existing condition of the society. Nay, they have both given great prominence to the idea. They would be undeserving the high rank we have assigned them, had they failed to do so.

§ 5. Both Comte and Spencer have recognized the increasing importance of the INDIVIDUAL, as contradistinguished from the society, as civilization advances, and have thus illustrated forcibly the SEVENTH of our seven main propositions. On this point, however, a marked difference is noticeable between the two reasoners, precisely illustrative of the characteristic difference, in this respect, between the Gallican and Anglican orders of mind and disposition—a difference in the main, or fundamentally, to the credit of Spencer. For while Comte, in common with nearly all Frenchmen, inclines to that system of thought which rather seeks to subordinate the individual to the society, nay, to *merge* the individual completely in the society, despite his recognition of the essential tendency of human progress in the opposite direction, Spencer manifestly belongs to the directly opposite system, which seeks to secure the eventual triumph of the individual over society.

In this respect these two authors illustrate well the opposite tendencies of their respective nationalities. For it seems to be the mission of the Gallican family, or the Celtic race, as represented by the Gallican family, to represent and carry forward the one of these two ideas, and that of the Anglican, or rather of the Teutonic, as represented by the Anglican, to represent and carry forward the other. Comte and Spencer may be accepted as the exponents and representatives, in part, of their respective nationalities in the fulfilment of these their respective missions or destinies.

In the performance of his part, however, which is undoubtedly the more important or paramount one, Spencer has committed far more serious errors than Comte. For he has asserted his idea altogether too unqualifiedly, while Comte, with more truly philosophical discrimination, has wisely qualified his idea with the distinct recognition of the counter idea, which Mr. Spencer has too unqualifiedly asserted.

So far indeed does Mr. Spencer carry the idea, to so vitally erroneous and injurious an extent, that he denies alike the right and propriety of any state provision for the maintenance of the poor, and, what is even still worse, for their education *—committing the vital error which the first propagators of every important idea are so apt to commit, of fixing their attention exclusively upon the idea, without regard to its qualifications—committing the error of concluding, that, because state provision for the poor and state education are not the best modes for accomplishing the ends so sought to be accomplished, as undoubtedly they are not, therefore they are not proper or right modes at all, and that they should not be resorted to, even as a last resort, when other and more proper modes have been neglected.

In this respect, as in some others, we must adjudge Mr. Spencer not by any means one of the most advanced thinkers, although, even in this respect, one of the most enlarged thinkers. For it is by reason of the very largeness of his views of society that he has committed the error in point. It is while recognizing and asserting the great general truth that human society is governed by the same stern and inevitable laws with the lower forms of nature, that he commits the error. In so far as the Poor Laws are concerned, he has committed the same error, although from a somewhat different stand-point, that Malthus committed, and which has been so strongly and justly censured in him.† But he

---

* See Spencer's work on Social Statics, Chapters on Poor Laws and National Education.

† For a complete exposition of the error of Mr. Spencer's reasoning in regard to Poor Laws, in common with those of Malthus, which, rightly interpreted or criticised, signify only opposition to a false and eminently defective system of Poor Laws, see the author's searching and totally exhaustive review of Mal-

has conjoined with this error the still more serious one, which Malthus never committed, and was very far from committing, of opposing state education.

§ 6. Both of these two eminent thinkers have exhibited the folly, the more remarkable in such grave and truly philosophical thinkers, of anticipating some great radical or organic improvement in the human condition, as involved in the natural order of "progress," as Comte styles it, or, of "evolution," as Mr. Spencer prefers to designate it. They have both virtually indulged the anticipation, in other words, that the time is coming when a horse will cease to be a horse, and become something more than a horse, or, what amounts to the same, when man will cease to be a mere man, and become something more than a man—*a faultless being.*

This is the essential significance of their reasoning on "progress" and "evolution"—more especially that of Spencer—in common with the vulgar mode of reasoning thereupon, although neither appears to have been quite far enough advanced in his perceptions in regard to this the very highest accessible branch of philosophy, to discern that such was the essential significance of his reasoning. They have both proved themselves infatuated, to some extent, with the popular delusion about "the good time coming," which has already so often "lighted fools the way to dusty death," and which will doubtlessly continue to light their way, until it shall have conducted the whole human race to its ultimate destiny—the grave of its existence and of its delusive hope.

This delusive dream of "the good time coming," or of some better time that is to come, which seems constantly to haunt the human imagination, in respect alike to the destiny of the individual and the race, has, most probably, like every other attribute of humanity, bad as well as good, its utility, and, not improbably, its latent and deep significance. It may be that it is a vague pre-

---

thusianism—if one may so speak of his own work—comprising the Fifth Part of the Series to which this work appertains, Chapter V. of that Part, in which the views of Malthus himself, and Dr. Chalmers, are particularly considered.

sentiment of a future life, in which the happy dream is to be realized; or it may be a dim prophetic foreshadowing of a higher order of beings that are hereafter to people this planet, an order as superior to man as man is to the highest order of his predecessors. When such a superior order of beings shall come to take the place of man on this planet, if such shall ever come, the anticipations which Comte and Spencer appear to have indulged, and which so many visionaries have explicitly avowed, may be realized. But until then it will be premature, as it is utterly unphilosophical, to entertain any such delusive and visionary anticipations.

§ 7. Comte and Spencer, strange to say, have both committed the palpable error, so constantly perpetrated by short-sighted reasoners in Social Philosophy, of inferring, from the undoubted progress which mankind have made, and from that further progress which they are undoubtedly capable of making, an unlimited capacity of progress, or at least a capacity of progress so great as to be utterly subversive of the very laws of human being, or utterly inconsistent with those laws. They have argued as if the course of human progress were steadily forward, and never backward—steadily upward, never downward—steadily on the advance, never on the decline. They have argued, in short, as if every human thing, and every other thing, tended only toward LIFE, nay, toward still higher life, never toward death. They have totally ignored, at least for all practical purposes, the law of DEATH, and its antecedent corruption and decline.

They have both totally ignored the idea—if, indeed, they were ever possessed of it—the eminently just idea, of Cousin, not less than of Fourier, that the life of the individual is the true type of the life of the race—nay, the still larger idea of Fourier exclusively, that this life is the type of every other, of universal life; and that everything, as we see illustrated in the life of the individual, has a beginning, a middle, and an end, in the natural course of its development—individuals, races, worlds, and systems of worlds.

If this be true, as indisputably it is, as that infallible reason, which manifests itself in man, under the instruction it receives from the suggestions of universal analogy, pronounces, with almost mathematical certainty, what becomes of this weak idea of the constant prattlers about "progress"—from which even as great thinkers as Comte and Spencer have proved themselves not to have been emancipated—this idea of unlimited progress, or steadily onward progress in human affairs?

If the life of the individual is indeed the type of the life of the race, as indisputably it is, then the progress of the race can only be carried to a certain point, to what we may call the ZENITH of the human race—and thereafter it must begin to decline, to go down towards death, and until it finally attain its death, either in some great convulsion of nature, or some gradual change in the physical conditions of the planet, which, coöperating with the moral degeneracy of man, will cause the gradual extinction of his species, as with the *dodo*, that is known to have died out within the historic period, or in one of those extraordinary transition epochs of the globe, that are distinguished by the introduction of a higher order of animals, when some such higher order in the scale of zoological existence shall appear upon the planet, before whose presence the degenerate descendants of the human race will slowly disappear, and be gradually sloughed off from the face of the planet.

§ 8. If we may assume, with the insanely dogmatical Fourier, that the life of the human race is to be just *eighty thousand years*,* and that it has now lived only some six thousand, it has yet some time before it, to be sure, within which to delude itself with those visionary hopes of "harmonic bliss," of which Fourier himself prated so absurdly, of "the final regeneration of humanity," of which Comte speaks so hopefully, and of "the evanescence of evil," and "the ultimate adaptation of humanity to its conditions," on which Mr. Herbert Spencer dilates with so much sophistical ingenuity.

---

* See Fourier's Passions of the Soul, as translated by Morell.
† See Spencer's Social Statics, Chapter on Evanescence of Evil, or Part I., Chap. II.

Nevertheless, truly sober-minded philosophers will be apt to believe that the first horse was a fair type of the last, and that the first man will be proved, in the end, to have been a not less fair type of the last man—that the past of human history will be found to afford a fair sample of its future history—that the world will never see truly wiser or greater men than it has already seen, although it will see, undoubtedly, far more enlightened men—that the first Plato was the true type of the last, and that the first state of civilized society was not less the type of the last state—that the last Plato, and the last state of civilization, will indeed be found standing upon *higher stilts*, in other words, upon higher knowledge, but that the real stature, the real character of the man, and of the society, will not be found to have been materially if at all altered thereby.

If the life of the individual be indeed a type of the life of the race, as indisputably it is, then the race will continue really to progress only until it shall have arrived at the age of *thirty-five*, or at most, *forty-five*, that is to say, accepting Fourier's dogma as to the lifetime of the race, until it shall have lived some thirty-five thousand, or, at most, forty-five thousand years, and thereafter it must begin, and continue thence onward, no farther to advance, but only to decline, decay, and totter towards its death.

§ 9. If the life of the individual be indeed the type of the life of the race, *a fortiori* is it the type of the life of a nation. And, as many individual lives pass away during the lifetime of a nation, so many national lives must pass away during the natural lifetime of the race. No individual can be expected to live as long as his nation, unless, indeed, some extraordinary casualty should prematurely carry off the nation. Neither can any nation be expected to live as long as the human race. If, then, the whole human race has but an allotted time to live, how much less time must every particular nation have to live? Within how contracted a period, therefore, must be developed that "progress," about which Comte and Spencer, in common with so many others, have beguiled their judgments to so serious an extent?

For, be it remembered, with a nation, as with the individual and the race, real progress, in the natural order of things, can only proceed during about one half of its natural life, and thereafter must begin the natural tendency to decline. This is the true natural order of that "Evolution," as applied to human affairs, which Mr. Spencer has made the basis of his whole system of Philosophy, and upon which he has built such large and delusive hopes. Yet he has looked at only one phase of the law of Evolution—the LIFE phase—and has totally ignored, at least in all his practical reasonings, the not less manifest and inevitable DEATH phase.

Spencer, not less than Comte, has regarded national progress, national improvement, exclusively in respect to the tendencies toward life, higher life, or further development of life, and has made no due or proper estimate of the not less inevitable tendencies to death—those tendencies to death which are indeed going forward, even at the very moment that the tendencies to life, and to higher life, are most active. It is strange that men of large minds should be insensible to a truth so manifest, and so important in its suggestions to the philosophical mind.

§ 10. Nations, like individuals, must die. Everything human must die. Whatever is born must die. Every organic existence must die; and before death must come decline, decay, weakening of the principle of life, and return to an inferior form of life. There is no unlimited progress for any form of life; and he is but a half philosopher who does not, in all his reasonings, bear in mind the two eternally co-ordinated principles of life and death, and shape all his reasonings accordingly. These two principles of life and death are, indisputably, as inseparably co-ordinated, and linked together, in the mystic chain of universal being, as are the principles of mind and matter —both indestructible, both eternal. There is no death to the principle of LIFE. There is no death to the principle of DEATH.

Nations, like individuals, must die. Every century brings us proof of it. It was but yesterday, as it were, that the Irish nation expired before the eyes of the world—before the eyes of the present generation. We beheld its last convulsive death-throes in the potato-rot—a disease totally incapable of carrying off so vigorous a nation, but for the concurrence of moral causes, and the weakening of the life-principle that had been slowly at work for centuries. With the reform measures inaugurated by the British Parliament, and consequent, in a great measure, upon that calamity, new life has, indeed, been infused into Ireland. A new nation will arise in that country, but it will no longer be the Irish nation. It will be an Anglican one mainly. The old Irish nation—the old nation of Milesian Celts—that old nation, with all its valor, wit, poetry and eloquence, will never live again.

The old nation of Milesian Celts is dead. But the Milesian Celts are not dead. They will yet live awhile. They have gone forth to commingle with other peoples, in other lands, and to contribute to new forms of national life. Like the disintegrated rocks of a former epoch, that have entered into more recent geological formations, the disintegrated masses of the old Irish nation have been swept abroad, by the *diluvium* of national death, and will there enter into newer *sociological* formations, in their turn to decay, disintegrate, and be destroyed. For nothing endures, nothing lives, beyond an ephemeral period, except the eternal principles of LIFE and DEATH—MIND and MATTER.

The old Irish nation is dead. On this point let none be deceived. The late Fenian movement in the United States and Canada, is but one of the spasms of the *galvanized corpse*.

It was but yesterday, too, that we saw the once great American nation, suddenly struck delirious with brain fever, rushing frantically towards the precipice of national ruin, and barely escaping, if indeed they have really escaped, the destruction which seemed inevitable. In the short interval of four years we saw that remarkable people move backward a thousand years on the dial-plate of history, and national existence. In that short interval we saw the Anglo-Saxon race in America hastily retreat from their far advanced position, and falling back to the age of

William the Conqueror, if not indeed to that of Canute the Dane.

It is true, so wonderfully recuperative are the capacities of the race, in its present state, which is that of vigorous manhood not yet on the decline, and with its highly advantageous surroundings, that we need not be surprised if we should see them recover the ground they have lost, and retraverse the vast distance of a thousand years, in the short period of a single decade. But these wonderful mutations of national destiny should admonish all how uncertain are the conditions on which depends the prosperity or progress of a nation. Yet Spencer and Comte have both argued as if these conditions were fixed and certain, or rather as if they depended only on the laws of life and progress, and not at all on those of death and decline.

§ 11. This oversight is the more remarkable in Spencer, because he distinctly recognizes the tendency to "Universal Death," as logically involved in the ultimate tendencies of his law of Evolution.* "After Evolution has run its course," Universal Death manifestly stares him in the face. From this gloomy vision of Universal Death, it is true, the tendencies toward Universal Life again manifest themselves to his view. And in this he is right, beyond all reasonable doubt. For the fundamental law of universal being is most probably typified in the old Egyptian fable of the Phœnix. From the ashes of a dead universe a new one seems inevitably destined to arise.

But while Mr. Spencer thus theoretically and remotely recognizes the tendency to Death, he does not practically or immediately recognize or estimate it. He postpones it to a remote, a vastly remote futurity—a postponement which may be legitimate as to universal nature, but not as to that complex, highly wrought, and short-lived phase of nature, which is manifested in man and his social organizations. For although the death of the universe is remote, that of man, of the whole human race, is proximate, is comparatively near at hand. Mr. Spencer should have remem-

---

* See Spencer's First Principles, Chapter XVI, or that on Equilibration.

bered this. He should have considered, that, although the death of siderial systems is probably very remote, the death of social systems is undoubtedly very near—near enough, at least, to render their natural and essential tendencies to death a proper and requisite element for philosophical consideration. In this respect he, and not less also Comte, have proved themselves at fault, in common with the multitude of superficial reasoners and declaimers, to whom they have proved themselves so far superior in many of their views, that it may well excite surprise to find them assimilated in this.

§ 12. Despite the obvious points of resemblance above indicated between these two eminent thinkers, and others not mentioned, objection has been made by Mr. Spencer to the classification of himself in the same category with Comte, or as appertaining essentially to the same school of thought.* But the exceptions which he has taken to such classification are altogether insufficient, nor are they by any means well taken. In this respect an author must allow others to be better qualified to judge of him than he of himself. The more especially should Mr. Spencer do so, when it is but too manifest that he has a disposition to disparage Comte, and set himself in opposition to his claims to be regarded as a controlling authority in the realm of thought. His impatience at being assimilated to Comte—his manifest desire to appear different from that great intellectual Titan of the modern world—his disposition to pick flaws in the reasonings of that august thinker—afford but one among many evidences, that Mr. Spencer has exhibited, of what we might venture to term *the small mind*, the more remarkable in one of so transcendent a genius, and of such prodigiously large thoughts, in the main, as he has proved himself indisputably to be.

We must, however, regard this error, or rather foible, of Mr. Spencer's, as merely an illustration of what his writings afford, abundant proof, that he is rather a vast and brilliant thinker, than

---

* See his Letter to the Editor of the New Englander for January, 1864, on Preface to First American Edition of his work on "First Principles."

a very accurate, or extraordinarily profound one. The chief merit of Mr. Spencer, indeed, consists in the vastness of his generalizations, and the brilliancy of his illustrations. The former quality, which is the more fundamental one, he has only in common with Comte. The latter, which is rather superficial, and appertaining only to the execution of his design, is peculiarly and preëminently his own. As a writer he is indisputably the superior of Comte. As a thinker he is indisputably his inferior, in so far at least as the practical applications of fundamental principles are concerned, which afford, after all, perhaps, the surest test of the most valuable thinker.

As a writer out of his thoughts, whatever they may be, right or wrong, solid or specious, wise or foolish, Herbert Spencer stands unsurpassed. As a thinker he has many superiors, although few, if any, that excel him in the correctness of his fundamental ideas and general delineations. It is only when he comes to the more particular ideas, or to the practical applications of his general and fundamental ideas, that his judgment fails him, that his perceptions appear to flicker, and lose the right direction. Nor is this to be wondered at. The very brilliancy of his thoughts tends to blind and deceive him. Who, indeed, could think as brilliantly as Herbert Spencer, and not be bedazzled by the splendor of his own thoughts? The lightning's flash is too brilliant to allow of one's seeing clearly by its light. It rather blinds and dazzles the vision.

In so far as artistic skill in rhetoric is concerned, in so far as relates to a clear, lucid, and brilliant style of writing, Herbert Spencer may well scout the idea of any comparison between himself and Comte. That field of glory is all his own. For he is as brilliant in composition as Comte is dull and prosy. While Comte discourses on the vast theme of universal science with the dullness and tedium of a professor of mathematics, Spencer makes the august theme almost as interesting as a romance. This is one of the chief merits of Spencer—his brilliancy of thought and illustration in regard to obscure and abstruse themes. But we must not be blinded or dazzled by his brilliancy, if we would rightly estimate his merits as a contributor to the domain of thought and true science. Rightly estimating him, in this respect, we shall find in him not a little of the sophist, and even of the *sophomore*. Calmly and critically reviewing him, we shall detect some vital errors in his Philosophy and mode of reasoning, more especially in regard to the Philosophy of Society—errors more serious in their practical significance than any we shall detect in the reasonings of Comte.

§ 13. It is very true that there are differences to be observed between Spencer and Comte. But those differences, in so far at least as relates to their reasonings on society, are in the main decidedly to the credit of Comte. It was not to Mr. Spencer's credit to exaggerate those differences, as he has labored to do. In his letter to the New-Englander, published in the Preface to the American Edition of his work on " First Principles," he says, " My own attitude towards Comte and his partial adherents has been all along one of antagonism." The greater is the pity that it should have been so. The more to be regretted it is, that, instead of seeking to harmonize the partial differences between himself and so great a thinker as Comte, he should have preferred placing himself in the attitude of " antagonism" toward him. The more to be regretted it is, that so valuable a thinker, and so brilliant an illustrator of thought, as Mr. Spencer, has not learned that the true philosopher is distinguished by the desire to detect points of *accord*, rather than of " antagonism," between himself and others.

The main difference between Spencer and Comte—that is to the credit of the former—is altogether fundamental, and relative only to their respective Theological tendencies. Comte is an intense materialist—*avowedly*, at least, which is, indeed, about the most that we can say of any materialist—while Spencer is not. Comte, in his *theoretical* reasonings, ignores all essence, all being, except matter, while Spencer, far more justly, recognizes both mind and matter. Comte ignores all scientific recognition of Psychology, and scouts all formal study of the laws of mind, except as certain manifestations of *cerebral activity*, while Spencer, far more wisely, makes Psychology one of the five main divisions of his Universal Philosophy.

But, after all, the essential difference between them in this respect is more apparent than real, more in theory than in practice. Like all fundamental differences of opinion, it is a difference in respect to terms, rather than as to ideas—a difference dependent on misunderstanding of each other, rather than of the subject on which they appear to differ. The difference between the atheist and pantheist is, indeed, exceedingly small; and one or the other every philosopher must be. It is narrowed down to the difference between one side of the razor's edge and the other, or between one color of the rainbow and the next. Comte takes the atheistic view of nature, Spencer the pantheistic. But what real difference does this make between them—in so far, at least, as practical aims or purposes are concerned? A man may avow himself an atheist, a mere materialist, an ignorer of all mind, soul, or spirit, as does Comte. But the avowal amounts to little. His practical reasonings give the lie to his fundamental postulate. There is no practical or real atheism. The atheist is simply one who rejects the vulgar idea of God—the wretchedly contracted theology which seeks to give Him "a local habitation and a name." There is no rejecting of the *idea* of God. The attempt to do so but illustrates the sentiment of Horace: "You may expel nature with a pitchfork, but she will return, she will break through all your shams, and assert her irresistible supremacy."* So it is with every great principle or truth. So it is with the *idea* of God. You may drive out the idea at the back door, but it will come in at the front. You may drive it out at both doors, and bar the doors against it; but it will break in on all sides. There is no resisting or rejecting it. The atheist vainly seeks to expel the idea of God from the universe. In resentment of his effort, it breaks out all over the universe. All nature becomes alive with the idea of God, spirit, all-pervading mind, which is

---

* See Epistles of Horace, passage, "Naturam expelles furcâ," &c. The precise reference the author cannot give, citing only from general recollection.

everywhere the true reality, and of which all tangible substance is but the outward habiliment.

We find this great truth strikingly illustrated in the reasonings of Comte. After rejecting all idea of God, as commonly received, he winds up with deifying man, with recognizing him as "the Great Being," a virtual return to the old Siamese idea of worshipping the white elephant—of recognizing God, or the Divine Idea of the world, in that form or manifestation of outward nature.

Not less manifestly does Comte falsify his theoretical atheism and materialism, in his more immediately practical reasonings. While he theoretically ignores all MIND, he practically recognizes it in all his reasonings, nay, to a far greater extent than does Mr. Spencer.

Such strange inconsistencies and paradoxes are constantly manifesting themselves in the reasonings of men. We find them strikingly illustrated in the contrast between these two great reasoners. Comte begins with denying God, spirit, or mind, altogether, and ends with making it supreme, or, at least, paramount and most fundamental in Social Philosophy. Spencer, on the contrary, begins with recognizing distinctly the idea of God—first and most fundamentally, under the title of "The Unknowable," and secondly under the title of "Laws of Psychology"—and ends with practically ignoring it almost entirely. Thus Comte, like a true Social Philosopher, distinctly recognizes the influence of RACE—which, rightly interpreted, signifies but the principle of MIND manifest in man—and places it first in the order of causes modifying national destiny, while Spencer virtually ignores it entirely, or weakly represents it as the mere result of "different conditions." To be consistent with their premises, Comte should have ignored the influence of race, and Spencer should have made it the paramount influence. But precisely the reverse has been the case. In this respect, as in so many others, the practical reasonings of Comte are more correct than those of Spencer.

§ 14. It was peculiarly unfortunate, too, for Mr. Spencer that, in his overweening desire to place himself in "antagonism" with

Comte, he should have undertaken to attack his "Genesis of Science,"* or rather his theory as to the true logical dependence of the sciences: for he has thereby shown his own lack of true philosophical discernment. He has thereby shown that he was ignorant, or at least not duly considerate, of the truth that all knowledge is manifested to the human understanding in a double view or twofold aspect—the analytical and synthetical, or in the order of development and envelopment. In other words, of more explicit import, he has failed to discern, or duly to consider, that the order in which the human mind advances to the discovery of knowledge is different from, nay, precisely the reverse, or the converse, of that which it pursues in proceeding to classify and systematize its knowledge, according to its true logical dependence and relations.

In the one case the mind proceeds from particulars to generals, in the other from generals to particulars. The latter is the true scientific mode, alike of classifying and considering the sciences. It is the mode which Comte has adopted, and Spencer too, in his actual classification of the sciences. Yet the latter has seen fit to attack the former for his mode of proceeding in this respect. And the ground of his attack is, that this is not the order in which we acquire our knowledge. It was necessary to improve our spy-glasses, for example—argues Mr. Spencer—it was necessary, in short, to make considerable attainments in optics, before we could make some of the most important discoveries in astronomy. Therefore, concludes this most hypercritically philosophical critic, Comte was wrong in placing astronomy first, or at least second, and next to mathematics, in his hierarchy of the sciences. He should rather, as we may infer, have placed it after optics—have made it logically dependent, forsooth, on the more particular science of optics. But enough of these general criticisms on Comte and Spencer. It is time that we should more particularly consider what they have done for the Philosophy of Society.

---

* This Mr. Spencer has done in his Essay or Article on the Genesis of Science, published in his Miscellany, entitled, "Illustrations of Universal Progress."

§ 15. The great merit, alike of Comte and Spencer, as contributors to Social Philosophy, is, that they have regarded the phenomena of society as but an appurtenance to the general phenomena of the universe, and have considered the science of human society in connection with universal science; nay, as logically and naturally dependent on all other science. Merit enough this is for any one man, or, as we may say in this connection, for any two men. Merit enough it is for any one man, for any one philosopher, at this epoch of the world, to have appreciated, as both of these great minds have done, the important truth, that, in order to master Social Science, we must handle it in connection with universal science. For this one merit we may well overlook many errors.

If, in the execution of this great design, Spencer has contributed less valuable suggestions, nay, if he has committed more serious errors than Comte, we must not impute it alone, if at all, to a less truly philosophical discernment on his part, but to the further fact that he has directed his attention, with a less absorbing or controlling view, to the phenomena of society. For he has rather considered the phenomena of society as incidental merely to his general view of the phenomena of the universe, has subordinated the former to the latter view, while Comte has rather adopted the converse mode, has rather considered the phenomena of the universe as incidental merely to his consideration of the phenomena of society, or has at least subordinated his view of universal science to his view of Social Science.

It is to be furthermore borne in mind that the views of Mr. Spencer, on the Philosophy of Society, have not been as yet fully developed. Comte has done his work, so far as he was permitted, and has gone from the stage of being, at least of terrestrial being, while Spencer yet remains, it is to be hoped for many years yet, to enlighten the world with his brilliant thoughts. We have, as yet, his views on Social Philosophy, only in so far as they are developed in his work on "Social Statics," his article on "The Social Organism,"* and incidental references to the science of

---

* See this splendid article in Mr. Spencer's miscellaneous work, entitled 'Illustrations of Universal Progress."

society, in his other writings. We have not as yet his more formal treatise on Sociology, comprising a part of his series on Universal Science. It is possible that in that treatise he may amend to a great extent the imperfections of his former disquisitions, although it is not at all probable that he will rectify some of his most fundamental errors, such as his notion that the diversities of Race, or of human character in general, are referable merely to "adaptation of constitution to conditions,"* and his puerile sophistry about "The Evanescence of Evil."†

For these errors seem to be ingrained in his order of thought, as they are, indeed, in the Anglo-Saxon order of thought in general, to which Mr. Spencer's evidently and most essentially belongs. For his is evidently not one of those exceptional minds, that we occasionally find scattered over the Anglo-Saxon formation of the intellectual world, analogous to those diluvial rocks of the geological world, which we occasionally find scattered over general formations with which they are associated, but to which they are evidently strangers, though destined, no doubt, for ultimate amalgamation.

These fundamental errors of Spencer evidently appertain to the Anglo-Saxon order of thought—to its essentially materialistic character and tendencies. He evidently has not that finer perception, that deeper insight, which readily penetrates through the outer crust of matter, through mere external forms, to those more interior energies, which are everywhere to be detected, everywhere to be found quivering beneath external forms, and which constitute the soul, the true life of the world. Had he possessed this clearer, deeper insight, he would not have committed the errors in question. He would have discerned that there are differences and defects in MIND, as well as in matter, not to be removed by a mere change of "conditions," and that what we superficially call "evil," can never be eradicated, that it is ingrained in the unchangeable constitution of the world, in the immutable laws of mind and matter.

§ 16. While Comte and Spencer have thus this common merit,

---

* Social Statics. Part I, Ch. II, § 2.   † Same. Same chapter in general.

of regarding the phenomena of society as intimately related to the phenomena of the universe, they are alike liable to this common criticism, that their views are, in the main, altogether too general, vague, and indefinite, for practical purposes. They are both liable to the criticism involved in the observation of Plato, that "The higher generalities give no sufficient direction; and the pith of all sciences, which makes the artist differ from the inexpert, is in the middle propositions, which, in every particular science, are taken from tradition and experience."* It is with the higher generalities, almost exclusively, that they deal. They have not concerned themselves about the middle propositions, the proximate principles, the practical ideas, and they, therefore, afford us no sufficient direction.

Comte and Spencer, indeed, furnish us rather with disquisitions on the *cosmogony* of society than on its *geology*. They dwell rather on hypotheses, or theories, as to the origin of society, and the modes of its progressive development, than on the causes which actually determine its condition at any given time. And as Lyell has properly excluded from the proper science of Geology all such disquisitions as to the probable origin of the world, all disquisitions on the cosmogony of worlds, so not less are all such disquisitions, as to the *cosmogony* of society, properly to be excluded from the science of Sociology.

The great leading and fundamental idea of Comte is, that the human mind, and likewise human society, which, in common with Cousin—of whom, however, he seems to be profoundly ignorant—he very righty regards as the mere reflex and counterpart of the human mind, pass successively through three grand phases—the *theological*, or fictitious, the *metaphysical*, or abstract, and the *positive*, or scientific. To this fundamental idea, which is doubtlessly in the main correct, notwithstanding the captious objections which Mr. Spencer has made to it, all his views of society are conformed and subordinated. To this idea the main brunt of his attention is directed. If other and more practical ideas are occasionally thrown out, they are too quickly run into the background, and this vague generality brought to the front.

---

* See Plato's Timæus.

The great leading and fundamental idea of Spencer, to which, in like manner, all his views of society, and of universal nature, are conformed and subordinated, is, "that all organic development is a change from a state of homogeneity to a state of heterogeneity."* This is his law of "Evolution," as contradistinguished from Comte's law of "Progress," which it may readily be seen is substantially but the same law, not by any means the vastly different law which Mr. Spencer, it seems, would have us to regard it. It is only a more general, vague, and indefinite statement of substantially the same law.

§ 17. In order to test the immediate value of the contributions of these two great thinkers to the Philosophy of Society, we have only to inquire what light do these great laws, which they have ransacked the universe to establish, throw upon the great practical question, to which the whole Philosophy of Society should direct its attention—WHAT ARE THE CAUSES ON WHICH DEPENDS THE WELFARE OF STATES, or, WHAT ARE THE CAUSES WHICH REALLY DETERMINE THE SOCIAL CONDITION OF MANKIND? Tried by this test, which is undoubtedly the true one, we shall have to adjudge their contributions of no great practical value, however important may be, and undoubtedly are, the fundamental ideas which they inculcate.

Their reasonings on the Philosophy of Society can hardly fail, indeed, to remind us of the language of a certain lawyer, in one of the back settlements of America, in ridicule of the argument of his adversary in a forensic controversy: "The learned gentleman has roamed with old Romulus, soaked with old Socrates, ripped with old Euripides, and canted with old Cantharides—but what, may it please your Honor, does he know about the laws of Wisconsin?" May we not aptly paraphrase this language in respect to these two eminent philosophers? May we not rightly say, they have roamed through creation, they have ransacked the universe in quest of information, they have brought the batteries of uni-

---

* We use here Spencer's own words, as expressed in his pamphlet on "The Classification of the Sciences."

versal science to bear upon the Philosophy of Society: but what light have they thrown upon the great practical question, what are the causes which determine the social condition of mankind, the causes which determine that one man shall be a peasant, another a prince; one a laborer, another a capitalist; one a slave, another a master; one a pauper, another a millionaire?

§ 18. Let us consider what light their teachings throw upon this great practical question. A pauper, who is the representative of one of the greatest ills observable in human society, presents himself, we will suppose, before the philosopher Comte, and asks why it is that he is denied all the comforts of life, while others are revelling in its luxuries. What is the reply he gets from Mr. Comte? Substantially this—"Miserable man! deplorable is your fate! But your case affords only another illustration of the great law which I have established in my system of Positive Philosophy, and my other writings, that the human condition, not less than the human mind, passes successively through three grand stages of progress—the *theological*, or fictitious, the *metaphysical*, or abstract, and the *positive*, or scientific. You have at length attained the *positive* state. Your destitution is decidedly *positive*. This is the scientific definition of your true position, in the *statical* aspect of society. Such is the positive result, so far as you are concerned, of all the *dynamical* modifications which human society has hitherto undergone."

So much for the explanation which Mr. Comte's great law affords. But, suppose one beggar, not satisfied with the philosophy of Comte, should turn to Mr. Spencer for explanation and satisfaction. What reply may he expect? Substantially this—"Unhappy man! you stand before me to-day a sad proof of the correctness of my great fundamental law of Evolution—a sad and convincing proof that all evolution is from the homogeneous to the heterogeneous. For whereas the human condition was originally *homogeneous*, and universally in that state of poverty in which you now are—as Mr. Senior, by the way, has wisely suggested to Mr. Malthus—it has now advanced to the *heterogeneous* state, in which a few are affluent, many are comfortable, and many remain destitute, as they were before. You, unhappy man, illustrate the worst aspect of the heterogeneous. But there is no immediate hope for your case. 'Humanity is being pressed against the inexorable necessities of its new position—is being moulded into harmony with them, and has to bear the resulting unhappiness as best it can. The process *must* be undergone, and the sufferings *must* be endured.'* No effectual relief can be assured for your condition, until mankind shall have attained that perfect state of morality delineated in my Social Statics—until 'evolution has run its course'—until the conflicting passions and interests of men shall have attained to a state of perfect 'Equilibration'—until, in short, the human constitution has become 'such as that each man may perfectly fulfil his own nature, not only without diminishing other men's spheres of activity, but without giving unhappiness to other men, in any direct or indirect way.' When humanity shall have attained to this blessed state, the inevitable tendency of the great fundamental law of 'Evolution,' then, but not till then, may we hope for any effectual relief to your distress."

§ 19. Such is a summary, in its most condensed form of expression, of the most essential teachings of Comte and Spencer, in regard to the great practical aspects of Social Philosophy. It may readily be discerned what insufficient direction they give—how little practical suggestion they afford.

It is due to Comte, however, to say, that he is *incidentally* much more explicit, that he *incidentally* furnishes, indeed, the outline in brief of the true Philosophy of Society, both in regard to its great practical aspects, and its true theoretical aspects, or fundamental relations. But, unfortunately, he does so incidentally only—he does not give due prominence to those incidentally expressed ideas—does not properly bring them to the front, but throws them rather to the rear of his more general and less valuable ideas. For he very correctly and explicitly states, in brief, the three grand causes which concur in determining the social destiny of mankind, as first RACE, secondly,

---

* The words embraced within the single quotation marks are precisely the words of Mr. Spencer, in his Social Statics, and the chapter on Poor Laws.

CLIMATE, thirdly, POLITICAL ACTION in its whole scientific extent. And to this perfectly just, though not faultlessly expressed, outline of causes, he adds this not less eminently just observation: "The political influences are the only ones really open to our intervention, and to that head general attention must be directed, though with great care to avoid the conclusion that that class of influences must be the most important, because it is the most immediately interesting to us."*

Comte would have spoken better, more comprehensively, and therefore more philosophically, if he had defined the three grand causes as, first, Race, secondly, Natural Environment, in its largest import, and, thirdly, Political Action, in its whole scientific extent. Climate is not by any means the only important natural circumstance tending powerfully to modify human character. Geographical configuration is scarcely less important. Nor is texture of soil by any means unimportant.

Thus expressed or defined, the three causes which Comte has stated, and in their true natural and logical order, afford us a correct outline of the true Philosophy of Society. It will be found, indeed, that the whole disquisition of the present author, as proposed, into the causes which determine the social condition of mankind, his whole system of Social Philosophy, is but an enlargement or expansion of these fundamental ideas, which, although entirely original with himself—in so far, indeed, as any human thought can be said to be original—have been, nevertheless, very clearly apprehended by the great French philosopher under review. Unlike Mr. Spencer, the present author has no disposition in any respect to disparage this great philosopher, or in any sense to put himself in an attitude of "antagonism" towards him, widely different as he, not less than Mr. Spencer, is from him, in some of his views, or rather apparent views of things. Far more ambitious to be simply true, than to be original, the author accepts with satisfaction, nay, hails with delight, this testimony of so great a thinker to the correctness of his own

---

* See Comte's System of Positive Philosophy. Book VI., Ch. III., or Vol. II., pp. 92–3. London Edition of 1853, as translated by Miss Martineau.

views, this clear recognition, in outline, of the true Newtonian Philosophy of Society, which it is his aim to inaugurate and establish.

Why should any one man, indeed, claim all the wisdom of the world for himself? Is it not as unnecessary and wanton an aspiration as it is unjust? Many brave men have lived before Agamemnon*—many brave men since. Are they any the less brave because Agamemnon was brave, too? Or is the same reasoning any less applicable as to wisdom than as to valor?

§ 20. Many valuable thoughts are to be found in the writings of Comte on the Philosophy of Society, or rather on "Social Physics," as he prefers to entitle his subject. But they labor under great disadvantage from his dry and mathematically abstract mode of expressing them, and under still greater disadvantage from the stand-point from which they are delivered, which is that, as already indicated, of the *cosmogonist*, rather than the actual *geologist* of society—a stand-point altogether too elevated and remote for immediately practical purposes. Some of his thoughts are, however, so valuable, so suggestive and expressive of new views in regard to Social Philosophy, or at least of more correct views than are commonly prevalent, that it would be a culpable omission to pass them by unnoticed, or uncited in brief.

How well does this great thinker express himself, for example, when he says: "If the statical analysis of our social organism shows it resting at length upon a certain system of fundamental opinions, the gradual changes of that system must affect the successive modifications of the life of humanity; and this is why, since the birth of philosophy, the history of society has been regarded as governed by the history of the human mind."† This, it will be seen, is but a diversified statement of Hume's famous aphorism, so copiously illustrated in our Sixth chapter, that all

---

* It may readily be detected that we here do but play upon the famous line of Horace—"Fortes ante Agamemnona vixere multi."

† *Positive Philosophy.* Book VI., Ch. VI., pp. 156-7. Vol. II., London Edition, 1853.

governments are founded in opinion." But it is a larger statement, a more copious expression, of this great truth, so little understood, so rarely considered.

Thus again to the same point, though in a different work, he says: "It becomes every day more evident how hopeless is the task of reconstructing political institutions, without the previous remodelling of opinion and of life."*

A somewhat different idea, that which we have noticed already as conspicuous in De Maistre and Buckle, the idea that human society is governed by fixed and immutable laws, not less than all the other forms of nature, he thus faultlessly expresses: "The phenomena of human life, though more modifiable than any others, are yet equally subject to invariable laws."†

To the same point, and still more nearly approximating the precise idea of De Maistre, that the laws of human society are, most essentially, beyond human control, in speaking of what he terms the objective basis, on which the harmony of our moral nature is to be established, he says: "That basis is, that all events whatever, the events of our personal and moral nature included, are always subject to natural relations of sequence and similitude, which, in all essential respects, lie beyond the reach of our interference."‡ Further on in the same paragraph he forcibly says of this basis, that, "It rests, at every point, upon the unchangeable order of the world."§

To the same point, and in the same connection, he says of this basis: "It teaches us that the object to be aimed at in the economy devised by man, is wise development of the irresistible economy of nature, which cannot be amended till it be first studied and obeyed. In some departments it has the character of fate; that is, it admits of no modification."‖ To the same point, yet again, he says: "We are powerless to create. All that we can do in bettering our condition is to modify an order in which we can produce no radical change."¶

---

* Comte's General View of Positivism, as translated by J. H. Bridges. London Edition, 1865. Introduction, p. 2.

† Same, Chap. I., p. 24.   ‡ Same, p. 28.   § Same.   ‖ Same, p. 29.   ¶ Same.

In illustration more explicitly of his idea that human society, and human destiny in general, are under control of natural laws, the following passage from the same work and chapter may be cited to advantage: "All knowledge is now brought within the sphere of Natural Philosophy; and the provisional distinction by which, since Aristotle and Plato, it has been sharply demarcated from Moral Philosophy, ceases to exist."*

§ 21. That Comte, not less than Spencer, looked to a higher standard of morality for the real improvement of society, and that he entertained more rational and sober expectations, in regard to that morality, than Mr. Spencer, is manifest from the following passage of the same work and chapter. In speaking of the combination between reason and sympathy, or the development of our affections and sympathies in accordance with the suggestions of reason, he says: "It will never, indeed, do away with the fact that practical life must, to a large extent, be regulated by interested motives. Yet it may introduce a standard of morality inconceivably higher than has existed in the past, before these two modifying forces could be made to combine their action upon our stronger and lower instincts."†

Mr. Spencer, on the contrary, has proved himself weak enough to suppose that practical life may eventually be regulated entirely by *disinterested* motives, or at least by interested motives so perfectly *equilibrated* with a just and benevolent regard for the rights and feelings of others, as will render them virtually disinterested, or as just and as beneficent, as if they were totally disinterested. Thus is the weak, puerile, and ridiculous idea of "the perfectibility of man" shadowed forth by Condorcet, and run to stark madness by William Godwin, and others, in the latter part of the *eighteenth* century, brought to light again by the specious sophistry of Mr. Spencer, in the middle of the *nineteenth*.

Yet it is evident, from a remark of Comte a few pages further on, and from the whole scope of his reasonings, that he, too, expects rather too much from the higher standard of morality to

---

* Same, p. 36.   † Same, p. 40.

which undoubtedly we are tending, *for a temporary epoch*, in the career of human development. For he says: "Sufficient for our purposes, if this incipient classification of our mental products be so far worked out that the synthesis of affection and action may be at once attempted; that is, that we may begin at once to construct that system of morality under which the final regeneration of humanity will proceed." So it would seem, that, according even to Comte, the grave, the stern, and mathematically rigid Comte, we are to have a "final regeneration of humanity." Eminently unphilosophical idea! Are we to have a final regeneration of horses, too? But when did a French philosopher, however great, or eminently wise, in the main, fail, in some part of his reasonings, to take leave of common sense!

§ 22. That Comte, not less than Spencer, recognized the tendency towards the larger play of Individualism, as civilization progresses, and that he took, at the same time, a much more rational, sober, and just view of this ultimate tendency than Spencer, who ran riot with the idea, as with nearly all his ideas, will be made manifest from the following passage of the same work, already so largely drawn upon: "When a pure morality arises, capable of impressing a social tendency upon every phase of human activity, the freer our action becomes the more useful will it be to the public. The tendency of modern civilization, far from impeding private industry, is to intrust it more and more with functions, especially with those of a material kind, which were originally left to government. Unfortunately this tendency, which is very evident, leads economists into the mistake of supposing that industry may be left altogether without organization. All that it really proves is that the influence of moral principles is gradually preponderating over that of governmental regulations."*

To the same point, he says, in a subsequent chapter: "Modern industry has long ago proved the administrative superiority of private enterprise in commercial transactions; and all social functions, that admit of it, will gradually pass into private manage-

---

* Same work. Ch. III., p. 177.

ment, always excepting the great theoretical functions, in which combined action will always be necessary."*

How much more just, more correct, is this qualified statement of the great leading idea, *that the essential tendency of all human progress is towards the ultimate triumph of the individual over society*, than that extreme, and almost totally unqualified assertion of the idea, which has been made by Mr. Spencer, who will not allow that government should have anything to do with provision for the poor, with state education, nor with sanitary provisions of any kind, whether relating to health of body or of mind. Mr. Spencer, indeed, would have the function of government rigidly restricted to "protection,"—protection to the community, and the individual. Very good. Rightly understood, and most essentially expressed, this is undoubtedly the legitimate function of government, or, at least, its main legitimate function.† But what then? Something is necessary to protection—is it not? What is necessary to protection, in its largest import—in its proper signification? Very evidently, under many circumstances, a good deal more than Mr. Spencer is disposed to allow. John Stuart Mill, beyond all question one of the most correct and valuable thinkers of the age, the grave, judicious, deliberate, many-sided Anglo-Saxon philosopher—who has never, indeed, shown any symptoms of *the Anglo-Saxon mud on the brain*, except in his slowness to appreciate the paramount influence of Race on national destiny, before criticised—in his valuable chapters on "The Functions of Government," has laid down, with admirable propriety, many of the important qualifications to which the great leading idea in question is liable, and which it will be found fully sustain Comte, and adjudge Mr. Spencer to be seriously in error.‡

§ 23. So much has been already said, in respect to the views of Spencer, by way of contrast as well as of assimilation, with

---

* Same. Chap. VI., p. 399.

† Mr. Spencer's definition of the legitimate function of government is substantially the same with that of the author, and hardly so rigidly expressed; but it is not duly qualified, as is the latter. See the author's unpublished work on "The Political School of Social Philosophy," or Part III. of this series, Chapter I.

‡ See Mill's Political Economy, Part V.

those of Comte, that we shall have the less need of dwelling at any length upon the separate and more particular consideration of those views, the more especially as they lie much more immediately open, than those of Comte, to the view of the Anglo-Saxon world, to which these thoughts are more immediately addressed.

The most essential and fundamental expression of the views of Spencer in his own words, an expression which serves at once to bring his merits and demerits, or deficiencies, as a fundamental thinker, most distinctly into view, the more especially from the sharp and clearly-defined contrast which it affords with the more profound thought of Comte, is to be found in the following passage from one of his miscellaneous works : "Social progress," says Mr. Spencer, " is supposed to consist in the production of a greater quantity and variety of the articles required for satisfying men's wants; in the increasing security of person and property; in widening freedom of action ; whereas, rightly understood, Social progress consists in those changes of structure in the Social organism which have entailed those consequences."*

Very profound, Mr. Spencer, undoubtedly ! But not quite profound enough. Rightly understood, and most essentially expressed, Social progress consists in those changes of fundamental OPINION, from which result " those changes of structure in the Social organism." Much more profoundly and correctly does Comte speak, in the passage which has been already quoted, in which he says, " the statical analysis of our Social organism shows it resting at length upon a certain system of fundamental opinions."†

Betraying the fundamental trait of his race, of which he is eminently representative, Mr. Spencer here rests his most fundamental thought upon the *outer* rather than the *inner* view of things—the grosser and more sensuous perceptions, rather than upon the finer and more essential ones—upon the *materialistic*

---

* Illustrations of Universal Progress. Article I., entitled, Progress—Its Law and Cause.

† See ante, § 20, p. 258.

rather than the *idealistic* metaphysics. He evidently has not penetrated to the great truth that mind everywhere precedes matter in the process of organization—that mind is the true motive power, the true organic principle in universal life, and that what he calls "changes of structure in the social organism," are but changes in the FORM OF THOUGHT, OR GENERAL CHARACTER, taking to themselves new forms of outward structure.*

§ 24. A much more creditable expression, in part, of his most essential views of society—nay, an admirable and faultless expression of a great fundamental truth of the most essential importance—does Mr. Spencer afford us where, in contrasting the social with the individual organism, he says: "It is well that the lives of all parts of an animal should be merged in the life of the whole; because the whole has a corporate consciousness, capable of happiness or misery. But it is not so with society, since its living units do not and cannot lose individual consciousness, and since the community, as a whole, has no corporate consciousness. And this is an everlasting reason why the welfare of citizens cannot rightly be sacrificed to some supposed benefit of the state; but why, on the other hand, the state is to be maintained solely for the benefit of citizens. The corporate life must be subservient to the lives of the parts, instead of the lives of the parts being subservient to the corporate life."†

This is an eminently just and valuable thought, deserving to be inscribed for all time in the temple of science. It is a clear, distinct, emphatic, and eminently scientific recognition and assertion of the great truth, that the society is subordinate to the INDIVIDUAL, the state to the CITIZEN, the government to the MAN—that, in short, governments are made for men, not men for governments.

---

* Mr. Spencer himself, in his more recent work on the Principles of Biology, virtually recognizes the same idea; for he there asserts that *function* precedes *structure*, which is but another mode of asserting that *opinion* or *desire* precedes *habit*, or social forms of any kind. For the laws of LIFE are the same, by his own reasoning, in individual and social organisms. . Principles of Biology, Vol. I., § 61.

† See Essay on The Social Organism, in Spencer's Illustrations of Universal Progress, pp. 396-7, N. Y. Ed. of 1865.

What a rebuke does this conclusive passage in Mr. Spencer's philosophy read to that madness which lately broke forth in American society—the last society on the globe in which it should have appeared—which sought to revive and give prominence to the counter-idea, the antediluvian idea, of Social Statics, that the individual is subordinate to the society, the citizen to the state, the man to the government—to the institution which is of his own creation, which is rightly his mere agent, his subject, his servant, his slave—nay, that madness which had the audacity to stigmatize the MAN, nay, millions of men, as "rebel," against a thing of his own creation, an arrogant abstraction, a rebellious abstraction, called "government," thus making the sovereign a "rebel" against his rightful subject, the master a "rebel" against his bonded slave.

For let it be for ever remembered—let it stand forth as an everlasting testimonial, or declaration of the truth, for all ages to come, that whatsoever government has, ever has had, or ever shall have, rightful authority over mankind, to any extent, holds such authority only in the name of MAN, for the benefit of MAN, of the individual MAN, by how many soever myriads the individual man is to be reckoned. Let it be for ever remembered that the British Queen, the French Emperor, the Russian Czar, the Sultan of Turkey, the Emperor of China, not less than the Stadtholder of Holland or the President of the United States, rightfully hold their respective authorities by the consent—implied, if not expressed—of the several peoples in whose names they respectively reign. Each and every one of those governments may be, and probably is, legitimate, rightful, and proper, under all the circumstances that surround it.

For be it furthermore remembered that it is of no great consequence that a few, or even very many, individuals, among each one of those several peoples, may be opposed to the existing government, provided such government truly represents the real interests of MAN. The discontentment of a few, or even of many, with their government, does not prove that such government is not the rightful representative of MAN, and does not reign by and through HIS righful authority. It is sufficient, very often, if such govern-

12

ment rightfully represents the most enlightened class of society—
the truly philosophical class—who always represent the true interests of the less enlightened classes, and very generally, indeed, their most essential will, even though it should be their unconscious will. For be it remembered again, that MAN, in the aggregate or individual, acts through his brain, and that the philosophical class constitute the true brain of humanity.

It should be manifest, therefore, that we can never actualize entirely, or fully attain the subordination of the society to the individual, or the triumph of the individual over society. We can only approximate it. Man is not capable of attaining to perfect justice, but only to approximative justice. In order to assure the liberty of many, we must curtail the liberty of some. Nay, in order to assure the rightful liberty of a few, it is sometimes necessary to curtail the wrongful liberty of many. In order to assure the liberty of those who know how to use liberty without abusing it, whether they be many or few, it is sometimes necessary to curtail largely the liberty of those who cannot so wisely use liberty. Hence, denial of liberty to men, to a certain extent, is sometimes, nay, too often, justifiable and necessary. But it is never so except for the sake of MAN—of the individual MAN—the rightful interests of individual MEN. It is never so for the sake of any such abstraction as society, or the government. Hence the late great war in America may possibly have been justifiable or excusable. But let it be distinctly and for ever understood, and borne in mind, that if it was so justifiable or excusable, it was so only as a war of the MAN of the North against the MAN of the South, to prevent the latter from unjustly depriving the former of some of his appropriate rights—not as the war of an arrogant and rebellious abstraction, called "government," against MAN, who is for ever the reality, the true sovereignty, the true divinity of earth, however distant he may be from heaven.

§ 25. Having thus highly eulogized the valuable idea of Herbert Spencer last quoted, it becomes now our less agreeable duty to note that the great practical error of his whole reasonings, on the Philosophy of Society, consists in the extreme application which he has attempted of this idea, and the plausible but flimsy sophistry of his theoretical reasonings, by which he has deceived himself into the imagination that the realization of this idea is possible, nay, is to be expected in the natural course of human Evolution. And this brings us at once to the consideration, more particularly than before, of his "Social Statics," his most elaborate disquisition, in fact his only formal treatise, on Sociology, as yet presented to the world.

This work, most essentially speaking, may be defined as a disquisition on the-perfect life for man, as an elaborate attempt to define what that life is—in other words, as an attempt to delineate the true standard of right to which men should conform their actions, more especially in regard to Social relations. This he virtually concludes is to be found in the perfect liberty of the individual, in short, in "the triumph of the individual over society," although he has not exhibited the genius, like Henry James, to express the idea with so much sententious brevity and terseness.

The practical conclusions of this work are, indeed, substantially the same with those of Godwin's Political Justice; although its theoretical reasonings, or its *diagnosis* of causes, are not by any means so superficial and ridiculously flimsy. For while Godwin was an extreme representative of the Political School of Social Philosophy, and, as such, pronounced GOVERNMENT the real cause of Social ills, Spencer, far more profoundly, recognizes the truth, though not so emphatically as might be desired, that their true cause is to be found in the constitution of the universe, of which the constitution of man is but an extension or ramification.

However much more profound in his fundamental ideas, or *diagnosis* of causes, than Godwin, nevertheless, the practical conclusions of Mr. Spencer, in his Social Statics, are substantially the same. They both tend to the denial of all government by the aggregate force of the society—to the abrogation of all political authority—to the unrestrained liberty of the individual. As already often before intimated, in these pages, this is indisputably a tendency in the right direction—the essential tendency of all advance in civilization, of all true human progress. But the error of Mr.

Spencer, only a little less conspicuous, in this practical point of view, than that of Godwin, is, that he carries the idea altogether too far, asserts it with far too little qualification—in short, without any adequate appreciation of the utter impracticability and hopelessness of the idea's ever being realized.

§ 26. In so far as Mr. Spencer's elaborately critical disquisition on *the true standard of right* is concerned, he has done no more than thousands have done before. There is no great difficulty in defining this standard. All men are fundamentally agreed about it, although they may adopt different modes of expressing themselves in regard to it. Mr. Spencer has only taken a very circuitous way to assert what any school-boy might have informed us, at least any school-boy in Jurisprudence. He has only taken a very roundabout way to tell us what we all knew before, that the true rule of Ethics, not less than of positive law, is, that " Every one may rightfully so use his own, and should so use it, as not to abuse another's," or, as the more terse Latin phrase expresses it, " Sic utere tuo, ut non abutere alieno." The world has known this all along. It did not require to be taught it even by Confucius, or Christ, much less by Mr. Spencer, at this late time of day. But the great difficulty has been all along, and will ever continue to be, to prevail on men to practise the doctrine. It is this great difficulty which Mr. Spencer so greatly underestimates. He talks learnedly and largely about the " evanescence of evil," and the ultimate " adaptation of humanity to its conditions," in which, as he argues, will consist the disappearance of all evil from human society.

When this result shall have been attained, of course, as he may very well argue, men may be left entirely free, they will need no governmental restraint ; for then " the human constitution must be such," to use his own language, " that each man may perfectly fulfil his own nature, not only without diminishing other men's spheres of activity, but without giving unhappiness to other men in any direct or indirect way."* Thus does this plausible and fal-

---

* Social Statics. Part I, Ch. III., § 2.

lacious, though brilliant writer, rehash the absurd idea of the "perfectibility of man," so absurdly foisted upon the world by Condorcet, Godwin, and others, in the latter part of the last century.

This is his ideal of the perfect man, and the perfect state of society, as portrayed in his Social Statics. To this ideal are all the reasonings of that work conformed. In short, Mr. Spencer, in his Social Statics, gives us little or no direction in regard to society as it is, but only in regard to society as it ought to be. He is the philosopher who, in his Philosophy of Society, treats of man as he ought to be, not of man as he is.

We did not need any ghost to tell us that ; in other words, to tell us what man ought to be, according to our superficial and contracted view of things. For about that we are all agreed, substantially at least. As to what man ought *really* to be, that is, in reality, quite another question. Had Mr. Spencer been a deeper philosopher than he has proved himself, he might have told us, perhaps, that man is already what he ought to be—that, as the more truly philosophical Pope tells us, "whatever is, is right."

Had he been a deeper philosopher he might have discerned, perhaps, that in reality there is no such thing as *evil*—that what we call *evil* is but the subversive phase of GOOD, or its converse phase—that it is an inseparable counterpart of GOOD, necessary to GOOD. He might then have discerned, perhaps, that what he is aiming to accomplish, what he hopes and vainly expects to see accomplished, the eradication of what he calls "evil," is not only impracticable, but happily so for mankind—that it forms an inseparable part of the vital economy of the universe—that the day which shall witness the extermination of evil, as we term it, must witness also the extermination of good—that the day which beholds the eradication of vice must behold also the eradication of virtue—that good and evil, virtue and vice, happiness and misery, are the inseparable antagonisms, the indispensable vital forces of the moral universe, without which it could no more live than could the sidereal universe exist, or live, without the inseparable and indispensable antagonistic forces which we respectively designate CENTRIPETAL and CENTRIFUGAL.

He who has not risen to the contemplation of these great truths has, most probably, mistaken the vital secret of the universe. But however this may be, and allowing that this vain conceit, this delusive hope, as to the eradication of evil, or the "evanescence of evil," as Mr. Spencer terms it, has some foundation in possibility, all will admit that the time is very remote, is very far distant, when the vain hope can, by any possibility, be realized. Yet Mr. Spencer bases his whole view of human society upon the hypothetical idea that this distant hope, this remote possibility, has been already realized, and gives no prescription for society in respect to its actual condition, except, indeed, to let it alone, to run its own course.

§ 27. The main and most essential criticism to be pronounced on Herbert Spencer, as he presents himself in his "Social Statics," is, that he ignores entirely the law of Evil, which renders his work a very admirable treatise on Ethics, but a very poor one on Sociology. He offers no prescription for society except upon the condition of its fulfilling the perfect law—nothing that will avail society until it shall have attained to that perfect law, which of course it will never do. He renders himself liable to the criticism or satire of the old orator Maynard, in the British Parliament, upon those rigid sticklers for form, who, even in the time of revolution, would do nothing except according to the prescribed forms of law, and whom he very aptly compares to the man who, having lost his way in the wilderness, stands crying, "Where is the king's highway? I will walk nowhere but on the king's highway."*

This fastidious moralist flatly tells us, in his Social Statics, that he has nothing to do with "expediencies," which, every man of common sense knows, are the very matters about which statesmen and true social philosophers have to concern themselves almost exclusively. He tells us that all he has to do is to inform us, what we all knew before, in the general and the abstract, what is "right"—to furnish us, in short, with the true ideal of human society, or the perfect life for man.

---

* See Macaulay's History of England. Vol. III., Ch. II., p. 24.

A penny for his thoughts on such a topic! The world is saturated, nay, water-logged, with disquisitions about that, quite as good as his. What we want in Social Science are some instructions, some clear directions, in regard to the great practical questions, how far can we safely or surely approximate this ideal of the perfect life, of the perfectly just—how far can men be rendered capable of approximating it—what can be done for men as they are—how can human institutions be so accommodated to human nature, as it actually is, with all its defects and imperfections, with all its follies, vices, errors, as to attain for mankind the best possible approximation to the ideal state.

Totally ignoring these great practical questions, conclusively showing himself incapable of meeting them, or of giving any very valuable or accurate and particular instructions in regard to them, he runs riot with his single idea about the perfect life, the perfect standard of right, the perfectly just, which he would have applied to all men, and to all societies of men, without regard, or any due regard, to their actual condition or their fitness to appreciate the perfectly just. Hence we find him running into the superficial fallacies of English Chartism—nay, far transcending them—and advocating universal liberty, universal "equal freedom," and "universal suffrage," nay, for women as well as men, even for England, when truly philosophical statesmen doubt seriously whether it is a safe franchise even for younger and more favorably circumstanced societies, in which the preponderance of destitution, and consequently hopeless ignorance, has not become as yet near so great as it is in England.

§ 28. This criticism on Herbert Spencer should sufficiently indicate how little merit he possesses as a practical instructor, or thinker, in Social Philosophy, despite the great value of his main fundamental ideas. But we should not duly estimate the superficiality and flippancy which has been strangely manifested by this eminent thinker, throughout the whole reasonings of his Social Statics, if we did not notice more particularly the flimsy sophistry with which he has revamped the absurd idea of the "perfectibility of man," or, what amounts to the same thing, in his own proper parlance, "the evanescence of evil." We may well feel the more called upon to do this, because the illustrious writer calls upon us to take exception to his reasoning thereupon, if we can—challenges us to do so, by saying, "If any one demurs to this, let him point out the error."

Let us see how the argument stands, which Mr. Spencer so vauntingly regards as triumphant and conclusive. Here it is:

"The inference that as advancement has been hitherto the rule, it will be the rule henceforth, may be called a plausible speculation. But when it is shown that this advancement is due to the working of an universal law; and that in virtue of that law it must continue until the state we call perfection is reached, then the advent of such a state is removed out of the region of probability into that of certainty. If any one demurs to this, let him point out the error. Here are the several steps of the argument.

"All imperfection is unfitness to the conditions of existence.

"This unfitness must consist either in having a faculty or faculties in excess; or in having a faculty or faculties deficient; or in both.

"A faculty in excess, is one which the conditions of existence do not afford full exercise to; and a faculty that is deficient, is one from which the conditions of existence demand more than it can perform.

"But it is an essential principle of life that a faculty to which circumstances do not allow full exercise diminishes; and that a faculty on which circumstances make excessive demands increases.

"And so long as this excess and this deficiency continue, there must continue decrease on the one hand, and growth on the other.

"Finally, all excess, and all deficiency, must disappear; that is, all unfitness must disappear; that is, all imperfection must disappear."*

Was there ever such an elaborate tissue of ridiculous sophistry before attempted to be formally and pompously foisted upon the

---

* Social Statics. Part I., Ch. II., § 4.

common sense of the world? Where was the professor of *logic* in whose school this artistic logician graduated, that he allowed his pupil to put forth such an exhibition of Sophomoric wisdom? We need not ask where was the professor of common sense; for surely there could have been no such professor in the college in which this transcendent sophist, not less than brilliant philosopher, took his diploma.

Let us abbreviate and simplify his logic, that it may be the more readily appreciated and confuted. It is substantially this. *All evil, or imperfection, is unfitness to the conditions of existence. But all unfitness to the conditions of existence has a constant tendency to die out or disappear. Therefore, all evil or imperfection has a constant tendency to die out, or disappear, and, consequently, must eventually die out or disappear.* Surely such absurdity is deserving of no other confutation than that of the *reductio ad absurdum*. Let us apply it. It may be rendered thus:

Death is the sum of all evils—the most dreaded of all, and that for which nearly all other human evils combined will readily be exchanged. It is the result of all the imperfections of organic being. Could all these imperfections be removed there would be no death, which is the mere result of those imperfections, of the unfitness of organism, whether vegetable or animal, to the conditions of their existence. But, as Mr. Spencer profoundly informs us, all unfitness to the conditions of existence has a constant tendency to die out, or disappear, and must eventually do so. Therefore all death must eventually die out or disappear. The happy time is therefore coming in which the trees will no longer die, the horses will no longer die, and, joyful to think, man will no longer die, but will be endowed with an immortality on earth—the very conclusion at which the ridiculous William Godwin arrived, in his delirious ravings about "the perfectibility of man," but which Mr. Spencer has not shown the acumen to perceive is the inevitable result of his absurd logic about "the Evanescence of Evil."

It is with regret that we have to take leave of so great a thinker, as Mr. Spencer undoubtedly is in the main, with such a discreditable exhibition of his reasoning. But what is here said to his disparagement cannot invalidate what we have already said as to his claims to distinguished consideration for the highly valuable ideas which he has so powerfully contributed to impress upon the thought of the world in regard to the true Philosophy of Society. The sun has his spots; Jupiter sometimes nods; and Herbert Spencer has occasionally played the fool with his great ideas.

§ 29. Before taking final leave of these two great thinkers, it may be well to notice, by way of contrast, the most essential difference between their great practical aim, the aim which is common to both, and that of the author of the present work. By these sharp points of contrast the real views of different reasoners come most clearly to the view. Comte and Spencer, though more especially the former, aim at the improvement of society—the author of this work aims merely at the improvement of the ideas or knowledge of men in regard to society. They aim at reforming the morals of the world—he at merely reforming the intelligence of the world. They hope, at least, and expect some radical improvement of the morals of the world—being altogether too great philosophers not to perceive that such improvement must come, if it come at all, in the natural order of "progress," or "evolution" —that it must come as a "natural growth," as Spencer has so clearly and beautifully shown. The author of this work hardly dares hope for any such improvement, much less expect it. When the religion of Jesus has failed, so sadly failed, what hope is there for man—that he can ever be rendered essentially better than he has heretofore been?* Has not all experience, indeed, tended to show that men grow in knowledge, but that, alas, in virtue or true wisdom, they for ever stand still? In this view the author has the entire concurrence of Buckle—a greater thinker than either Comte or Spencer—who regards intellectual progress as the only real progress of which mankind are capable.

While Comte and Spencer both aim, or at least hope, to change, in some essential respects, the system of society, the writer of these pages aims and hopes simply to explain it. In this, he respect-

---

* That the world has been somewhat improved by the religion of Jesus, see the chapter on Christianity in the author's unpublished work. Part II. of this series.

fully submits, that he more nearly represents the true Newton of Sociology. The Newton of Astronomy did not aim, did not presumptuously aspire to change, in any respect, the system of worlds, but simply to explain it. Scarcely less presumptuous is the attempt of the Social Philosopher to change the system of human society, which is, in fact, the logical conclusion derivable from the premises of both Comte and Spencer, not less than of Buckle, though they do not, like Buckle, strictly adhere to their premises.

There is, to be sure, this important difference between the system of worlds and the system of human society, that the knowledge of man concerning the former cannot exert any influence whatever upon it, while it may and must have some necessary influence upon the latter. And this is the only ground of hope entertained by the writer of these pages.

In so far as improvement of men's knowledge, concerning the true principles of human society, must exert a necessary influence in modifying their conduct, so far and no farther is there any reliable hope of human improvement. And when it is considered that right knowledge tends to teach men, not only how to do right, but that it is their true interest to do right, considerable hope of improvement from this source may not unreasonably be entertained. But let it not be too much over-estimated, as it is too apt to be by that class of reasoners who, like Godwin and Spencer, are capable of being led away by the absurd idea of human perfectibility. Men are not governed by their judgments alone, but to a great extent also by their appetites and passions. These repeatedly lead men to do wrong, against their own convictions, nay, their very desires to do right—so that it is emphatically true, as the poet has expressed it—

"I see the right, and approve it, too,
Despise the wrong, and yet the wrong I do."

Men habitually do wrong against their own interests, and against a certain general desire to do right, and to abstain from the wrongful acts which they habitually practise. What drunkard, gambler, or debauchee, so lost to all sense of right and virtue as not to know that it is not his interest to continue in the practice of those vices which he habitually practises? Yet he continues to practice them, and will continue to do so. If men will thus knowingly do wrong, even to themselves, against their own interests, what hope is there that they can ever be prevented from doing wrong to others, by the mere knowledge that it is their interest not to do so?

There is no hope of it. There is no hope for the eradication of evil from the human constitution, or what to our contracted view so appears. There is no hope for any radical improvement in the human condition. Passion will ever be more potent than reason, and that passion will ever prompt men to do what reason disapproves. It has ever been so. It will ever be so. The past is the true type of the future. There is no fundamental change to be expected in man, or in any race of plants or animals.* It is utterly unphilosophical to expect it.

Let all delusive hopes of any great or radical change in the human condition be dismissed from philosophical contemplation. Let no one fondly dream that human life, at least in its terrestrial phase, can ever be rendered essentially different from what it has ever been—a great battle-field of antagonistic principles—a battle-field in which truth and error, good and evil, virtue and vice, happiness and misery, will continue to wrestle together in mortal agony "unto the last syllable of recorded time."

---

* Cousin well says, "Man changes much, but not fundamentally." See work so often quoted. Lec. VI., p. 189.

CHAPTER XIII.

THE AMERICAN CONTRIBUTION TO SOCIAL PHILOSOPHY BRIEFLY CONSIDERED—WEBSTER, CALHOUN, AND HENRY JAMES PARTICULARLY NOTICED—THE LATE GREAT WAR GLANCED AT, AND THE LESSONS IT INCULCATES.

§ 1. As the two writers, considered in the foregoing chapter, stand at the head of the column of most advanced thinkers in Social Philosophy, so American society stands at the head of the column of most advanced experimenters in that philosophy, if, indeed, it may not be said to stand at the head of the column of advancing humanity. Relatively speaking, where Comte and Spencer stand theoretically, American society stands practically. As they stand in the world of thought, that society stands in the world of action.

It has been well and beautifully said by Victor Cousin: " In universal life nothing perishes ; everything is metamorphosed and appears anew ; mechanics and physics reappear in chemistry, and chemistry in vegetable physiology, which again finds a place in the economy of animal nature." Nor is this observation any less true of the moral than of the material realm, of the world of mind than of the world of matter.

The former thought and effort of the world, in regard to the improvement of society, have not been lost. They are preserved essentially in American institutions, and live in the society which embodies those institutions. American society is the lineal outcome of all antecedent society, and of all anterior theories, speculations, reasonings, and experiments in human society. It is the latest product of the combined wisdom of all the past.

With all its imperfections and errors, with all its omissions of what is good in the past, and adoptions of what is bad in the present, or its premature adoptions of what appertains more properly to the future than the present of human affairs, American society may be regarded as the nearest approximation that has ever yet been made, on any large scale, towards the realization of that state for which the aspirations of the human soul are constantly yearning, and towards which all true Social Philosophy must ever direct its aims—that state which has been so justly defined by Rousseau, and to which he has contributed so little that is really valuable—the state which joins "the considerations of natural right and public interest, so that justice and utility may never be disunited."*

Our review of the most advanced ideas in Social Philosophy would evidently, therefore, be very incomplete, if it should omit all reference to American society, and whatever contribution it may have made, either theoretically or practically, to that philosophy. For in America practical results must be important in their suggestions, if not accompanied by corresponding speculation, or an order of thought competent to deduce the most important conclusions from such results. It is to America, indeed, that the world should look for instruction in Social Philosophy. It is there that we should naturally expect to find the true Newton of Sociology. For where the highest experiments are attainable, there the highest attainments in science are properly to be anticipated. "To whom much is given, of them will much be expected."

§ 2. The student of human society enjoys many advantages in America—advantages which cannot be obtained in any other part of the world. There the anatomy of all anterior social life lies open to his view, in the higher organism which it has at last attained in American society. Through that highly wrought organism he can look down through all the lower stages of social life—down to the PROTOZOIC, which Mr. Spencer very justly recognizes in the society of the Bushmen.† As it has been said that the modern school-boy could teach the most renowned geographer of antiquity a good deal about geography, may it not be said that the American school-boy can teach the most eminent

---

* Social Contract. Book I., Ch. I., p. 1.

† See article on the Social Organism, in Illustrations of Universal Progress, p. 399. Am. Ed., 1865.

Sociologist of other lands some important lessons in Sociology? Can he not teach him how vain and fallacious are the calculations which they make, the high expectations which they found, upon the improvement of the mere political institutions of a people?

Of how many errors may the student of society be saved who enjoys the advantages of regarding it from the high stand-point of American society! Of how many miscalculations, delusive remedies, and vain hopes, may he save himself the anxiety! Of how much error and miscalculation might as eminent thinkers even as Comte and Spencer have been delivered, had they enjoyed these advantages! They have built large hopes for humanity, to a great extent, at least, although not exclusively, upon nothing more than what has been enjoyed in America for nearly a century— upon political institutions and civil rights, which have been so long enjoyed and regarded as well settled there, among the white race at least, that they had lost their value in common estimation, and were recklessly thrown away by the people in their late insane war—it may not unreasonably be hoped, not as yet finally or irreclaimably thrown away.

We might almost say that American society begins where the speculations of Comte and Spencer on the Philosophy of Society end. These reasoners may be almost said to rest from their labors where those of the American statesmen practically begin. Equitable government, equality of political franchises, equality of civil rights—political authority founded on the consent of the governed, universal suffrage, universal "equal freedom," as Mr. Spencer expresses it—seem to have constituted the great practical ends at which they aimed—the ends, at least, from which they hoped great things. But of what avail, asks American society, would be the realization of these desired ends? What use are mankind going to make of these blessings when they obtain them? American society affords but too faithful an answer to these questions. America threw away all that just a day or two ago.

§ 3. A practical and familiar acquaintance with American society might have suggested an important idea or two to these too hopeful philosophers—especially to the specious, the plausible, and visionary Spencer, with his fantastic absurdity about "the evanescence of evil." It might have taught them both, and especially Mr. Spencer, who needed the lesson most, where the real difficulty of any great improvement of human society lies. It might have taught them that the difficulty amounts to impossibility. It might have taught them, too forcibly to be mistaken even by Mr. Spencer, that the difficulty does not lie in man's "conditions" alone, as he so systematically and superficially argues, but in MAN himself. They might have found in American society a great practical illustration of the way in which mankind may be expected to treat the very best institutions, the very greatest blessings, that the wisdom of man, combined with the rarest favors of Fortune, can confer upon them. They might have learned that mankind are ever too apt to treat such blessings like the base Athenian who voted to ostracize Aristides because he was tired of hearing him called "the just."

This much, at least, one may learn from the study of American society, if nothing more. Practically, indeed, much may be learned from a critical survey and examination of that society, although theoretically or speculatively but little. Thought or speculative inquiry has been but little directed to Social Philosophy as yet in America, except in relation to mere politics. The American contribution to Social Philosophy, from the theoretical point of view, for the most part, indeed, appertains exclusively to the Political System of thought, and, as such, has been already noticed in the previous work of the author devoted to the review of that system. In so far as its theoretical contribution to any higher system of thought is concerned, we are without any formal treatise or systematic effort to direct our inquiries, unless, indeed, we may except the masterly work of Calhoun on Government, which may be regarded as a mere incidental effort to the great business of his life. Such contribution is to be found rather in the mere droppings, if we may so speak, from the larger thoughts of the larger minds of America.

We take no notice, of course, in this connection, of some pretentious efforts that have emanated from the American press— such, for example, as the ridiculous effusions of Mr. Henry C.

Carey, first published in 1837, under the title of "Principles of Political Economy," subsequently revamped, and published in 1848, under the preposterous title of "The Past, Present, and Future," and still more recently again revamped, and published to the world in 1858, under the pretentious title of "Principles of Social Science." The author has already wasted time enough in exposing the ridiculous absurdities of these successive effusions of diluted balderdash, in his chapter on the Anti-Malthusians,* of whom Mr. Carey is most essentially one, although he founds his ridiculous reasonings upon the conjoint endeavor to overthrow not only Malthus on Population, but also Ricardo on Rent, with some incidental exceptions to the indisputable truths established by Adam Smith. These ridiculous and hugely voluminous effusions belong exclusively to the illimitable realm of VERBIOLOGY, and have no place whatever in the realm of THOUGHT.

§ 4. The larger minds of America have hitherto devoted themselves almost exclusively to practice rather than theory, to art rather than science, to business rather than philosophy—in short, to the world of action rather than the world of thought. The only noteworthy departures from these general tendencies, besides the masterly disquisitions on the Principles of Government, already considered in our review of the Political System of Thought, are to be observed in the department of History, in which America has already presented to the world some admirable specimens. The historical compositions of Irving, Prescott, and Motley, deservedly outrank the arid pages of Hume, the pompous strains of Gibbon, and the tediously brilliant effusions of the constantly overwrought Macaulay. Nor should we, perhaps, omit from this category the highly meritorious Bancroft, although somewhat less resembling the true Herodotus.

Incidentally, however, some of the larger minds of America have thrown out some valuable ideas in regard to the Philosophy of Society, which it is the leading design of the present chapter to notice. Omitting all reference to valuable ideas, rare gems of

---

* See Part V. of this series, Ch. IX.

thought, that occasionally drop from the political press of America, and attest the undeveloped capacity for a higher system of thought than has hitherto prevailed in regard to the phenomena of society, we shall notice only some thoughts that have escaped from three preëminent intellects, two of the political realm, and one of the theological—Webster, Calhoun, and Henry James.

When we contemplate the wonderful proportions of those two colossal intellects of the political realm, we can scarcely refrain from exclaiming regretfully how much might have been gained for science if they had expended their power on the world of thought, instead of squandering it on the world of action What a blessing, indeed, would it be for mankind, if they could only attain to a little more *thought*, and a little less *action !* It is an old proverb, "think twice before you speak once." Of how many incalculable ills might mankind save themselves, if they could only be prevailed upon to think *thrice* before they *act* once.

§ 5. The American public have been so much accustomed to hearing another great name associated with those of Webster and Calhoun, that with them it may appear odd to hear those two mentioned without the other. Clay, Webster, and Calhoun were the three great contemporary magnates of America, who can scarcely ever be named except in connection with each other. They were the living TRINITY of American statesmanship. They were the great TRIUMVIRATE, whose parliamentary conflicts were appropriately referred to in the contemporary press of the day, as "the war of the giants." Of these three the first named was undoubtedly the greatest, as an orator, a leader, and practical statesman. His was the intellect to which, in great emergencies, all looked for direction. His was the clarion voice before which all others became silent. His was the creative energy which spake the word, and it was done. Practically he was the superior of both his illustrious compeers. Theoretically he was their inferior. In moral power, on which successful action far more depends than on purely intellectual, he was incalculably their superior. In intellectual power he was decidedly their inferior.

There are three kinds of great men—the great in thought,

speech, and action. Clay was the great man alike in speech and action. He was the great orator, the great actor, the great MAN to plan and execute, and, of course, *to think*, so far as relates immediately to the exigencies of the crisis. Webster and Calhoun were great in thought. They looked into the past, they penetrated the future, and regarded the present in relation to both, to a far greater extent than their great compeer seems to have done, or perhaps was capable of doing. They appreciated principles much more thoroughly—he their practical applications only.

Henry Clay was the great man of his day and generation; but he has bequeathed no great thought to posterity. Daniel Webster and John Caldwell Calhoun have left thoughts that will live after them—not such rare or valuable thoughts, indeed, as might have been expected from such highly endowed intellects, but sufficiently so to arrest a passing notice. Hence it is that we have some special remarks to make here on these two great ones, and none on the other.

§ 6. It is remarkable that the most valuable thought ever uttered by Webster, having any direct relation to the Philosophy of Society, was thrown out informally and casually at a public dinner. Had all else that this great statesman ever spoke or wrote been lost, the world would have been no great loser thereby; because all else that he ever said, the world had been repeatedly and eloquently told before. But the thought embodied, however imperfectly, in that dinner speech, the world has been too seldom told, and its value, as in so many other cases, is in proportion to the limited extent of its circulation, and familiarity to the common view. In a speech delivered at a public dinner in Baltimore, on the 18th of May, 1843, this great statesman said: "Depend upon it, gentlemen, it is change and apprehension of change that unnerves every working man's arm in this section of country. Changes felt and changes feared are the bane of industry and enterprise."*

Here we have a partial and imperfect expression of the great

---

* See Nile's Register for 1843, or Vol. LXIV., p. 219.

fundamental truth, which constitutes one of the four grand corner-stones of the true system of Social Philosophy, that, *the essential nature of the* IMMEDIATE *evils of all bad government is* UNCERTAINTY—the uncertainty which they beget in the public mind as to the future—the impression which they create that no dependence can be placed on the action of the government and the stability of its policy—the inevitable consequence of which is a general and wide-spread *paralysis* of national industry and enterprise. It is but an approximative expression, to be sure, of this great truth, but so nearly approximative as readily to suggest it, or, at least, open the way towards it.

Look where we may, and we shall find verification of this great law. Look where we may, and we shall find proof, not only that " changes felt and changes feared are," as Webster has so justly said, " the bane of industry and enterprise," but that the essential nature of the *immediate* evils of all bad government is resolvable into this influence—the influence of UNCERTAINTY, and apprehension of CHANGE.

We speak not here of any other evils of bad government, than those that are IMMEDIATE in their influence. We speak not of indirect or remote evils or influences. We speak not of that influence which the government of states may exert, and must inevitably exert, to a greater or less extent, in moulding the character, and thus indirectly shaping the destiny, of nations. We speak only of direct and immediate influences, and such as the vast majority of mankind concern themselves about, almost exclusively. And we say, let these influences only be *stable, fixed,* and *certain*—let us only know what they are going to be, and it matters not what they may be, or matters but little. Let us only know what the action of government is going to be, in respect to taxation, or in any other respect—let us but know whether the government is going to tax us to the extent of *five* per cent. on our net income, or *twenty-five* per cent., and we may triumph over its action however burdensome, and prosper under it all—provided always, and, of course, that the burdens of taxation be not so great as *to paralyze industry or enterprise.* For when it does this, then it strikes into the very vitals, alike of individual and national prosperity. Then it strikes into the very SOUL of man. And there it is, as we shall ever find, that the true sources of his prosperity lie. Paralyze not the industry or energy of man, by imposing too heavy burdens upon it, however certain and fixed, much less by bewildering it with UNCERTAINTY as to what the burdens are to be, and you still leave open to him the door of hope—you still leave it morally and socially possible for him to prosper.

Give us but an industrious, intelligent, provident people, and a STABLE government—a government whose action can be depended on, can be calculated on—and you give us all the essential elements of national prosperity, in so far as they lie open to the view and admit of calculation. It matters not IMMEDIATELY, again we say, what sort of government it may be, provided only it be *stable* —provided only it be fixed and certain in its policy. It matters not what may be its form, or outward appearance. "The forms of government let fools contest." A man may prosper under any form of government—under one government as well as another— under the government of England as well as under that of Massachusetts; and under the government of Russia as well as under either, provided only the government, in each case, rigidly adheres to its legitimate business, of simply protecting the individual in his honest industry, of simply letting him alone itself, and guaranteeing that he shall be let alone by others—in other words, provided it only insures to him stability, or CERTAINTY, in so far indeed as CERTAINTY is attainable by man.

§ 7. What then!—it may be asked—is the government of a state a matter of no importance, except in respect to the stability or certainty of its action? Undoubtedly it is, but not *immediately*. Indirectly and remotely it is of essential importance in other respects. For, be it remembered, as already stated, that one of the conditions of national prosperity, of social well-being, nay, the grand main condition, is, an industrious, intelligent, and provident people. Now are not some governments more favorable to this condition than others? Undoubtedly; and such governments are, *cæteris paribus*, the best. Most essentially speaking, indeed, that is the best government for a people which, under all the circumstances, is the most favorable to this condition.

Is a republican government preferable to a monarchical one? It is precisely because it is a government most favorable to the development of industry, intelligence, and providence, among the people. It is the government most likely to foster self-reliance, which is the true parent of success in life. It is the government most favorable to the development of those qualities on which success in life mainly depends; although, unhappily, it is not the government for which all people are properly qualified, which all people are capable of using without too greatly abusing.

In this connection, too, we may readily see why it is not well for a people to be heavily burdened with taxation, however stable, certain, and fixed that taxation may be. It is because the moral effect of it, the *remote* effect, is bad. It is because it strikes, like every form of bad government, at the SOUL of man, and the inmost fountains of his prosperity. It has therefore been well said, by that profound observer and philosopher for all time, Sir Francis Bacon, "The blessing of Judah and Issachar will never meet: that the same people or nation should be both the lion's whelp and the ass between two burdens; neither will it be that a people overlaid with taxes should ever become valiant or martial."* Nor less significantly to the same point has he spoken, where, in the same connection, he has said, "that no people overcharged with tribute is fit for empire." Let the overtaxed nations ponder this.

§ 8. Let us not, however, lose sight of the important idea which the great name of Webster has been here invoked to substantiate or illustrate, that the IMMEDIATE evils of all bad government are, most essentially, resolvable into the influence of UNCERTAINTY, and that, consequently, if we would find a true measure or standard by which to estimate the immediately injurious influence of government on the social condition, we may find it in the formula, or problem, *how far is such government* UNCERTAIN *in its action*. This truth is the more valuable because of its rarity, because it is so

---

* Essays of Lord Bacon.

little known or considered, or rather, because it is so wholly unknown and unconsidered. As with every other great fundamental truth, mankind are slow in coming to its recognition. For here, as elsewhere, we find the great law verified, that the most fundamental truths are always the very ones that come last into view.

But it is assuredly time that mankind had come to the recognition of this important truth. THE CLOCK OF TIME HAS STRUCK TWELVE. We are in the afternoon of human existence. It is high time that mankind had come to know something about the real nature of those ills against which they have been constantly clamoring since the world began. It is high time that they had come to know that it is not high taxation that really oppresses them, but UNCERTAINTY of taxation—that it is not anything which stands permanently established in human society, in political forms, governmental action, or the like, that really or necessarily and directly tends to their injury, but that which is forever unsettled, uncertain, and bids defiance to all attempts to calculate what it will be.

It is high time that we had come to know, and understand, that it is in the power of a people to triumph over every other evil emanating from their government except instability, uncertainty, constant apprehension of change, an abiding sense that nothing can be depended upon—that, if they have within themselves the requisite moral energies to insure success in life, they can triumph over every other political ill but this, and that the fault is therefore with themselves if they do not succeed and prosper, provided only they have this one grand and indispensable political desideratum—stability, certainty, permanent security against arbitrary and capricious molestation, either on the part of state authority or that of individuals.

This great truth has been already appreciated to some extent, and in respect to some kinds of government; but, by a too natural obtuseness of vision, it has not been discerned that it applies even more forcibly to other kinds of governments, and such as are apparently of a diametrically opposite character. It has been commonly enough recognized in regard to Democracies; and we have accordingly heard quite enough in regard to the evils, in this respect, of the turbulent Democracies of Greece, that voted hemlock to their heroes one day, and statues on the next. But it has not been so commonly recognized, nay, it does not seem ever to have been suspected, even by so great a statesman as the one immediately under review, that it applies still more forcibly to another kind of government, and that it is precisely for this reason that a worse kind of government is possible than an unlimited Democracy—namely, an unlimited Monarchy.

Why are unlimited monarchies, generally speaking, and subject only to some few qualifications and exceptions, the worst of all governments? Most essentially speaking, it is precisely because they are the most capricious, unstable, and uncertain in their action, of all governments. The very opposite of this is, indeed, the view commonly entertained. Superficial reasoners, sentimental philosophers, represent absolute monarchies as the most stable of all governments. They speak with tremulous horror of what they well enough term "the calm of despotism," and seem to regard it as the synonym of stability. But they are most essentially mistaken as to the real nature of this "calm." It is the calm not of stability, but of instability—the calm resulting from a fatal UNCERTAINTY as to the future, which rests like a deadly spell upon the public mind, and paralyzes all its healthful energies.

Why that death-like calm which pervades all Russia? Is it the result of stability, with the corresponding sense of security, so indispensable to the true welfare of states? Or is it not rather the result of a fatal insecurity, a disastrous UNCERTAINTY what an hour may bring forth? In an hour, in a moment, at any moment, an order may come, like a thief in the night, to any Russian—"Prepare to leave. It is the Imperial ukase. Your orders are—to Siberia. The Czar Nicolai wills it. Let no man dare inquire why."

What is the great bane of all countries cursed by Turkish despotism? It is the fatal sense of insecurity, the disastrous UNCERTAINTY which pervades all minds. Look at Egypt, the former granary of the world, more fertile than the richest garden of other lands! Why lies it now waste—crawled over by vermin, rather than men? It is the fatal insecurity, uncertainty, which paralyzes all industry, all energy. It is because nothing is fixed, nothing stable, in the action of the government. It is because the Pacha of Egypt does not exact of his subjects any fixed rate of taxation —not one-fourth, one-half, or even three-fourths of the crop—but just as much as he may feel inclined to take—it may be all—it may be whatever his rascally subalterns can lay their hands on. It is obvious enough what must be the inevitable effects of such a condition of society upon the general habits, as well as character, of a people. It is very obvious that, under such circumstances, men will have no adequate motive to labor for anything, except what they can hide from the government. What must be the state of things in a society where industry and enterprise are thus fettered, restricted, and paralyzed? Very evidently, just what we find it in all countries cursed by Turkish rule.

§ 9. The most essentially valuable ideas of the great American statesman John Caldwell Calhoun, that have immediate relation to the Philosophy of Society, are most concisely, and, at the same time, most systematically expressed in his able "Disquisition on Government," a work of some 107 pages, octavo, published at Charleston in 1851, and evidently intended, though not so expressed, as an introduction to his more particular "Discourse on the Constitution and Government of the United States," which immediately follows it in the same volume. Most essentially considered, this work may be defined, in brief, as a powerful reaction or protest, springing up in the very heart and centre of the great democratic spirit of the age, against the false, though commonly received idea, THAT THE MAJORITY HAVE THE ABSOLUTE RIGHT TO RULE THE MINORITY. The grand leading aim of the illustrious author in that work evidently was to ascertain how the rights of MINORITIES are to be protected in republican governments.

Somewhat differently, somewhat more generally, and less explicitly, does he express his object, where he defines it as consisting in the endeavor to determine the question:—"How can those who are invested with the powers of government be prevented from employing them as the means of aggrandizing themselves, instead of using them to protect and preserve society?"* Somewhat more explicitly, though not quite explicitly enough, does he define his object a little further on, where he says: "What I propose is—to explain on what principles government must be formed, in order to resist, by its own interior structure—or, to use a single term, *organism*—the tendency to abuse power."†

Neither of these definitions, however, so essentially and explicitly expresses the real aim of the author in question as does that which we have given above. For here again we have to note the truth, that men do not always, nor even generally, appreciate the full significance of their own utterances, reasonings, or aims. To do this is, indeed, the consummation of philosophy, and must come last—must come towards the close of a long and brilliant train of researches and reasonings in every science—as did the *Principia Mathematica* of Newton.

§ 10. The plan by which the great statesman under review proposed to accomplish this great desideratum, of protecting minorities, and preventing governments from abusing the powers confided to them, was, *to take the sense of the community on every question by its separate component parts, or separate distinguishable interests—to take the vote by concurrent majorities—so that each separate component part, or distinguishable interest, may hold in its hands a check against the action of the others.* "All constitutional governments," he very justly remarks, "of whatever class they may be, take the sense of the community by its parts—each through its appropriate organ; and regard the sense of all its parts, as the sense of the whole."‡

Hence his peculiar views, so rarely appreciated, and so extensively unpopular, in regard to "state rights" in the American system of government. Here we detect the philosophy of those views, or the fundamental idea on which they rest, as far as that idea was appreciated by him. In order to protect minorities, in order to represent every distinguishable interest in the vast confederacy of American states, he proposed to give to each state a negative upon the action of all the rest—an ultimate negative, or

---

* Discourse on Government, p. 8.   † Same, p. 11.   ‡ Same, pp. 36–7.

negative, as a last resort; nay, he maintained that such right existed in accordance with the federal constitution. This was the right of "Nullification," so much discussed in American politics.

Suffice it to say here, where we can touch but briefly these great questions of political science and practical statesmanship, that the views of this great statesman, here presented, are partly true, and, perhaps, partly false. Theoretically, or rather fundamentally, they are indisputably true. Practically, or, rather—to speak with more truly philosophical precision*—in *practical* theory, as contradistinguished from *fundamental* theory, it is by no means so clear that they are true; that is to say, that they admit of practical recognition or assertion to so great an extent as is involved in the doctrine of state nullification.

For here we have to confront the fact, so little appreciated or considered by superficial and visionary theorists, that the most fundamental or essential ideas can never be actualized or practically attained. The perfect idea can never be realized, but it must be rightly and duly appreciated. Perfect justice exists only in theory. But it must, nevertheless, be kept constantly before the view in practice. The North Pole can never be reached, but the mariner must keep it constantly in view, and take his reckonings by it. So of truth, reason, justice.

Hence the great business of the statesman, or Social Philosopher, is twofold. He has first to ascertain the right—the true and perfect idea—and, secondly, to decide how far it can be approximated—with a clear understanding that it can never be attained. He has to consider first the RIGHT, secondly the EXPEDIENT. He has to concern himself with both RIGHTS and EXPEDIENCIES, and has at last, however reluctantly, to merge the right in the expedient, that is the perfectly right, or the fundamentally right. For the expedient then becomes the right—the right as far as it is attainable by man, under existing circumstances. Hence, again, the great practical concern of the states-

---

* The author desires here, as elsewhere, to emphasize and rebuke the fool's idea, so widely prevalent—to the shameful discredit of the thought of the age—*that a thing may be right in theory, and yet wrong in practice.* All right practice has indisputably its appropriate theory—its own right theory.

man. or Sociologist, is with EXPEDIENCIES, but nevertheless with expediencies conformed to right—fundamental right—perfect right—as far as under all surrounding circumstances may be found possible.

And here again we catch a clear and distinct view of the fallaciousness of the aims of Mr. Herbert Spencer, in his work on Social Statics, reviewed in the foregoing chapter. For in that work, he considers exclusively the idea of the perfectly just, or perfectly right, in the institutions or laws of human society, without any reference at all to the great truth that this idea can never be realized, and without throwing any light whatever upon the great practical question, to which all true statesmanship has always to address itself—what is, under all the existing circumstances, EXPEDIENT, or, in other words, what is the nearest possible approximation to the perfectly just or perfectly right.

§ 11. It is in respect to the valuable contribution which the great American statesman immediately under review has made to this the primary and fundamental idea for the statesman—the idea of the perfectly just or right, in the arrangement of human society—that we have to commend highly his clear and cogent reasonings. In regard to the practical applications which he has made of those reasonings we are not prepared, by any means, so highly to approve, or even to enter assent. His tendencies in regard to that primary and fundamental idea are in the right direction. They are in identically the same direction with those of Mr. Spencer, as already shown, and those of Mr. James, to be presently more particularly considered. They are identically in the direction in which all really advanced thinkers in the Philosophy of Society are tending—*towards the largest play of* INDIVIDUALISM, *and the eventual triumph of the individual over society.*

Here again, too, we have to note the momentous fact that men, very great men, nay, even the greatest men, or greatest thinkers, of their day, do not fully appreciate or perceive the full and true significance of their own great ideas. This great American thinker, as we have before had occasion to remark,* did not by

---

* See Chapter VI.

any means fully or duly appreciate the essential significance, the true drift, and ultimate tendency of his own reasonings on the true principles of government. Not from lack of capacity, however, did he fail in this; but rather because he considered these great questions only from the stand-point of practical statesmanship, and not from that of fundamental philosophy.

§ 12. It was not given to John C. Calhoun to see that, in his able, though exceedingly brief, "Disquisition on Government," he was developing those germs of thought which naturally expand into the idea of complete Individualism, or the triumph of the individual over society. He saw, indeed, that the true end of government was to protect the weak, of which the minority is but one manifestation, and, consequently, that one of its main ends was to protect minorities. But he did not see that the MINORITY, to be protected by human society in its ultimate analysis, is reducible to *one*—that the individual is the ultimate integral atom or molicule—the true elementary social idea to be conserved—the true sovereign, whose rights are to be protected, vindicated, and maintained.

He saw, indeed, that in order to protect minorities, it was necessary to give them, to some extent, a negative power in the action of majorities. But he did not see that in order to vindicate the idea at which he was thus aiming, to its most complete, thorough, and elementary or radical extent, it was necessary to give each individual in society a *negative* upon the action of the rest—as we see illustrated in the organization of *juries*—to invest each citizen with the *quasi* character of a Roman tribune—to ordain, in short, that no governmental action, except, indeed, what relates to the *mala per se*, shall be of binding force in society unless it obtain the UNANIMOUS CONSENT of the society— the consent, at least, of every one of the citizens composing the society, and regarding as such, at least, every adult male person over the age of twenty-five, who is of sound reason and sound average honesty.

This is the true radical idea of Social Statics, in regard to JUSTICE, or the theory of RIGHT. This is the ultimate result of the true Principia Mathematica Philosophiæ Socialis, as attained by the *resolution* of the forces which appertain to the idea of THE RIGHT. But what is the true idea in reference to practice, to EXPEDIENCY, or the nearest attainable approximation to the perfectly right? In other words, what is the result of the true Principia Mathematica Philosophiæ Socialis in its practical conclusions, or in its *composition* of forces, with a view to the great practical idea of attaining the best possible results, or the great ends of expediency? This is the question in regard to which the reasonings of Calhoun go as far beyond the truth, perhaps, as they fall behind it in respect to the elementary idea of right.

§ 13. Every one will readily see that it is utterly chimerical to expect that human society can ever realize the perfect elementary idea of right, that government shall be founded upon the *unanimous* consent of the governed. The nearest possible approximation that can be made to this idea, is that which Calhoun immediately aimed at, namely, that government shall be founded on the unanimous consent *of all the separate distinguishable interests of the society.* This is certainly a just idea, and one not chimerical or visionary to calculate on, as an attainable possibility. But whether it would be expedient, and therefore RIGHT, to attempt to enforce this idea, to the extent at which he aimed, essentially if not avowedly, in regard to a grand confederated government like that of the United States—to the extent of regarding every state of the confederacy as a separate distinguishable interest, and requiring the unanimous consent of all these separate states to the validity of any act of the general government of the confederacy—we may safely assert is more than doubtful, at least, in the present age and condition of the world.

True statesmanship, however, true Social Philosophy will readily discern that some decided approximation to this arrangement in such large political organizations as that of the United States, might be safely attempted, nay, would undoubtedly conduce to good, to harmony, to quietude from too much legislation, to a just restraint on the too great tendencies of mankind to encroach on the just rights of others, under the forms of law. It might be advisable, in such a large confederacy as the American, to recognize as many as two or three, if not four or five, separate and distinguishable sectional interests, and to give to each a check upon the action of the rest, or to require the unanimous consent of the majorities in all of these sections to the validity of every act of the general government.

Some such arrangement as this was actually proposed in the American Congress during the year 1860, by a statesman of no inconsiderable ability, Mr. Clement L. Vallandigham, as a means of harmonizing those great sectional strifes which were then tending rapidly to their too natural ultimate results. Had his project been adopted, it might not only have averted the disastrous war, which has occasioned so much suffering to humanity as well as so much regret to the humane, but taught the world, by practical illustration on a large scale, the most impressive mode of instruction, some highly important lessons in the science of government.

In all such arrangements, however, as that here alluded to, for arresting or restraining the action of government, and constraining it to seek the unanimous approval of society, or approximative unanimity, every wise statesman will readily appreciate the importance of bearing in mind the eminently just observation of Rousseau, that " the more grave and important the deliberations, the nearer ought the determination to approach to unanimity," and that " the more expedition the affair requires, the less should unanimity be insisted on."*

§ 14. The most noteworthy idea presented by the thoughts of Mr. Henry James, is that which we have so often before had occasion to cite, and which is to be found in his essay on Moralism and Christianity, where he says : " This is the last great triumph of humanity, the signal for the complete inauguration of God's kingdom on earth—the triumph of the individual over society." All his other thoughts, that have any direct relation to the Philosophy of Society, are but diversified statements, illustrations, or verifications, of this great idea, so vividly expressed.

---

* Social Contract, Book IV., Chap. II.

This happy expression is destined to an immortal renown, not less, perhaps, than the memorable lines in Gray's Church Yard Elegy, concerning the flower "born to blush unseen and waste its sweetness on the desert air." We cannot refrain here from making some small contribution towards bringing the immortal sentiment into its merited notoriety. It furnishes us, as before stated,* with the true POLARITY by which to take our reckoning as to the true position or drift of human society, in any quarter or age of the world. The position which it describes can never be reached, it is true, any more than the North Pole—we might almost say than the North Star. But it furnishes us, nevertheless, with the guide, by which we may safely take direction in political navigation, and yet larger explorations of the great seas of human destiny.

Do we wish to ascertain how far any state of human society has drifted from the true direction, either by false navigation, or inevitable stress of weather? We have only to inquire *how far is such society distant from that condition in which the individual is triumphant over the society.* Russian society, we shall find, for example, is at a vast distance from that condition†—American society very considerably advanced towards it—Frankish society holding an intermediate position.

§ 15. Let no superficial or short-sighted critic object to this brilliant idea of Henry James, that, more properly, we should accept the very opposite condition, as the true ideal of human society, in its ultimate statical aspects—the condition that may be described as that in which the society is completely triumphant

---

* See Chapter VI.

† In illustration of the true position of Russia, in relation to the idea in question, we cannot forbear quoting the remarks of the Marquis de Custine in his Travels in Russia. "There results from such a social organization," he says, "a form of envy so violent, a stretch of mind towards ambition so constant, that the Russian people will needs be incapable of anything but the conquest of the world. I always return to this expression, because it is the only one that can explain the excessive sacrifices imposed there upon the individual by society."—Travels in Russia, in 1839, Chapter XVI., p. 206.

over the individual. The splendid idea of Henry James, rightly interpreted, and as he evidently intended, is expressive of both ideas. The triumph of the individual over society, as he intended it, is, at the same time, the triumph of society over the individual. It may be more faultlessly defined, indeed, though less brilliantly, as consisting in the complete harmony between the individual and the society. It does not consist in what Robert Owen has stigmatized as "repulsive individualism," as opposed to what he calls "attractive union,"* but in *individualism* completely harmonized with *communism*—an individualism duly subordinated to the general good of society at large—an individualism, so highly enlightened, so wisely instructed, that it recognizes the great truth, towards which all true civilization is constantly tending, THAT THE GOOD OF ALL IS INDISPENSABLE TO THE HIGHEST GOOD OF EVERY ONE.

Thus are the two ideas, apparently contradictory, perfectly harmonized. Is not all truth, indeed, harmonious? Does not all true knowledge tend to the harmonizing of apparent discords? Said we not rightly, often before in these pages, that he alone is the true philosopher whose system comprehends and harmonizes all systems? It is only, the little, narrow mind, that is forever cavilling at the ideas of others, attempting to excite opposition and beget strife in regard to them. The true philosopher finds only harmony where the simpleton finds only discord.

Justly was it remarked by Aristotle, in his famous work on Politics, that "the best test of a happy mixture of a democracy and an oligarchy"—which he wisely regards as the best of governments—"is found when one may properly call the same state both a democracy and an oligarchy."† Not less justly may we make a similar remark concerning the two great model governments of the present age—those of Britain and America—either of which may be rightly described as either a limited monarchy, or a limited democracy—the king in one, it is true, being elective, but exercising the greater powers, for that very reason, and the democratical element in the other being less obviously manifest,

---

* See Owen's " Book of the New Moral World," p. 263. Am. Ed. 1845.
† Aristotle's Politics, as translated by Walford. Book IV., Ch. IX.

but hardly less potent. To the same point, substantially, we may not less correctly—perhaps somewhat more correctly—describe these two great model governments—the one as a highly aristocratical republic—the other as a highly democratical one.

These examples should illustrate clearly enough how apparent discords may be substantially harmonized, and render it less difficult to understand how the triumph of the individual over society may be in entire harmony with the triumph of the society over the individual, although apparently antagonistic ideas.

§ 16. Entirely in harmony with the great idea just noticed, which Henry James has contributed to the world, are his more particular reasonings on government, as expressed in his essay on "Democracy and its Issues." In that splendid and intensely penetrative essay he clearly recognizes the great idea, already suggested while reviewing the ideas of Calhoun on Government, that the real tendency of all true human progress is towards the denial of all government that does not express the *unanimous* will, or consent of society—which is evidently, still more essentially to speak, the denial of all government by the aggregate force of the society—all government except that of the individual over himself, which is, most essentially defined, TRUE SELF-GOVERNMENT.

His lucid words, in illustration of this great truth should be incorporated immediately into the great body of the now forming and ultimate Philosophy of Society. On this point, he says: "Democracy, then, is still imperfectly embodied, even among us;" —meaning of course Americans—"monarchy asserts the rule of one man; aristocracy the rule of a minority. Our institutions assert the rule of a majority. These latter, consequently exhibit a very decided advance upon the old institutions, but are by no means conclusive. They indicate the progress of the democratic idea, but are very far short of giving it a complete expression. If the rule of a majority be valid against that of a minority, much more must the rule of the whole be valid as against that of a mere majority; and so far, accordingly, sustain and subserve the sentiment of democracy. But when the sentiment becomes fully acknowledged, or attracts the universal homage of mankind, it will disown our present political institutions, no less than all past ones. It will disown, in fact, all merely *political*, and claim purely social manifestations."*

We must close our brief review of this eminently suggestive thinker, with the remark that he seems, in the passage last quoted, to anticipate, as an attainable result, a state of society which the true Social Philosopher must ever regard as a merely ideal state, by which the validity of principles and the utility of tendencies are to be tested. It has been justly remarked by an eminent political economist, Nassau William Senior, that "Political Economy does not deal with particular facts, but general tendencies."† Nor is the observation any less applicable to the larger science of Sociology, of which Political Economy is but one of the handmaids, and which it is the business of Social Philosophy to cultivate and improve. Not as indicative of any probably attainable state of society, therefore, let it be understood that the foregoing words of Mr. James have been quoted approvingly; but rather as indicative merely of TENDENCIES by which actual states of society are to be considered and estimated.

§ 17. Our brief review of American society and its teachings, should not be concluded without noticing the signal lesson it has practically afforded, by its late great intestinal war, of one great truth in Social Philosophy, often before asserted in these pages, but by no means generally accepted, *that it is the* MAN *that makes the* INSTITUTION, *not the institution that makes the man*—that mankind are the architects of their own fortunes, and the true *proximate* cause alike of their own enjoyments and their own sufferings.‡ If there were any doubt remaining, as to this truth before, it must be dispelled by the signal teachings of this extraordi-

---

* Lectures and Miscellanies of H. James, article on Democracy and its Issues, pp. 6, 7.

† Senior's Political Economy, p. 102, Ed. 1854.

‡ The author must request that he be understood explicitly, as speaking here of proximate and not original causes—as speaking, in short, in a merely *physical* sense, and not in a *metaphysical*, or the highest philosophical sense. Other-

nary and gigantic war, with all its stupendous train of consequent evils.

If the earth should suddenly experience a grand convulsion upheaving a continent, and submerging other extensive portions of land, the real process of geological transformations, as they are often effected, although seldom, if ever, on so large a scale, could not be rendered more manifest, than that of sociological transformations has been rendered by this war. It constitutes one of those grand transition epochs in human history, that has been consummated so quickly and vividly to the view, that there can be no mistaking the true motive power by which it has been immediately effected. It was clearly the work of the people themselves, who had the power in their own hands, and wantonly threw it away —that power, which in aftertimes they will be vainly seeking to reclaim, and clamoring against the injustice of denying to them, when it was their own reckless hands that threw it away, or madly lavished it on political tricksters and military tyrants.

This was not one of those slow movements, obscured by the night of barbaric ages, the true operation of which could not clearly be discerned, and concerning which there could be no conclusive contradiction to the specious assertions of ignorant brawlers, and canting, hypocritical, shallow demagogues, that the pure and innocent people had been robbed or cheated out of their rights, by the superior force or strategy of the few, without any fault on the part of the many. This was done in the daylight—in the daylight of the highest civilization—almost in a single day; and there can be no mistaking its real agency and causes.

The people themselves did it. The people have been in this case, as in nearly all others, the responsible agents of their own ruin. They rushed madly on their own destruction. They threw away the noblest institutions ever enjoyed by mankind with their own rash and reckless hands. They threw away a

---

wise a palpable inconsistency in his philosophical system, as developed here and elsewhere, even in these pages, might be inferred. Really, most essentially, most fundamentally, man is not the CAUSE of anything. He is a mere EFFECT, a mere phenomenon, or grand CONGERIES of effects or phenomena.

government founded upon the noble idea of the consent of the governed, and substituted in its stead a government of force, of arrogance, of insulting *coercion*. In order to oppress others they become willing to be oppressed themselves. In order to deprive others of their rights, they were willing to be deprived of their own. In order to gratify their malignant hostilities toward their neighbors, they invoked principles that must bring down destruction upon their children and their children's children. In their demented zeal for liberty they trampled out the most sacred principles of liberty. Avowing their abhorrence of slavery, they proved, by their acts, that the only slavery they really abhorred, was that which deprived them of the liberty of doing just whatsoever they pleased, without regard for the rights or liberties of other men.

Such is the nature of man. The acts which we here condemn in the American people cannot properly be imputed to them in particular. They are the acts of humanity, and such as mankind in general are constantly prone to commit, under like circumstances, and when losing nearly all sense of reason, they are carried away by highly-excited passion. The American people were as little likely to act so unwisely and culpably as any others, under the like extraordinary circumstances. No people have ever been more generally possessed of the requisite qualities for the highest form of civilization. No people have ever been endowed with a more liberal spirit, a more generally enlightened judgment, or more truly humane sentiments. What hope is there, then, of man, when such a people, a people upon whom so many cherished hopes were centred, and with such good grounds, have acted so unwisely, rashly, fatally!

The satire which we here pronounce directly against the American people, or rather the dominant party of that people, is, therefore, to be regarded as a satire on man, of whose real nature American society has exhibited, in the acts under review, but too faithful a portrait. The censure falls immediately upon the people of the North, or rather the adherents of the Federal Government, whether North or South; but, *mutatis mutandis*, it may be applied with almost equal justice to those of the South, except, indeed, that the highly culpable follies of that section were confined to a minority of the people. But under like circumstances there is no reason to suppose that they would have acted any less culpably than the people of the North. They were the minority section, the weaker party, by far. And the wonder is that, being such, even a minority, so large a minority, could have been found among them advocating so insane a policy as that which has mainly shaped their course for the last quarter of a century—a policy which, instead of seeking, by extraordinary efforts, to conciliate opposition, sought rather to browbeat the rest of mankind into acquiescence with their peculiar, and in many respects extraordinary, views in regard to slavery—a policy so well calculated indeed to exasperate their opponents as to afford much palliation, though surely no justification, for the gigantic follies and crimes of the North.

§ 18. Never before in the history of the world have a people made so rapid and great a descent from the height of prosperity. Occupying the highest position ever attained by human society, on so large a scale, they have come down, in the short period of *half a decade*, to the level of some of the most oppressed nations of the globe, in many important respects. Never before have a people inflicted such great injury upon themselves, and so manifestly by their own folly. Blessed beyond all former example, they have wantonly thrown away their blessings. Strangers to national debt, on any considerable scale, and almost unacquainted with taxation, they have brought down upon themselves and their posterity a stupendous debt with its necessary incubus of taxation, to fetter their industry, and demoralize their virtue. And this they have done under the pretence of necessary war, when a few gentle words of wisdom and of peace, on the part of those in power, would have settled all the difficulties without sacrificing one drop of blood, or one dollar of treasure.

Holding in their own hands, to a far greater extent than any other people, the reins of authority, the direction of their own affairs, they have, by their own acts, transferred them, to a dangerous extent, to the hands of a contrivance called " the government," where all experience has proved they are most liable to be abused. Enjoying political institutions that were the highest result of the accumulated wisdom of ages, and for which their own immediate ancestors had struggled and fought during at least a thousand years, they sacrificed those noble institutions on the unholy shrine of their passions—their partisan furor and sectional hate. For a government nobly resting on the consent of the governed they have wilfully substituted a government resting on the sharp points of the longest bayonets. For the legitimate government of America they have substituted the government of Russia; and over nearly one half of the once great confederacy they have substituted for sovereign states, conquered provinces.

Was it for this that all the toils, struggles, and sufferings of former ages have been endured in order to afford to mankind in America the best government ever yet found to be attainable? Yes, it was only for this. It was only that on having attained it they might by their own follies and crimes wantonly, recklessly, throw it away. This is only in accordance with the great law of human destiny, from which there is no appeal. One generation amasses wealth in order that another may recklessly squander it.

§ 19. Happy might it be for mankind if the evils that have been already inflicted in this mad affair of internal strife, that has rent and torn the great American family, were the last or even the greatest. Happy might it be if the difficulties thus sought to be adjusted, were really settled, as the deluded advocates of those unworthy measures have sought to persuade themselves. Happy might it be, if those who have been the immediate agents of the mischief that has been already done, could themselves escape similar mischief. But there is no ground for any such hope. The eternal laws of justice are not so easily to be evaded. There is an "even-handed justice," not to be escaped, which eventually "commends the ingredients of the poisoned chalice," which we have administered to others, " to our own lips."

In the stern economy of the moral universe there is no such anomaly as "forgiveness of sins." Men cannot escape the consequences of their own acts. They who sow the wind must expect to reap the whirlwind. They who wrong others must expect to be wronged themselves—still more, to have it requited to them *measure for measure.* They who commit murder must expect, in one form or another, to suffer its penalties. And the sacrilegious assassins who immolated the noblest system of government that the world ever saw, upon the altar of their unhallowed passions, need not hope to escape the terrible atonement which, in some form or other, must be their inevitable allotment.

It is but one side of this bloody picture that we have as yet seen. It is but one act of this eventful tragedy that has been as yet enacted. The proscriptions of Sylla have indeed very nearly run their course. But those of Marius are to follow. They who have spent their own rage need not expect to trammel up the rage of others. They who have enjoyed the game of war and "coercion," just so long as it played into their own hands, need not indulge the delusive hope that, so soon as the fortune of the play begins to turn against them, they can arrest its progress by crying peace, peace, there has been enough now of the war game, the coercion policy. The time for peace was before the dragon's teeth had been scattered broad-cast over the land. Acteon may call on his trained dogs to desist. But it will be all in vain, after he has lost the control. Nor will his unavailing cries save him from the doom of being devoured by his own hounds.

"His blood be upon us, and on our children," once cried a wicked rabble, concerning a noble victim whose blood they demanded. Useless invocation! The blood of the slain will rest uninvoked upon the heads of the guilty and their descendants. The sins of the fathers will be visited upon the children. Future generations will mourn the crimes of the present, in sackcloth and ashes, and they will often have occasion to exclaim with anguish, like the murderous woman of the play, in her distempered dream: "HERE IS THE SMELL OF THE BLOOD STILL. NOT ALL THE PERFUMES OF ABABIA WILL SWEETEN THIS LITTLE HAND. OH! OH! OH!"

§ 20. Such is the teaching of the late great war in America in regard to the CAUSES from which really flow the ills of society.

But is there not any correspondent lesson to be deduced in regard to the agency by which those causes are to be counteracted, or at least combated? If we have learned an important lesson from that great event, in regard to the true DIAGNOSIS of social disease, can we not derive any lesson in regard to its THERAPEUTICS? We shall be obtuse observers, poor Social Philosophers, if we cannot.

The great practical lesson which may be deduced from that extraordinary and ever-memorable event in human history, is precisely that which the theoretical teachings of Spencer, Calhoun, and Henry James, as we have already seen, inculcate, and towards which all true Social Philosophy, and all real progress in society, are constantly tending—the importance of imposing greater restraints upon the political authority of states, of restricting the limits of their activity, and requiring, as to many acts of government, the approval of a much larger portion of the community than a bare majority—of a majority approximating UNANIMITY. It inculcates the lesson that a very large majority of the people, a great deal more than a bare majority, should be obtained before the government shall be at liberty to raise its audacious hands in violence against any considerable portion of its disaffected citizens for merely political offences—for mere appeal to the great fundamental right of revolution.

Consider the absurdity and monstrous iniquity of allowing a bare majority to bring down upon the whole of society such stupendous calamities as were involved in the late great war in America. Suppose it had required a majority of at least *three-fourths*, if not *four-fifths*, of both houses of Congress, to inaugurate civil war, on the part of the general government against any one state, or at least any three coterminous states, that had resolved, by the formal action of a majority of their several peoples, to resort to revolutionary measures, either by secession or otherwise. Does not every candid mind see, that if such had been the constitutional law in America, and that law had been respected, all these late terrible calamities would have been avoided—that there would have been no civil war, and no secession, no successful or permanent secession?

Such a constitutional provision would have compelled a compromise of those difficulties, which were the gradual accumulation of *seventy years* of American life—a compromise that would have settled those difficulties. Or, if it had not done this, the secession fever would have soon run its course, and quietly subsided. Or, if even this had not occurred, the worst event would have been a violent effort of the *minority*, in the great conservative states of Virginia, North Carolina, Tennessee, Arkansas, and Missouri—which had refused, by large majorities, to secede, until the insolent policy of " coercion" had been adopted—to force those states out of the Union. This would inevitably have inaugurated civil war within those states; and had the Union party proved too weak, they would undoubtedly have invoked the aid of the general government, which, in that event, would have been entirely legitimate, and unexceptionable to all reasonable men. Thus would the great end, for which the gigantic war was invoked, avowedly at least, have been effected without any great war, if any at all. For without those more conservative and more important states of the South, the more impetuous states that had seceded, before " coercion" had given them really good ground for doing so, would undoubtedly have receded from their unwise position, and fallen back again into the old confederacy.

§ 21. It is indeed a remarkable fact, deserving of more particular consideration here, that the great civil war in America was inaugurated and forced on the people by the minority—by a minority party. The party holding the reins of government at Washington during this war had been elected—although in accordance with the forms of law, and with an indisputable constitutional majority—by an actual *minority* of the people merely. A majority of at least *one million* of the American people were opposed to them. Yet they had the audacity to adopt a policy which even a majority should not have dared to assert, which even a majority should not have been constitutionally allowed to adopt or assert.

By a singular oversight in the wise and provident framers of the American constitution, it was not only allowable that a President might be elected, with a large majority of the people against him, but that he might inaugurate the most momentous measures, not less than ordinary ones, with no larger concurrence of the popular will. So imperfect in some of its features, is that justly-admired constitution. So imperfect and defective are some of the noblest works of man. So much do all human efforts need amendment and reform.

CHAPTER XIV.

GENERAL SUMMARY—THE PRESENT STATUS OF SOCIAL PHILOSOPHY MORE EXPLICITLY DEFINED IN BRIEF—ITS COMMENDABLE THERAPEUTICS—ITS IMPERFECT DIAGNOSIS—ITS COPERNICAN IDEA DISTINCTLY DEFINED—ITS NEWTONIAN IDEA SUGGESTED RATHER THAN DEFINED—CONCLUDING REMARKS.

§ 1. WHAT, then, is the present status of Social Philosophy? Speaking generally, we may say it is in a transition state, or in what a French philosopher might term a provisional state; in which old ideas have, to a great extent, lost their vitality, but the new ones have not as yet acquired sufficient consistency and force to direct thought, or control action, to any important extent. It is in that state in which former systems of thought have been overturned, but no new system has as yet been organized.

§ 2. Still speaking generally, but somewhat less so, we may say that Social Philosophy is, at present, in the condition in which the religious idea was, in the time of the great reformer who has given his name to the present epoch of the world; in whose time men did not so much need any new suggestion in regard to that idea, or to what Mr. Carlyle has well designated as man's "vital relations to this mysterious universe," as some determinate direction for the many suggestions they had already received.

The august mission of that great reformer of thought and feeling, in regard to the religious idea, or the Divine Idea of the world, as interpreted by himself, was accordingly "not to destroy but to fulfil," although, in a certain sense, it was indeed to do away with "old things," and to "render all things new." It was not so much to introduce new ideas as to remodel the old, and accommodate them to the larger ideas of a more advanced humanity; which is in truth for the most part the sole significance of the work of every reformer, however great.

He, indeed, who attempts to do much more than this generally fails to do anything. He who advances too far ahead of his age generally disconnects himself from all sympathy with his age, and thereby loses the power to control or modify it, to any important extent. Accordingly very great thinkers, who seek to reform the thought of the world, as we may readily detect, are very cautious how they utter many of their greatest thoughts, and very manifestly dare not communicate them to the full extent of their significance. This we see strikingly manifested in the teachings of Jesus, although he communicated enough of new truth, enough of his own transcendent inspirations, to cause him to be immolated on the altar of truth, as Socrates had been before, and so many have been since.

The world, in the time of Jesus, was not by any means wanting in the ideas out of which to construct a larger theology, and a higher, a grander morality. There were the sects of the Pharisees, Sadducees, and Essenes, among the Hebrews, who had been discussing those great questions for more than a century, and who were possessed of all the fundamental ideas that mankind have ever been able to obtain, or probably ever will, on these profound mysteries. There were also the schools of the Academics, Epicureans, and Stoics, among the Greeks, who had been discussing them for a much longer time, and which were but different phases of the same forms of opinion that were represented respectively by the Pharisees, Sadducees, and Essenes. For the forms of thought are substantially the same among all nations, and in all ages of the world, and are but few in number.

The Pharisees were substantially the Academics of Hebrew philosophy, the Sadducees were the Epicureans, while the Essenes most essentially represented the Stoics.* This is a substantially a correct classification of those ancient sects and schools, although, of course, not entirely unexceptionable. In some respects the Essenes more nearly resembled the Cynics, while in some the Pharisees resembled much the Stoics.

---

* See Josephus' Antiquities of the Jews, Book XVIII., Chap. I., for the different ideas of the three great Hebrew sects.

It is noteworthy that among all these Hebrew sects, except the Sadducees, and all the Grecian schools except the Epicureans, prevailed the idea of a future life for man. Among the Greeks it was styled the immortality of the soul, among the Hebrews, the resurrection from the dead. It was only necessary, therefore, to combine this hopeful idea of the resurrection, or future life, so strongly insisted on by the Pharisees and Essenes, not less than by the whole Platonic school of Greece, with the extreme piety, rigid morality, and more spiritual form of worship, inculcated by the Essenes, and baptize it with "the fire out of Heaven," derived from that grand old Hebrew tradition of the Messiah, that was to appear about that time, and Christianity was organized, and began its eventful career. In short, the sect of the Essenes was, to all intents and purposes, the *embryo* of Christianity. It only required the Divine inspiration of Jesus to breathe it into life.

§ 3. The ideas, then, were not wanting in the time of Jesus. It was only the designing and combining mind, with a certain degree of new and higher inspiration, or with some few additional and more comprehensive ideas, superadded to the old, that was requisite to commence the great revolution which was then inaugurated in the moral destinies of the world. And this is all that is now needed by Social Philosophy, and in order to effect a great revolution, not indeed in the social condition or political destinies of the world—for that is not to be hoped—but in the *understanding of* MEN in regard to the causes which determine that condition, and control those destinies.

It may have been with reference, in part to the fact here stated, that the great teacher, whose example is here cited, made his expressive observation, "The harvest indeed is plenty, but the laborers are few," which may be interpreted, either as meaning that there was much work to be done, and but few disposed to do it, which is the common interpretation, or, that that there was much work that had been already done, that the harvest of ideas, feelings, and hopes, was abundant, but that laborers were wanting to turn them to proper account. Such at least is the present condition of Social Philosophy. The harvest of ideas is plenty, but the reapers are wanting, who know properly how to gather in the ideas, and store them away in their appropriate garners. It is not so much new thought, as proper systematization of thought, that is needed in this, as in many other departments of knowledge.

Some new ideas it was indeed the mission of Jesus, as of every great reformer of thought, to announce. How beautifully and sublimely did he teach that the time had passed when God was to be worshipped in this mountain or in that, and when He was to be regarded, rather as the inhabitant of the whole world—nay, moreover, that the time had passed when He was to be regarded as dwelling in an outward tabernacle, and when the human soul was to be regarded as the true tabernacle in which the Divine presence is manifested to man; "for lo," he says, "the kingdom of heaven is within yourselves."

How just as well as beautiful an illustration, by the way, does the teaching of this august reformer in this respect afford, of the teaching of true Social Philosophy! The time has passed, says that philosophy, when men are to look to this place or to that, to this man or to that, to this law or to that, to this institution, this form of government, or some other, for their true prosperity; and when they should come clearly to understand that the kingdom of this world, not less than the "kingdom of heaven," is within themselves—that the real sources of their prosperity, either as individuals or nations, are to be found in their own industrial, moral, and intellectual energies. So much for our general answer to the question—what is the present status of Social Philosophy.

§ 4. Speaking more particularly, we may say, Social Philosophy is at present in the condition it which medical philosophy, or medical science, as it is more commonly styled, finds itself when it has attained to a very correct THERAPEUTICS, for the treatment of any disease, but is as yet very imperfect in its DIAGNOSIS of the disease. For this is, almost precisely defined, the present *status* of Social Philosophy.

It has attained to a correct THERAPEUTICS for social disease, in so far as it admits, in common with physiological diseases, of any remedy; but its DIAGNOSIS of causes is very imperfect, meagre, and wretchedly contracted. Hence, while it has made considerable practical attainments, in short, nearly all it can ever make, it is very backward in its theoretical attainments; which is perfectly in harmony with the great general law, that *correct practice everywhere precedes correct theory;* or that the observation and instinct of men lead them in the right direction, long before their rational faculties have been sufficiently developed and enlightened to discern the grounds of its propriety.

Social Philosophy has already attained to the great practical conclusion that the only sufficient and reliable remedy for social ills in so far indeed as they admit of remedy, is to be found IN THE ELEVATION OF THE MORAL AND INTELLECTUAL STATUS OF MANKIND—for which conclusion, as has been often before stated in these pages, it is immediately indebted to Malthusianism, or to the great conflict of thought to which that doctrine has given rise. Vague recognitions, indistinct and imperfect expressions of this great truth, had indeed been asserted before—nay have appertained more or less faintly to every age of the world. But nowhere have they been so distinctly and emphatically expressed as by the Malthusian philosophers. Nowhere else have they been asserted with sufficient distinctness and emphasis.

There is a great difference between the loose and merely casual assertion of a truth and its formal announcement—between its merely poetical recognition and its scientific assertion. The former we have had before. The latter we have obtained only from the Malthusians. The former assertions have availed but little, as is the case with such loose, indistinct, and disconnected assertions generally. How many glimmerings of the truth do we faintly catch before the whole truth blazes on us! How many streaks of the morning shoot upward from the horizon before the effulgent sun looms upon the world! The former announcements of this great idea were but glimmerings of the truth. Those which the Malthusian philosophers have made afford us the genuine and effulgent sun-light.

The most emphatic and noteworthy assertion of the great truth under review, as before remarked, is to be found in the thought and expression of Dr. Chalmers and John Stuart Mill—the former an *original*, and the latter a *later* Malthusian.* "Everything, in fact," says Dr. Chalmers, "short of a moral economic check on the multiplication of the species, and that through the medium of the people's education and improved habits, will turn out but an ephemeral expedient for enlarging their means of enjoyment, and raising their status in the commonwealth."† Nor less to the same point says the same great thinker: "Nothing, in fact, will save the community at large from the miseries of an oppressed and straitened condition, but an elevation of the popular character and mind."‡ Nor less pregnant, expressive, and comprehensive, is the language of Mill, so often before quoted: "No remedies for low wages have the smallest chance of being efficacious which do not operate on and through the minds and habits of the people."

On these two expressions of Dr. Chalmers and J. S. Mill rest the highest practical attainments as yet of Social Philosophy. In them may be said to consist the present STATUS of that philosophy, in respect at least to its conclusory ideas as contradistinguished from its fundamental ones. In these expressions, moreover, is contained, in general form, and in its most condensed essentiality, the true Therapeutics of Social Philosophy.

§ 5. It should not be necessary to halt here to meet the question, which may be raised by superficial criticism, what can be the utility of further inquiries in Social Philosophy if it has already attained to a correct Therapeutics, or to just ideas concerning the practical ends to which it should conform its efforts. Sufficient it should be to reply, that it is highly important, for many reasons, practical as well as theoretical, to attain a correct

---

* For the important distinction between *original* and *later* Malthusian, see the author's unpublished work on that system of thought, and more particularly Chapters IV. and VI. of same.

† Chalmers' Pol. Eco. Ch. X., p. 242.   ‡ Same. Ch. XI., p. 282.

DIAGNOSIS of CAUSES, not less than a correct THERAPEUTICS of practice, concerning every efficient science, not less than every purely theoretical one. Sufficient it should be to reply, that the end of every science—its true and proper end—at least its true *scientific* end, is simply *to know*, without reference to the practical applications of that knowledge.

The very name of science comes from *scio*, which signifies to know. Its true scientific object or end is, therefore, *to know*—to know everything—everything, at least, that can be known, which is preciously little, to be sure—to know especially CAUSES, as far as they can be ascertained, or LAWS, as Mr. Comte prefers universally to call them. This is the immediate object of science, its true or proper object, its purely scientific object.

If, then, we wish to master the science of Sociology—if we wish, in short, to establish a thorough Social Philosophy, adequate to the great work which appertains to it, of perfecting such a science—assuredly we must penetrate to CAUSES, to the fundamental LAWS, which give rise to phenomena, and which have to be counteracted or coöperated with, in order to produce any desired end by human instrumentality. This is necessary not only with reference to the purely scientific end of Social Science, but also in reference to its efficient or practical end.

It is not sufficient for the purposes of science that right conclusions should be arrived at. The right reasons for those conclusions are also requisite. Science demands not only the truth, but the true reasons for the truth. By these we shall not only be best assured of the truth, but most likely to insure their general reception. Nay, they are often, and always to some extent, necessary to that end. No truth, indeed, can be regarded as scientifically established until its scientific reasons have been discovered. Before that time it will be, and may properly be, regarded, as merely empirical truth, needing further and truly scientific verification, which consists in establishing its essential connection with some great fundamental law, already accepted, or susceptible of demonstration.

This is the true reason why so little real progress has been hitherto made in Social Science. It is the true reason why even the great practical conclusions, which have been just now announced, in the words of Dr. Chalmers and J. S. Mill, have not as yet been so generally accepted or widely disseminated as they ought to be. There has been no fully sufficient reason presented, no overwhelming demonstration afforded, of the grounds on which rest those great practical conclusions.

This observation reveals the true great want of Social Philosophy in its present state. It is the want of a true and thorough DIAGNOSIS OF CAUSES—a true, thorough, and exhaustive exposition of THE CAUSES WHICH DETERMINE THE SOCIAL CONDITION OF MANKIND.

This is what the author of the present work proposes specifically to accomplish for Social Philosophy. He accepts the great practical conclusions which the highest thinkers have already attained, as well as many of their fundamental ideas, or reasonings on CAUSES. But he cannot, by any means, accept their diagnosis of causes as complete, thorough, or sufficiently fundamental and comprehensive. There has been as yet no distinguishable organization of thought, except upon the fundamental grounds presented by the three systems already designated as the Political, the Politico-Economical and Malthusian. These imperfect and superficial systems—in so far as they have adapted their reasonings to the great fundamental question, *what are the causes which really tend to depress the social condition of mankind,* or to militate against the welfare alike of states and individuals—have essentially, and virtually, if not avowedly, maintained that the real cause is, either that there is something wrong about the GOVERNMENT, or political institutions, as the one represents; or that there is some deficiency of WEALTH, as another represents; or some excess of POPULATION, as the third system avowedly proclaims.

Very manifestly neither of these systems affords a sufficient or complete diagnosis of causes. It would be chimerical to attempt to found a correct or thorough system of social science upon any such meagre induction of causes. As well might it have been attempted to found a correct and thorough system of astronomy upon Kepler's laws, as to the harmony of planetary distances, without the aid of the PRINCIPIA MATHEMATICA.

§ 6. Speaking still more particularly than before, we may say, the present status of Social Philosophy is that in which sidereal philosophy was, when it had attained its Copernican idea, nay its Copernican and Keplerian ideas, but had not as yet discovered its Newtonian.

In thus representing Social Philosophy, however, as having already attained its Copernican idea, we should remark that it is only with a somewhat questionable propriety that we can make the representation. For although the idea has been asserted, and repeatedly, it can hardly be said that it has been as yet fully attained.

The attainment of an idea properly consists, not in its bare discovery or assertion, but in its just appreciation. Malthus was the real founder of Malthusianism—the true discoverer of the great Malthusian idea,—an idea to which he has rightly given name, as to the natural tendency of all animated life, man included, to increase beyond the means of subsistence. He was the true discoverer of the idea. He it was that made this important attainment for Social Philosophy; simply because he was the first adequately and justly to appreciate the idea—in fact to overestimate its importance, as the discoverers of new truth are so apt to do. It was not because he was the first to discern or assert the idea, for he was not. Aristotle and Plato, besides many others, both in ancient and modern times, had discerned the truth, and casually asserted it. But Malthus was the first to discern its great importance, its momentous bearings on the social condition and destiny of mankind.

Nay, the Copernican idea of astronomy was not asserted, for the first time, by Copernicus. It had been conjectured before by Pythagoras, and distinctly recognized by the Egyptian astronomers, in so far as the revolutions of two of the planets were concerned.* What Copernicus did was to demonstrate the truth, scientifically to establish it, to put it beyond all question, to discern the universality of its applications, and extend it to all the planets. Very manifestly no one has as yet accomplished this, for what we have designated as the Copernican idea of Sociology. No one has as

---

* These were Mercury and Venus.

yet shown that he duly appreciated the idea, or discerned its true relations to Social Science. To have truly discovered the Copernican idea of Sociology, to have fully attained it indeed, it was requisite that the asserter of the idea should have discerned that it was the Copernican idea—that it was related to Social Science as the idea developed by Copernicus in his treatise *on the motions of the Celestial Orbs*, was related to astronomical science.

This assuredly no one has as yet done. Hence it is, that the author of the present work may, not unreasonably, claim to be the true contributor to Social Philosophy of its appropriate Copernican idea, although he has not been by any means the first to assert it, and although he has been to a far greater extent aided and sustained than Copernicus was, by the previous reasonings of others.

The Copernican idea of Sociology has undoubtedly been asserted, and asserted repeatedly, although it cannot properly be said to have been as yet fully attained, formally inaugurated, or rightly appreciated. In a certain sense, and to a qualified extent, Social Philosophy has had many Copernicuses. Nor has it, certainly, been wanting in its Keplers, its Galileos, and its Tycho Brahes innumerable, with their vast array of important observations. All that it now needs is the designing and combining mind, the penetrative and comprehensive reason, to discern and apply the great remaining and undiscovered fundamental law, or laws, which comprehend and harmonize all former observations, which explain and systematize all the facts.

This is what the mind of Newton accomplished for sidereal philosophy. It is what some mind, not less comprehensive in its reasonings, however much less gifted with natural strength, must accomplish for Social Philosophy. For, be it ever remembered, that lack of natural talent may be largely compensated by a greater and more earnest spirit of inquiry, and by that intensely skeptical cautiousness in drawing conclusions, which, however bold, original, and independent, in relying on its own intuitions and ratiocinations, yet dares not finally accept its own conclusions, until it has verified them by the accumulated wisdom of ages, as well as by all the known facts, and until it has brought to bear upon its own particular science, the concentrated batteries of universal science.

We have already pronounced Sismondi the Copernicus of Social Philosophy, or rather the inquirer who is the most deserving of that appellation—the most nearly approximated to the true Copernican idea that is to be attained. But we have already seen how far short of the true idea he has come—how imperfectly he appreciated it.* Sismondi's appreciation of the Copernican idea of Sociology was, in fact, very little more thorough than was the old Egyptian astronomers' appreciation of the Copernican idea of astronomy. They discerned it only in regard to the revolutions of two of the planets, Mercury and Venus, which they discovered to revolve around the sun. But they had no idea that the earth did the same, and all the other planets.

In like manner Sismondi discerned the Copernican idea of Sociology in regard to Political Economy, but not in regard to any other realm of the vast science of Sociology. He saw and loudly proclaimed, to his distinguished credit, that it was fallacious—at least, with any immediate view to essentially important ends—to fix attention, mainly or directly, on WEALTH, and the abstract laws of its production, distribution, and consumption. He saw and loudly proclaimed that attention should rather be directed mainly and directly to MAN.

To this extent, but no farther, does he appear to have discerned the great truth that MAN is the true CENTRE of the social universe, and that around HIM revolves all his social destiny—his wealth, his laws, his political institutions, his religion, and the general part he plays in the great drama of human existence. For this is what we have termed, and again term, the true Copernican idea of Sociology.

As Copernicus taught that, in order to master the laws of sidereal motion, it was necessary to disabuse our minds of the vulgar and merely apparent idea that the earth is the centre of the universe, or at least of our own solar system, and fix our

---

* See Chapter X.

minds *outside* of this world, and upon the sun, as the true centre of motion and cosmical destiny, so the true Copernican idea of Sociology teaches, that, in order to master the laws of sociological motion, we must, by a directly converse process, disabuse our minds of the vulgar and merely apparent idea that the political institutions of mankind, or any mere external conditions or surroundings, are the centre or real controlling influence of the social system, and fix our minds *within* ourselves—on MAN himself—on those physical, moral, and intellectual energies which underlie his mere physical frame, and constitute the real MAN, as the true centre of all sociological motion, and all human destiny.

This we say again is the true Copernican idea of Sociology, which, although many have approximated or partially asserted, none have as yet fully attained or thoroughly perceived; although it has been nearly enough approximated, or asserted in its full significance, to justify us in regarding it as already virtually attained by Social Philosophy. For here, as elsewhere, the writer of these pages is disposed to accept the assertions of eminent authorities, in their full significance and utmost logical import, to enlarge rather than to restrict the meaning or rendition of their ideas.

Nor shall we stop here to repel exceptions, to the similitude here instituted, which might be taken by such captious and hypercritical critics as Mr. Herbert Spencer, who would doubtlessly object to the assertion that the earth is round, because Chimborazo and other mountain peaks rise many thousand feet above the sea level, and who appear totally regardless of the proverb of Coke, that "no metaphor runs on all-fours." In coming to develop more particularly, as it is proposed to do in the following Part of this Series, the laws which most fundamentally determine the social condition of mankind, we shall have occasion to notice and explain some objections that might be made to this designation of the Copernican idea of Sociology.

§ 7. Thus it appears that, aided by the expressions of anterior thinkers, and the interpretations and enlargements of the thought involved in them that are here contributed, we have the Copernican idea of Sociology. But what is the Newtonian idea, which we need in order to complete the Philosophy of Society, and furnish all the elements of a thorough Social Science? For we need not stop to inquire what are the Keplerian or Galilean ideas. It would only be by an overstrained effort at similitude, indeed, that we could designate as such any of the ideas appertaining to Social Philosophy.

It would be foreign to the purposes of the present work to respond to this question. To do so would be to communicate the thoughts which are claimed by the writer, as more peculiarly, if not exclusively, his own. These appertain to the work or part of the series immediately following this. It is the aim of the present work to notice, and bring prominently into view, only the valuable thoughts of anterior thinkers, however partially and imperfectly expressed. No thinker as yet appears to have discerned the true Newtonian idea, or as we should rather say, the true Newtonian principles of Social Science.

Of all former thinkers, Comte appears to have most nearly approximated these principles. Very nearly does he approximate them, when in speaking of the "objective basis," on which is to be established "the harmony of our moral nature," as he expresses himself, he says, "It rests at every point on the unchangeable order of the world."* In this expression, however, Comte conducts us only towards what may be termed the universal law of social gravitation, or the centripetal force of the Social Cosmos. It does not conduct us toward the *centrifugal* force, nor indicate the direction in which we are to look in order to find it.

The Newtonian idea, or the principle which it involves, does not relate merely to the universality of the laws of gravitation or centripetal force, as seems to be commonly supposed. It relates rather to the universality of the laws of MOTION, in their double aspect of centripetal and centrifugal. These we must find, and

---

* See Comte's General View of Positivism. Ch. I., p. 28; also ante, Ch. XII. of the present work.

clearly estimate, in regard to the Social Cosmos, if we would attain the true Newtonian idea of Social Philosophy, or its true *principia mathematica*.

This much, however, we may well enough here say, in regard to the idea in question—thus far we may here go towards its full expression. We may state the idea in its most general form, and also present the specific formula of the problem to be solved, in order to attain its full and complete development.

Most essentially and most briefly expressed, the veritable idea of Newton, which perfected astronomical science, was the universality of the laws of motion, and the consequent identity of the causes which regulate the movements of an atom and a world, the smallest or the largest masses of matter. Most briefly and simply expressed, therefore, the problem which Newton had to solve was: What are the laws which regulate the movements of an atom, or the smallest considerable body, as an apple, a stone, or a cannon-ball?—What are the laws which regulate its movements, when impelled by any exterior or centrifugal force, and determine whether it shall continue for ever after to maintain the centrifugal force it has received, and *revolve in an orbit of its own*, like the worlds, or whether that force shall be entirely counteracted by the centripetal, and the body return again to a state of rest? For, given these, we have the laws which regulate, only on a larger scale, the gyrations and movements of worlds.

A cannon-ball, for example, fired in a horizontal direction with its usual velocity, even in the absence of atmospheric resistance, as if discharged beyond the limits of the atmosphere, we shall find, would soon expend its force and fall to the earth, as not having enough *momentum* within itself to maintain the imparted motion. But give it a velocity of *five miles a second* and it would never revisit the earth, but continue, as the astronomer Vaughn informs us, to revolve around it as a satellite, or miniature world in itself.*

---

* See Daniel Vaughn's Popular Astronomy, pp. 55-6, Cincinnati edition, 1858. We prefer to cite here the authority of this highly meritorious philoso-

Such is, in brief, the Newtonian idea of astronomy—one of its simplest illustrations. The Newtonian idea of Sociology is precisely analogous. It asserts the universality of the causes, or laws, which determine the social condition of mankind, and the consequent identity of the causes which determine the social destiny of an individual and a nation—of the humblest individual in the human family and of the most exalted—of the pauper as well as the millionaire—of the laborer as well as the capitalist—of the peasant not less than the prince.

§ 8. Most briefly and simply expressed, therefore, the problem which the Social Philosopher has to solve, the main fundamental problem, as contradistinguished from the innumerable particular and practical problems that claim his attention, is : What are the causes or laws which determine the social destiny of the individual, which determine in the long run, and in the absence of extraordinary disturbing causes, whether he shall be prosperous or the contrary, whether he shall be a pauper or millionaire, a laborer or capitalist, a peasant or prince—which determine, in short, whether his own internal momentum or *centrifugal* force shall be overpowered by the potent gravitation, or *centripetal* force, which is constantly prostrating human efforts, or shall enable him to maintain an independent position, and REVOLVE IN AN ORBIT OF HIS OWN. For, given these causes or laws, we have precisely the causes or laws, which determine the destiny of nations, the rise and fall of empires. Thus do we in Sociology not less than in Astronomy, nay, not less than in universal science, by the same laws or principles, solve the simplest and the grandest problems.

§ 9. Surely these few observations in regard to the true Newtonian idea of Sociology, however general and abstract, must be sufficient to suggest to scientific or philosophical thought, the whole *principia mathematica* of Sociology. Should the work of

---

pher precisely because he is so little known and appreciated. He is one of the world's many unknown heroes. Happy world! how much richer is it in intellectual treasuries than it knows of, or, alas, cares to know!

the present inquirer, therefore, end here, it will not have been entirely in vain that he has devoted the best hours of his brief existence to the development of that system of thought, of which the thoughts here presented are but disjointed fragments.

Nay, flippant criticism and superficial reasoning may exclaim, in reference to the most essential teachings of the new Social Philosophy, how simple is all that—what great difficulty is there about it—who did not know that much before—who did not know what are the causes on which depend the welfare of an individual? The only reply to which reasoning, that need be offered here, is—so spake they about the EGG, and how easy it was to set it up on the end.

Easy enough it was, doubtless, to sail westward until they reached land. But why did they not do it before Columbus led the way? Easy enough it is too to discern, when one looks the matter squarely in the face, that the causes of the welfare or decline of states and individuals, are identical, and that, so regarded, the solution of the main fundamental problem of Social Philosophy becomes simple enough. But why have not mankind discovered the simple though grand truth before, applied it to the great practical issues of society, and drawn from it its vast and far-reaching conclusions? Why have they not, in all their discussions and contentions for the last *two thousand years* and upwards, elicited the idea? Or, if they may have happened, now and then, in some of their conflicts, to stumble upon the idea, why have they not had the sagacity to appreciate it, to seize upon it, to appropriate it, to elevate it into due prominence, and make it the basis of that new, more enlarged, and correct system of thought, in regard to the destinies of society, which, to the justly discerning mind, it may readily suggest?

Simple truths! Yes, simple, plain, and familiar truths, when most essentially rendered, are those which the writer of these pages is most solicitous to bring prominently into view, and to stereotype upon the thought and brain of the world. For it is precisely these truths that mankind are constantly prone to ignore, and to lose sight of, in their larger reasonings. Simple, plain, and familiar truths, most essentially considered, they are, and therefore they are true.

Let none despise the simple truths. They are the true types, the exact miniatures, of the large ones. The true function of the philosopher, or true man of genius, is ever to bring men back to the simple truths, from which they are constantly prone to wander and go astray. The greatest triumphs of philosophy often consist in merely bringing men back to a more just, clear, and thorough apprehension of some of the simplest and most familiar truths. Extremes everywhere tend to meet. The smallest and the greatest men are alike distinguished by their simplicity and humility. The smallest and the greatest truths lie near together. A dew-drop is a miniature of the ocean. An atom is a sample of the universe.

True philosophy delights in simple truths. It deals in them. Its true business is to go back to the most simple, elementary, and fundamental truths; which are to be found almost everywhere cropping out, in the world of thought like the primeval rocks of the terrestrial world, and with which the humblest minds are to some extent familiar.

The course of true philosophy is like the course of the individual man—the true or model man, if we may assume such to exist—in his course of life. It begins with simplicity and ends with simplicity. Mark the course of man in his earthly development. How simple and unaffected is the prattle of childhood—with its deep questions, now and then thrown out, that puzzle the profoundest philosopher! How turgid, frothy, and grandiloquent, is juvenility, when it has just begun to smatter in learning, and has become intoxicated with its "first fevered draughts of the Piercan Spring!" How simple again becomes the conduct and conversation of true manhood, when "deeper imbibations" have sobered it again! The Chinese have a proverb, that "the truly wise man never lays aside the simplicity of a child." Might we not almost make the same observation of a truly wise philosophy? Like the truly wise man, in his general conduct and conversation it ends as it began with the simplicity of childhood. Said we not rightly before, the smallest and the greatest truths lie near together? Extremes must ever tend to meet. The origin and the end of all things are the same.

There was once at Rome an orator of such rare merit, that when he spoke, though all listened with the utmost attention, all were prompted to exclaim, when he had finished, how plain, simple, and obvious, is all that he has said—who could not have said just what he has told us. Yet there was no other man in Rome that could speak as this man.*

Is not this again an apt illustration of the talk of true philosophy? It conducts us through some of the greatest difficulties that can possibly be surmounted by the human understanding, and does it so simply that, in many cases, one can hardly help exclaiming, what is there that it tells us that we did not know before? It conducts us to some of the grandest and most important conclusions, by simply extending and carrying forward, to their true logical conclusions, ideas which are familiar to the minds of all.

§ 10. According to the plan originally intended by the writer of these pages, the preliminary work, entitled *Review, Historical and Critical, of the Different Systems of Thought in Social Philosophy*, of which the present work forms part, would properly end here, at the close of that which is properly the Sixth Part of that Review, or Series of Reviews. It was the original intention to add, in a Seventh Part, the general reasons which demand a new system, and to indicate merely the general drift or tendency of the new system—reserving, however, any presentation of the distinguishing fundamental ideas of that new system, for the subsequent and main work of the author, his *Inquiry into the Causes which Determine the Social Condition of Mankind*.

As the preliminary work, however, proceeded, amid many difficulties, discouragements, and interruptions, expanding continually in volume with unanticipated expansion of thought, and extension of observation, on the part of the writer, apprehension be-

---

* Will the editor of "Notes and Queries" inform us who this orator was? For it has escaped the author's recollection. It was not Cicero or Hortensius, but some one of an earlier date.

gan to arise that this mere preliminary undertaking might prove unintentionally the labor of a lifetime, and that death might overtake the laborer, before he had got to the proper commencement, even of his own peculiar work. Thus would he be expending his life in bringing before the world the thoughts of others, which it already had, while his own, which it had not, would remain unannounced—a labor indeed not unworthy of a lifetime, although not fully equal to that which the workman had proposed to himself. For the thoughts which the world already had, on the momentous questions here dealt with, though many of them of great value, lay so scattered, and disconnectedly, over the field of discussion that they were not duly appreciated, nor even understood. The work which the present laborer had undertaken, in this preliminary enterprise, of systematizing and arranging, in somewhat logical order, those thoughts, could not but prove a valuable one to the scientific world—nay, we might venture to say, as valuable to the student of the world of thought, however much less entertaining, as the work of the historian Gibbon, at least, to the student of the world of action.

This, however, was not precisely, nor properly, what the writer aimed at. It was to get his own thoughts before the world, that he mainly proposed, and merely as means to this end, as a most proper mode of introducing his own thoughts, he sought to present a systematic and condensed statement of the substance of all anterior thought. How was this important preliminary work, then already far advanced, to be carried forward, without sacrificing the main object—the very end to which it was originally intended as a mere means? The thought then occurred, and the resolution was formed, to embody in the Seventh and last part of the preliminary work, that which yet remains to be written, not only the general drift or tendency of the main work, but a complete SYNOPSIS of its main ideas, and OUTLINE of its plan. Thus would be rescued from oblivion his main ideas, even though death should cut short his career, and his arduous and unrequited labor of life would not have been wholly in vain.

In short the writer found himself, metaphorically if not literally, somewhat in the condition of the great geographical discoverer, when on his homeward voyage, driven by stress of weather and apprehending shipwreck, he wrote a brief narrative of his discoveries, and, enclosing it in a cask, cast it into the sea, hoping that it might reach some civilized coast, and rescue from oblivion the important discoveries he had made. When he considered the uncertainties of life, the difficulties of the voyage on which he was embarked, the frailness of the hulk to which his destinies for the voyage were committed, beaten by many storms, and sorely pressed by stress of weather, he despaired of ever reaching land, with his cargo of thoughts, and resolved to write out a brief outline of those thoughts—of his observations, discoveries, and conclusions—and enclosing them in this preliminary work, commit them to the deep of human thoughts, trusting that they might be picked up, or drift to some enlightened shore, and suggest to some more favored explorer, those discoveries which, as it seemed, he was not to be permitted to communicate.

Animated with this purpose, his labors were prosecuted with renewed energy. But even in this he seems to have been doomed to disappointment. The magnitude of the preliminary work has expanded beyond all calculation—threatening the dimensions of two closely-packed volumes, of the largest sized octavo, *seven hundred* pages each—and the expense of publishing has expanded accordingly—a consideration of no small moment with a work far above the comprehension of the masses, wholly inappreciable by the generality even of scholars, and having no hopes of even the smallest consideration except from the few, the very few, who most essentially constitute the world of thought—the truly philosophical world—THE ONE IN THE MILLION.

Thus has it become doubtful whether the writer will be permitted, by that inexorable fate which so unrelentingly and mercilessly pursues some men, to get even his preliminary thoughts before the world, with the condensed statement which they embody of his main thoughts. Thus does it again appear probable that he will be overtaken by death before he shall have been permitted to make known, even in very small part, the objects for which he has lived.

Apprehending this fate, disgusted with so much delay and so many discouragements, constrained moreover by a sense of duty to others—whose interests he does not feel at liberty to sacrifice at the neglected shrine of TRUTH, as he is willing to sacrifice his own —to forego, for the future, much more than in the past, the thankless pursuit of KNOWLEDGE, for the more appreciated one of *profit;* he has resolved to submit at once the few thoughts and observations in this small volume contained, comprising the Sixth Part only of his entire preliminary work, to the consideration of the world, or the very few of the world whom they can ever directly reach.

In prosecuting this resolve, in preparing this brief volume of thoughts and observations, he has kept steadily in view the former purpose, of rescuing from oblivion his own main ideas, and, with that view, of imitating, although on a much smaller scale than before intended, the example of THE ILLUSTRIOUS NAVIGATOR, as already cited. In communicating the higher thoughts that he has discovered in others, with which this volume is mainly freighted, he has taken care so to weave around them his own thoughts and observations, or actually to superadd them, by way of addendum, as in this last chapter, that subsequent inquirers, future explorers in these seas of thought, can have no great difficulty in recovering the observations, and repeating the discoveries which he has made, apparently to so little purpose. These he now commits to the uncertain waves of human inquiry and activity, trusting that in some future age, if not in the present, they may drift to some enlightened shore, and be rightly applied to human good.

Having done this he feels relieved of a great anxiety, is inspired with the hope that his labors may prove to have been not wholly in vain, is consoled by the reflection that, although it is but little he has done, he has done the best that he could, under all the many disadvantageous circumstances by which he has been on all sides surrounded, and is enabled, with some satisfaction, to take leave of the world, at the very moment of first intruding himself upon its attention.

In one noteworthy respect, beside others not less important, it may be worth while to add, the *mariner* who here throws overboard, from his too heavily belabored bark, this brief suggestion of his discoveries, differs from the GREAT MARINER whose example he thus seeks to imitate. Not like that illustrious and more favored navigator, did he set sail, on the voyage of discovery, with any great expectations, plans, or purposes—still less under the protection of royal navies and exchequers. For the mariner who attempts to explore these SEAS OF THOUGHT must furnish his own outfit; and should his poorly provided craft founder at sea, or be wrecked upon the reefs, no royal *gazette* regretfully announces his disaster, or even notifies the world in what latitude or longitude the unregarded craft was steering her way, when she was last seen struggling with the waves.

Not with any large intentions, nor with views the result of long and mature reflection, did this navigator of the seas of thought begin his voyage of discovery. But unexpectedly he has been drifted into far larger explorations than he had originally intended—explorations so large, indeed, that, had he known such would have to be undertaken, he would scarcely have ventured to set sail. How often are men unconsciously drifted into their destiny! How little do they discern the ends of those endeavors, of which they plan, at most, only the beginnings!

Some twenty years ago, or somewhat less, this weather-beaten mariner of these seas of thought, set sail on a youthful adventure, following the drift of one only of the many important questions,* which had been much discussed, concerning the *deeps* of Social Philosophy. Unawares he was drifted far out to sea, which, however, he feared not to attempt. Nor had he long been at sea before he found himself drifting on the great GULF-STREAM of human destiny. Unable to resist the mighty current, of which before he knew but little, and far less inclined to do so, he lent himself to the momentum, and was carried along with it. On, on, he

---

* This was the Malthusian drift.

sped, passing often in review the floating fragments of former empires, and the more numerous wrecks of individual fortunes.

When at length the mighty current had swept him through many degrees of latitude and longitude, he began to take his reckoning. Then, with far larger ideas, and more extended observations, he discovered that his original purpose would be of little avail, to very small purpose. Then he discovered that it would be of little or no use to present partial observations or suggestions, concerning such vast seas of thought—that the world had already had enough of such partial work—that what it now wanted were comprehensive, systematic, and conclusive observations—that it no longer needed mere charts, showing the directions of a few winds or currents—that it needed rather a comprehensive map, compassing the whole of this vast comprehensive sea of thought, showing all its main currents, winds, harbors, headlands, and reefs, with their respective bearings and relations to each other, and thus presenting in general outline the whole field for investigation, leaving, of course, large spaces for future and more particular observations.

This, which we have long had in physical geography, it became evident to his mind was not less needed in SOCIAL geography. This was the comprehensive, large, and systematic work, which he saw clearly the world now needed. It was precisely the work which accorded with the natural propensities of his mind. For large enterprises, or none at all, could arouse its ordinarily sluggish energies. Through and thorough work, searching complete and exhaustive efforts, or none at all, were precisely what his mind required. Such was all it was capable of executing, except in a most slovenly and indifferent manner. Large and thorough efforts it sought and longed for. Small work of any kind was not possible to it.

What then was he to do? Was he to abandon the enterprise on which he had embarked, and sailed so far, without accomplishing anything? Not readily—least of all when the work demanded, by the requirements of the world, was precisely that for which he was the best adapted, and when he found himself, thus unexpectedly, drifted into the very position for which Destiny seemed to have intended him. What then was he to do? Evidently go forward, and execute the work into which he had been drifted, as it were, almost wholly without any agency of his own.

He resolved to make the attempt. He spread his canvas to the breeze. He sailed onward. He courted every wind. He drifted with every current. He traversed every sea, and coasted every shore—sailing landward or seaward as occasion seemed to demand. He has availed himself of the most approved charts of former navigators, and superadded extensive ones of his own, revising and correcting former ones by his own more recent observations. He has thus not only visited every sea and coast, of any note, ever visited by former navigators, but many a sea where no navigator has been as yet reported, and many a coast where no trace of human footstep before has been discovered.

After a cruise of nearly twenty years, thus directed, in these seas of thought, the toil-worn navigator finds himself now homeward bound. Gladly would he reach the yet distant shore, and report at large his extensive observations and discoveries. But can such good fortune be destined to attend him, and his hitherto wholly unrecognized labors, trials, and self-sacrifices? It is not now to be hoped. The bark on which his life destiny is freighted, frail at best, has been beaten by too many storms, and is now too sorely pressed by heavy stress of weather. The ship has nearly run her course. It is not to be expected that she can successfully encounter the difficulties which must yet be endured before she can hope to reach the port.

What then? Shall all his explorations, toils, self-denials, life-sacrifice, for the cause of knowledge and human advancement, prove for naught? Shall he perish, with his many unspoken thoughts, and dearly purchased observations, and the world not know, even in part, for what he has lived—for what he has remained so long unreported? Nay, shall mankind at large gain nothing by his loss—his life-sacrifice? Shall they learn nothing of that, which he has expended his life, in order that they might learn? Shall they know nothing of all that which he has remained *unknown* in order that they might *know?*

It is devoutly hoped not. To prevent this result—this saddest consummation of life-trials—this little volume of thoughts, this small envelope of observations and reflections, hastily prepared, and under pressing exigencies, is now committed to the waves of trouble that surge around. It is cast forth as a solitary WAIF, evidently destined long to float unobserved upon the watery waste. Some day perchance it may be picked up, and suggest to some more favored explorer those tracks of inquiry which it seems not intended that the present explorer shall be permitted to make known.

Is it not possible, moreover, in these days of so many sail, of so much navigation, that some mariner traversing these seas, discerning this WAIF, and deciphering its import, may have his attention turned in the right direction, and bring relief to the distressed mariner? No such possibility is to be anticipated. Such relief comes only to the distressed mariner of the briny seas. They who navigate the SEAS of THOUGHT must sail on their own hook, and at their own peril.

There is no such possibility. But may not the hope be cherished that, while the mariner is cast away, his cargo of ideas may be preserved in part—that the thoughts now cast upon the waters may not be lost, but drift at length to some appreciative shore? Actuated by this hope, he now commits this little WAIF, —this brief suggestion of his observations and reflections—to the great SEA of HUMAN THOUGHTS. Let it drift whithersoever the WINDS and CURRENTS may impel.

www.ingramcontent.com/pod-product-compliance
Lightning Source LLC
Chambersburg PA
CBHW031856220426
43663CB00006B/648